Prohibition an.
in the American West

ALSO BY JEREMY AGNEW
AND FROM MCFARLAND

*The Electric Corset and Other Victorian
Miracles: Medical Devices and Treatments from
the Golden Age of Quackery* (Exposit, 2021)

*The Landscapes of Western Movies: A History
of Filming on Location, 1900–1970* (2020)

*Healing Waters: A History of Victorian Spas* (2019)

*The Age of Dimes and Pulps: A History
of Sensationalist Literature, 1830–1960* (2018)

*Crime, Justice and Retribution in the
American West, 1850–1900* (2017)

*Spanish Influence on the Old Southwest:
A Collision of Cultures* (2016)

*The Creation of the Cowboy Hero:
Fiction, Film and Fact* (2015)

*Alcohol and Opium in the Old West:
Use, Abuse and Influence* (2014)

*The Old West in Fact and Film:
History Versus Hollywood* (2012)

*Entertainment in the Old West: Theater,
Music, Circuses, Medicine Shows, Prizefighting
and Other Popular Amusements* (2011)

*Medicine in the Old West:
A History, 1850–1900* (2010)

# Prohibition and Bootlegging in the American West

JEREMY AGNEW

McFarland & Company, Inc., Publishers

*Jefferson, North Carolina*

ISBN (print) 978-1-4766-8833-6
ISBN (ebook) 978-1-4766-4812-5

Library of Congress and British Library
Cataloguing data are available

Library of Congress Control Number 2022047025

© 2022 Jeremy Agnew. All rights reserved

*No part of this book may be reproduced or transmitted in any form
or by any means, electronic or mechanical, including photocopying
or recording, or by any information storage and retrieval system,
without permission in writing from the publisher.*

On the cover: This postcard from 1899 shows
Nogales divided into two towns. The international
border runs through the middle of the photograph, with the
dry United States side in Arizona on the right and the wet side
in Mexico on the left. Some saloons were built straddling the
border and patrons could enjoy either soft drinks or hard liquor,
depending on which end of the building they were drinking in
(author's collection); *background* © Shutterstock

Printed in the United States of America

*McFarland & Company, Inc., Publishers
Box 611, Jefferson, North Carolina 28640
www.mcfarlandpub.com*

For Larry and Tani,
my mentors for things alcoholic

# Table of Contents

**A Moonshiner's Poem**

(John Kobler, *Ardent Spirits: The Rise and Fall of Prohibition*, 225)

Mother's in the kitchen
Washing out the jugs;
Sister's in the pantry
Bottling the suds;
Father's in the cellar
Mixing up the hops;
Johnny's on the front porch
Watching for the cops.

# Timeline
# of Prohibition Events

1830s: First stirrings of the Temperance Movement.

1858: The popular play *Ten Nights in a Bar-room* spreads the message of the evils of drink to theater-goers across the country.

1874: Woman's Christian Temperance Union founded.

1876, 1880, 1887: Constitutional amendments for prohibition of alcohol presented to Congress, all defeated.

1880s: Temperance workers campaign vigorously against "The Demon Rum" and other alcoholic beverages.

1893: Organization of the Anti-Saloon League in Ohio.

1895: Anti-Saloon League re-formed as a national organization.

1913: Webb-Kenyon Bill passed to prohibit the transport of alcohol to dry states.

1914: Start of World War I in Europe.

1917: United States enters World War I; passage of the 18th Amendment to the Constitution of the United States.

1919: War Prohibition Act goes into effect; 18th Amendment ratified; Congress passes the Volstead Act.

1920: The National Prohibition Act (the Volstead Act) starts the so-called "Noble Experiment"; Prohibition goes into effect.

1929: Stock market crash; Wickersham Commission appointed.

1931: Final report of Wickersham Commission published.

1933: Ratification of the 21st Amendment to the United States Constitution ends Prohibition.

# Preface

*"For chemists, alcohol is not a problem, it's a solution"*
—anonymous

DRINKING FERMENTED BEVERAGES has been a part of human culture as a pastime and pleasure since before recorded history. But from the 1830s until 1920, supporters of temperance marshaled their forces to rid the United States of alcohol, generically known then as the "Demon Rum."

This fervent desire to ban alcoholic beverages was not new. The trustees of the British colony in Georgia experimented with imposing prohibition in 1735, though for various reasons they abandoned the idea in 1742. Further attempts to ban hard liquor in the United States started in the 1830s and 1840s in several states in the East. These efforts mostly ended in failure and faded from public interest when the beginning of the American Civil War in 1861 diverted the attention of reformers and legislators to other more important issues.

The Temperance Movement and its ideas returned in full force in the late 1800s. Those in favor of banning alcoholic beverages enlisted the support of evangelical religious leaders and, as a result, drunkenness became equated with damnation and a lack of salvation. The supporters of prohibition finally succeeded in forcing the Eighteenth Amendment to the Constitution of the United States that created a total ban on alcohol from 1920 to 1933. This amendment was unprecedented in that it restricted the activities of the people, unlike the rest of the constitutional amendments which limit the activities of the government.

As the United States tried to forget the dreadful events of World War I that ended in 1918, the country entered a more carefree era in the 1920s. The grim horrors of the recent war and its unprecedented new ways of conducting hostilities and killing gave way to the new freedoms of the Roaring Twenties. But a shadow loomed over this new-found happiness in the form of a total ban on alcohol.

The work of the Temperance Movement reached its goal with National

1

Prohibition, which went into effect on January 1, 1920, as an attempt by self-appointed moral guardians to improve American society by removing alcohol. This legislation banned the manufacture, transport, and sale of alcoholic beverages in the United States.

Enforcement of the Eighteenth Amendment turned out to be virtually impossible in practice as the country entered the decade of the Roaring Twenties. Even though liquor was banned during these years, the ingenuity of mankind to achieve what is wanted resulted in a wave of illegal alcohol that washed over the country to meet the demands of thirsty drinkers. One of the results was that illegal stills were in use everywhere. Liquor smuggling, speakeasies, and rum-running became popular. For the first time men and women drank together. And physicians wrote more than 11 million prescriptions for medicinal alcohol.

Among the unexpected and unintended results of Prohibition were an actual increase in drinking, the increased liberation of women, the emergence of flappers, the popularity of speakeasies, and a crime wave that surrounded liquor. Prohibition created bootleggers who, in turn, contributed illegal alcohol to the Twenties, together with an undesired increase in dope pushers, gamblers, rumrunners, prostitutes, pimps, gangsters, and hit men.

The overall history of Prohibition has been told in a wide variety of books. Similarly, the histories of specific individuals who were involved in bootlegging, from the stories of leading criminals who operated the largest illegal alcohol businesses to the history of specific local families, can be found in various places. Why, then, another history of Prohibition? The simple answer is to provide a different perspective. The story of what happened during the years of National Prohibition has typically been told from the viewpoint of the historical and political events that occurred in the East and Midwest of the United States, particularly the criminal activity that accompanied prohibition in New York and Chicago, as they were violent centers of bootlegging, law-breaking, and illegal behavior. Eastern newspapers were filled with reports of gangster killings, liquor wars, bootlegging, clogged courts, corruption, and crowded jails. The story of what happened in the western half of the United States, however, is usually not described or is described only briefly. The goal of this book then is to tell the story from the viewpoint of the western states, an aspect of Prohibition that has not been explored to any great extent.

Prohibition and bootlegging in the western United States were different than what occurred in the eastern half of the country. The ban on alcohol in the East spawned violence, gangsters, and crime in the big cities, a combination that culminated in the slaughter of five mobsters and two accomplices who were executed gangster-style in the St. Valentine's Day Massacre at a garage in Chicago in 1929. In the wide-open spaces of the Western states, by contrast, moonshining and bootlegging consisted mostly of small-time booze-makers and low-key activities associated with the manufacturing and distribution of illegal alcohol.

"Moonshine" was the popular name for liquor manufactured illegally or smuggled from elsewhere because such alcohol was supposedly distilled at night to avoid the smoke from the still being seen, and it was transported by the light of the moon to avoid detection by law enforcement agents. The distribution of illicit alcohol was called "bootlegging" because the illegal product was originally carried in bottles hidden in the tops of the boots of early whiskey smugglers.

Much of the bootlegging in the West was on the order of a small cottage industry, rather than the large-scale operations of the East. Western moonshiners and bootleggers were mostly considered to be neighbors and friends, and were often thought of as local folk heroes, rather than vicious criminals. Certainly there were large centers of illegal alcohol importation and manufacturing on the West Coast, such as in Los Angeles and San Francisco, but even this was not on the scale of bootlegging activities in major cities of the East.

As well as being manufactured in countless small stills and backyard operations, illegal alcohol in the western half of the country flowed down over the country's northern border from Canada by car, truck, and airplane, and similarly up across the Mexican border into Arizona and California, occasionally even carried by such unusual methods of transportation as rafts and mules.

Like the East Coast, the West Coast also had its own "rum row," a line of ships that steamed off the coast in international waters while smaller boats ferried their cases of illegal booze to shore. This influx of liquor arrived on large ships that transported alcohol from Mexico, Canada, Tahiti, and even as far away as the Bahamas, to meet the demands of the thirsty, and then transported it from international waters to hidden coves and waiting customers on shore via speedboats, yachts, rowboats, and other small craft. Cases of illegal liquor were then rushed by truck and car to distribution centers in the large cities of the West Coast, such as Los Angeles and San Francisco.

Though the text describes what happened in the West between 1920 and 1933, the years during which National Prohibition was in effect, this book is not a comprehensive history. This has been addressed elsewhere in numerous books. Instead, this book focuses on the popular history of moonshining and bootlegging in the western United States and why this was different from the East.

Expectations for Prohibition were high. William Ashley Sunday was a baseball player before he found religion. In 1890 he became an evangelist and went on to become one of the most successful American preachers of his time, spending forty years in the pulpit. Heralding the arrival of Prohibition, evangelist Sunday joyfully proclaimed at a revival in Norfolk, Virginia, "The reign of tears is over. The slums will soon be a memory. We will turn our prisons into factories and our jails into storehouses and corncribs. Men will walk upright now, women will smile, and the children will laugh."[1]

As we shall see in the following pages, that was not at all what happened.

# 1

# The Saloon Must Go!

Prohibition in the United States and the banning of alcohol from 1920 to 1933 had its genesis in that venerable old American drinking place, the saloon. Without saloons and their impact on the drinking public, both perceived and real, there would have been no pressure to ban alcohol. Thus to understand the basic causes of Prohibition, it is necessary to understand the old-time saloon and its functioning.

The stirring of the Temperance Movement that led to Prohibition started when social reformers realized that more alcohol per capita was consumed in the United States between 1790 and 1830 than at any other time in its history.[1] Drinking was indeed one of the few pleasures of America's working class who labored hard in dirty, low-paid, low-skilled jobs. In addition, until the 1830s, most Americans thought that strong alcoholic drinks were a healthy foodstuff and a necessary accompaniment to any hard work. Alcohol and drinking were an important part of the social structure of early communities and played a role in local cooperative activities, such as barn-raisings and communal harvesting.

Whiskey was also considered to be an admirable and reliable medicine that would ward off fevers, illness, colds, and even snakebite. Contemporary popular opinion was that any alcohol was good for the health, whether it was beer or whiskey. And admittedly, beer and whiskey were probably safer to drink than much of the available drinking water that had been polluted by various animal, human, and industrial wastes.

In rural areas of early colonial America, places to find a drink started as "ordinaries," later called "taverns" during the Revolutionary Period. These were establishments where a traveler could purchase an alcoholic beverage, find a meal, and enjoy lodging for the night. As competitive businesses emerged to provide food and lodging, a further outgrowth of the taverns were establishments that specialized in supplying only drink, where people gathered for relaxation at the end of the day and to discuss local news and current issues. These were the saloons. In large cities these businesses eventually evolved into places to relax and have a sociable drink

5

while discussing the latest events of the day and passing on gossip in a congenial atmosphere. The lower-quality variety of saloons became known as "groggeries" or "grog-shops."

The word "saloon" that came into nineteenth century usage was derived from the French word *salon*, which was the name used to describe a large public meeting hall that was intended for receptions or entertainment. The designation had a somewhat more elegant ring to it than "tavern" and the name "saloon" for a drinking place was in the popular vocabulary by at least 1840.

The use of the French name implied the elegance and sophistication of the French *salons* to avoid the seamy implications of the eighteenth-century names of tavern, taproom, and grog-shop. The word was eventually corrupted into "saloon." It was also combined with other words to include "dining saloon," "billiard saloon," and "beer saloon," as owners tried to make their establishments sound more dignified and exotic than they really were. The general meaning of the word "saloon" eventually came to include any establishment where drinks were sold to be consumed on the premises, such as a barroom independent of an inn for lodging.

Around the turn of the nineteenth century, the United States experienced a flood of immigrants from southern and eastern Europe, many of whom did not share the Protestant religion or Puritan attitudes of much of mainstream America. These were foreigners in a strange land and these working men often sought refuge in saloons where they could congregate and socialize with fellow immigrants. These were not always very elegant places and many contemporary woodcuts of early American taverns include in the background the figure of some helpless drunk throwing up.

In the post–Civil War era, the proliferation of neighborhood saloons was fueled by the creation of an increasingly industrialized urban workforce. Saloons where workingmen could meet became popular social places to gather together away from the workplace and from life at home.

## Saloons in the West

Saloons were a ubiquitous feature of the expanding frontier of the American West. As the American frontier extended westwards, saloons were typically among the first businesses to be established in a newly-established town, mining or logging camp, or cattle town, and were often the focal point for the activities necessary to establish any new community. In spite of a cultural difference between the East and the growing West, in many ways saloons were similar across the country and the saloons of the West closely resembled their Eastern counterparts.

A saloon-keeper was often one of the earliest residents to arrive at a new settlement in the West and establish a tent or building that was dedicated to drinking. Early saloons in a newly-founded town or mining camp were often housed in only a portable canvas tent brought in on the back of a wagon. This was the cheapest and easiest way to start a saloon and was the smartest way for a saloon-keeper to protect his investment. If a fledgling settlement prospered and grew into a permanent town, the saloon could be easily moved from the tent into a more substantial wooden building. If the camp did not survive, the saloon-keeper simply packed his tent back into his wagon and moved on to the next prospective new town. Some enterprising saloon-keepers simply served drinks off the tail-boards of their wagons until they decided if they wanted to erect a more permanent structure.

For a businessman who could afford it, a saloon was a good investment and provided a reliable source of income for the owner. All that was required was a bartender, a few glasses or tin cups, some tables, a few spittoons, and a keg of alcohol. Owning a saloon was one of the most profitable professions in the Old West and was considered to be highly respectable.

The saloon often served as the hub of an infant town. On a few occasions, however, the process happened in reverse. The town of Arland, Wyoming, for example, was established specifically to supply local cowboys with whiskey and women. The entire town consisted of a dance-hall, a brothel, a store, and the local post office.[2]

Economy, speed, and simplicity often marked early drinking establishments. In the proprietor's haste to start serving eager customers, the bar might be a makeshift affair consisting of a rough-sawn board thrown across two whiskey barrels or beer kegs. The men in mining and logging camps were often so impatient to drink that the tin cups or mugs used to serve the local brew were constantly in use with no time to wash them between customers. Luckily the alcohol in whiskey had some antiseptic properties that cut down on the spread of germs between drinkers. Non-drinkers, or those who might have taken a temperance pledge, could order ginger-ale, non-alcoholic ginger beer, lemonade, sarsaparilla, mineral water, soda water, or other non-alcoholic beverages.

Many early Western saloons were constructed with a wooden floor and partial wooden walls, perhaps three or four feet high, with a canvas tent stretched over the top. These structures were not very substantial, and strong winds or heavy snows could cause them to collapse. Early saloon buildings were often put together so rapidly that daylight could be seen through the cracks in the walls.

A typical permanent saloon in an early frontier town in the West was a narrow, deep, log building with a long wooden bar that stretched from

Reformers who wanted to abolish the old-time saloons claimed that, among other undesirable features, they were hotbeds of crime and the hangouts of criminals. To some extent this was true. In the forefront is Jefferson Randolph "Soapy" Smith, a dedicated con man and gang leader at his headquarters in a saloon in Skagway, Alaska. Smith met an untimely demise in 1898 at the hands of city engineer Frank Reid when Smith's myriad gang activities became too much for the local citizens (Library of Congress).

front to back along one of the longer side-walls. The interior of the building typically consisted of a large, open, low-roofed room that ranged in size from fifteen feet wide by thirty feet deep to perhaps thirty feet wide and eighty feet deep. The first saloon in Deadwood, South Dakota, was a fourteen by twenty–foot log building located on Main Street.

The floor might be hard-packed dirt and the walls unfinished logs. The swinging batwing doors popularized by the movies were not in general use in most Western saloons, particularly in the cold climates of the mountains of the West or the Pacific Northwest, where there was a need to keep the heat inside. Standard double doors were more common, though sometimes they were never closed, such as in some Kansas towns during the cattle-shipping season. Batwing doors were, however, sometimes mounted inside the regular doors to block the view of the inside of the saloon and its activities from respectable town residents passing by on the street.

As the early towns matured, saloons quickly added gambling in order to provide entertainment for patrons between drinks. Gambling was always a popular activity and it substantially increased the saloon's profits. Most saloons offered games such as poker, faro, keno, three-card monte, and various dice games. Some games were friendly, others were more serious and could generate hard feelings and turn into fights.

As temporary mining camps matured into established, permanent towns, the early tent saloons made from wood-frame and canvas evolved with the rest of the buildings, and the saloons became permanent structures constructed with logs or rough lumber. If a town lasted long enough and business was good enough, the saloon evolved into a more ornate building with finished boards on the outside. Saloons in two-story wooden buildings were common, and often had false fronts to give them a substantial and imposing air.

But the mission still remained the same. Drinking. One apocryphal story that made the rounds concerned a man with nothing better to do, who watched a teamster unload twenty barrels of whiskey and one sack of flour for a store in Deadwood, South Dakota. The watcher shook his head and asked a fellow lounger what he thought the store was going to do with all that flour.[3]

As saloons became more permanent, the bars themselves became fancier. Early bars made of rough boards evolved into elaborate wooden counters with ornately-carved fittings. Cherrywood, walnut, oak, and mahogany bars were popular. Elaborate back-bars were carved to match the counter, with inset mirrors to store and show off elegant bottles, glasses, and perhaps a few ornaments. The ultimate expression of ornate bars was reached in the late 1800s and building them became a significant industry that employed many skilled craftsmen.

These elaborate bars were very expensive. Back-bars made by the Brunswick Company of Chicago sold for around $500, with the counter in front costing almost as much. As a saloon matured, tables and chairs, and eventually pictures, mirrors, and fancy glassware, were added.

Men at the bar drank while standing up in front of it. There were no bar stools, though most saloons featured a brass rail that ran along the front of the counter for patrons to rest a foot while drinking. Towels were usually hung every few feet along the front of the bar counter, so that patrons with moustaches could wipe off any foam from their beer. Needless to say, this communal practice contributed to the spread of many infectious diseases, such as tuberculosis and pneumonia, that were prevalent in that era.

Placed at strategic intervals alongside the rail were brass cuspidors; however, photographs of the interiors of early saloons show that the aim of the tobacco-chewing patrons was notoriously inaccurate. Under the influence of alcohol, most men underestimated their ability to aim, plus their ability to judge long-range accuracy. To counteract the many misses, the floor was often liberally sprinkled with sawdust to soak up drips, foam, and spills from beer glasses, as well as dropped food, poorly-aimed tobacco juice, and anything else that might end up on the floor. Even when dirt floors were replaced by plank construction, sawdust was still spread on the boards to soak up beer, tobacco spit, and other debris.

The selection of drinks in early tent saloons was usually limited. Often the only choice was whiskey ladled into unwashed tin cups out of a nearby barrel. Beer was very popular with men, but was slower to arrive in many early towns because of the difficulty and expense of freighting it across the West. Beer was too bulky, fragile, and inexpensive to be shipped for great distances until the arrival of the railroad provided cheap freight rates. To solve this problem, enterprising businessmen usually started a brewery soon after permanent structures were erected in town and made beer locally. San Francisco had a brewery by 1850 and Denver had one as early as 1859.

The exterior appearance of a saloon depended on the building materials that were available locally. At a mining or logging camp where trees were readily available, early saloons were typically a low-roofed, dark, log-walled building. On the plains of the Midwest, where trees and wood were scarce, the saloon might be a dug-out with sod walls and a sod roof. In the desert Southwest, the walls might be adobe, stone, or mud and brick.

The dark, gloomy inside of a saloon was dimly lit by oil lamps that hung from the ceiling and gave off black soot-filled smoke and greasy fumes. The patron entering one of these establishments was greeted with a characteristic aroma that was a combination of unwashed customers, stale beer, coal oil fumes, and the smell of strong tobacco.

## The Saloon as a Social Center

During the early development of a town in the West, the sawdust on the floor might also double as bedding. Because there was typically a shortage of housing as a new town boomed, saloon tables and floors were often rented out after closing hours to new arrivals or transients. The typical charge was twenty-five cents a night for accommodations on the floor, and a dollar to sleep in a chair. The more advanced saloons chalked off spaces on the floor in order to more efficiently pack additional patrons into the available space. The practice of sleeping on the floor, coupled with the unsanitary habit of patrons spitting on the floor or at the stove to hear the sizzle, was a cause of the rapid spread of various lung diseases, such as tuberculosis, among many of the new arrivals.

As the entertainment center for early towns, the saloon was a place where a man could have a drink, relax among friends, play a friendly game of cards, and conduct his business. Some saloons incorporated a post office, or at least offered mail boxes where customers could receive and send letters. There might be a bulletin board, where "help wanted" or "for sale" notices were posted. Medical emergencies, such as a gunshot wound or a broken bone, might be treated while the patient lay on a gaming table after swigging whiskey from the bar to serve as a crude anesthetic.

The saloon was also the information center of a town. This was usually accomplished by word of mouth in the form of gossip, but the saloon might have copies of the local newspaper, if one was available, which might appear only weekly.

If there was no bank yet in a fledgling town, a saloon might have a safe that could be used for protection of customer valuables. This might be done as a favor to the customers, or in some cases, for a small fee. The saloonkeeper might be the only source of a short-term loan for someone needing to pay off debt or finance a loan to tide a person over until the end of the month. These services were not totally altruistic, as the saloon-keeper figured that customers with available money were likely to spend some of it in his saloon.

In an infant town there was usually no church building, so preachers often temporarily used saloons for religious meetings. Before permanent churches were established in the West, the religious needs of many of the early frontier communities were served by itinerant preachers who rode from camp to camp by stagecoach or on horseback, stopping to preach and take up a collection at each settlement. When a preacher came to town, drinking was temporarily suspended and the gambling tables were discreetly covered up during the services. Many saloon-owners felt that it was their civic duty to allow the use of their buildings as makeshift churches, and they were pragmatic enough to know that after listening to a fiery preacher for an hour or two, the audience usually had parched throats that needed to be wetted. After the preacher left, the gaming tables and paintings on the wall were uncovered again, and the saloon continued the business of offering excitement, recreation, and relaxation for hard-working young bachelors.

In addition to filling the obvious roles of a drinking and gambling establishment, saloons often served other functions in a newly-founded town. They were used as meeting halls, trading posts, employment agencies, courtrooms, temporary mortuaries, post offices, for political campaigning, and as hotels. Saloons and their bartenders were gossip centers for the latest news or the newest joke making the rounds.

Some saloons featured a barber or bath facilities at the back of the building. The arrangement was such that customers who stopped in for a shave, a haircut, or a bath had to pass the bar and might be tempted to have a quick beer on the way to the back. Also, customers who publicly denied drinking could go in for a haircut and down a few quick drinks at the same time. Another hypocritical aspect of the saloon that was aimed at closet drinkers was that some accommodating bartenders would sell small bottles of whiskey labeled "medicine" to those who did not want it publicly known that they drank.

The other feature of saloons that was objectionable to reformers was the employment of women in various capacities. These women were not necessarily prostitutes. They might serve only as waitresses, dancers, or entertainers. Their primary purpose was to hustle drinks, and most of them did not routinely offer sexual services. Some of the women were married and trying to make ends meet while their husbands worked as cowboys, miners, or loggers. Some were widows trying to support themselves. Some were young and unmarried, and could find no other type of employment. The primary function of these women was to smile at the customers, to talk or dance with them, and to flirt with them, while constantly trying to sell them more and more drinks.

Many of these women, however, were indeed prostitutes who were either employed by the saloon or used the saloon as a place to meet potential customers. If a man needed additional persuasion, dancing with a woman might decide the issue. From the customer's viewpoint, dancing with these bar girls was often the only way that a lonely bachelor could put his arms around a woman.

As well as the basic necessities from the customer's viewpoint of drinking, gambling, and the availability of women, an enterprising saloon owner might stage other masculine entertainment to draw in customers. Cock fights and dog fights might be arranged as special events, along with wrestling matches, boxing bouts between bare-knuckled pugilists, and any other event that the saloon owner thought would attract customers, such as plank-walking contests, temperance lectures, minstrel shows, and bear-baiting.

## The Saloon as an Economic Force

Even when saloons were considered to be a bad influence on the male portion of the population, they were often tolerated because of their economic influence and benefits for a town.

As immigrants surged westwards to populate the prairies, deserts, and mountains, drinking, the number of drinkers, and the number of saloons proliferated. In a booming town in the West there always seemed to be room for another saloon, and the measure of a town's success and wealth was usually judged by its number of saloons. The faster saloons were established, the more successful a town was considered to be. Most early towns were proud of their saloons. Contemporary guide books often listed the number of saloons in a town as an indicator of the community's success, along with information about churches, hotels, and banks.

By 1859, just a year after its formal founding, Denver had thirty-one saloons and dancehalls. By 1860 Denver's saloons had grown to thirty-five and the population to 4,749.[4] Minot, South Dakota, had twelve saloons by the time it was only a few weeks old. In 1881, the rowdy silver-mining town of Kokomo, Colorado, had a hundred saloons along its main street. In Colorado, in June of 1879, the Leadville *Daily Chronicle* reported that the town, which soon gained (and probably deserved) its reputation as the most wide-open boom town on the Rocky Mountain mining frontier, proudly boasted 10 dry goods stores, 4 banks, 31 restaurants, and 4 churches, along with 120 saloons, 19 beer halls, and 118 gambling halls. At the end of 1880, Leadville had 249 saloons, which made up the third largest type of business after mining and banking. One single block on West Second Street in Leadville, which was known to the locals as "whiskey row," had twenty-four buildings on one side. Fourteen of them were saloons.

By 1867, the rowdy town of Hays City, Kansas, had twenty-two saloons and three dance halls, along with one grocery store and one clothing store.[5] Bodie, California, founded as a gold-mining town in 1860, had 15,000 residents by 1870, consisting mostly of thirsty miners who were served by three breweries and thirty-five saloons that were open around the clock. A year after its founding, Sawtooth, Idaho, had forty-one retail stores, of which twenty were barrooms.[6] Deadwood, South Dakota, had seventy-five saloons by 1877.[7] Lake City, Colorado, founded in 1875, had twenty-nine establishments selling liquor by July of 1877.[8]

In 1876, Dodge City, Kansas, had nineteen establishments selling liquor. In all fairness, though, this many were needed during the summer and fall months when the ranks of the town's 1,200 permanent inhabitants were swelled by hundreds of transient cowboys and cattle buyers, along with the professional gamblers and prostitutes who flocked in to grab their share of all the cattle money floating around.

Most cattle towns during the boom days of the great cattle drives had twice as many saloons as other businesses. Not many were of the Hollywood variety with ornate bars with a mirrored back-bar and beautiful saloon girls in short skirts and with bare arms. Most saloons were long, narrow rooms poorly lit by smoky oil lamps, with a small and simple bar, and a few tables and chairs. They smelled of tobacco, stale beer, horse manure, sweat, and kerosene.[9] In winter, cowboys lounging around with nothing to do amused themselves by spitting at the stove to hear the crackling noise it made when their aim was successful.

In 1853, the young town of San Francisco had 537 saloons. By 1890, this had increased to an amazing 3,117 licensed establishments selling beer and whiskey.[10] In 1883, a year after its founding, Livingston, Montana, had a population of 3,000 and thirty-three saloons.[11] By 1900 the Colorado gold mining town of Cripple Creek had seventy saloons, many of them on Myers Avenue, alongside the cribs and brothels of the red-light district.

License fees and fines on these many saloons, gambling houses, dance halls, and brothels by a town's courts was a dependable source of public income. Leadville, Colorado, derived about two-thirds of its municipal revenue from saloon fees during its early years. By 1875 the city was collecting about $35,000 a year in liquor license fees.[12] Silverton, Colorado, relied on liquor licenses for about 90 percent of the city income. Thus, when Victorian moralists wanted to close the saloons and brothels in order to protect the values of their homes and churches and to maintain a civilized town, this created a dilemma for many city fathers. Growing towns wanted, and needed, the fees, fines, and taxes that came in from the saloons, the saloon-owners wanted the profits that they made from drinkers and those seeking female companionship, and town boosters wanted a vigorous local economy.

## Hell-on-Wheels Towns

Some of the worst saloons in the West were to be found in the so-called "hell-on-wheels" towns. These were temporary mobile construction camps that were built to house and feed railroad workers for the Union Pacific Railroad during construction of the eastern section of the transcontinental railroad. The popular name of "hell-on-wheels" referred to the fact that sometimes the shacks were mounted on wagons or railroad flatcars for the ultimate in portability

When President Lincoln authorized the building of a transcontinental railroad in 1862, the final contracts for construction went to the Union Pacific Railroad and the Central Pacific Railroad. The Central Pacific started building eastward from Sacramento in January of 1863, while the Union Pacific started westward from Omaha, Nebraska, in December 1863. The two railroads finally joined at Promontory Point, Utah, in 1869.

Railroad construction on the eastern side of the mountains spawned many short-lived boom-towns that provided diversion and entertainment for the railroad workers in the form of women, drink, and gambling. As the railroad tracks pushed their way westwards from Omaha, temporary construction camps followed to house and feed the workers. As the tracks advanced, these camps were periodically torn down and re-built at a new location a few miles further down the track. Temporary railroad saloons might consist of a wooden platform for the floor, board walls three or four feet high around the sides, and then heavy tent canvas supported by a rough wooden framework for the roof and upper walls.

Many of the "buildings" were tent structures for maximum portability, because the entire town was expected to last for only a few weeks, or at the most, a few months. When a particular section of track was finished, and the construction camp moved on, the associated town packed up the tents, disassembled the shacks, and followed the rails to start again at the new end-of-track. Because the temporary towns consisted mostly of tents and wagons, they were called "moving towns." These temporary towns ballooned rapidly from nothing to entertain the railroad workers, then disappeared into nothing just as fast when the end of the tracks moved further west and the next hell-on-wheels town was erected.

The principal amusements for the inhabitants of these temporary boom towns were brawling, getting drunk, fraternizing with saloon women, gambling, and generally raising hell. Saloons and brothels were the mainstays of the hell-on-wheels towns, and so they attracted gamblers, saloonkeepers, thieves, con-men, pimps, and prostitutes. Every sort of vice was available around the clock and was freely used to separate the tough railroad laborers from their pay as fast and thoroughly as possible.

As the Union Pacific pushed its rails to the west, temporary end-of-the-track towns sprang to life every sixty miles or so, mushroomed, and then disappeared when the forefront of the railroad moved on. Kearney and North Platte in Nebraska, Julesburg in Colorado, and Cheyenne, Laramie, and Green River in Wyoming were some of the toughest and wildest hell-on-wheels towns in the West. These were not necessarily small camps. Julesburg in 1867, for example, had nearly 2,000 temporary inhabitants. In a similar manner, the Kansas and Texas Railway (affectionately known to locals as "The Katy") spawned the towns of Denison in Texas, Muskogee in Oklahoma, and Coffeyville and Parsons in Kansas, all of which were noted for brawling, gambling, boozing, wild women, and frequent homicides.

The town of North Platte mushroomed from essentially nothing to 5,000 inhabitants during the winter of 1866–67. The "town" consisted of a collection of canvas tents housing gambling dens, places of prostitution, saloons taverns, and dance halls. Whiskey flowed like water and crime was rampant. Fights and murders were common, even during broad daylight, and nearly all the men carried weapons. The death rate was reported to be as high as a murder every day.

Interestingly, on the other side of the mountains, where the Central Pacific Railroad struggled over the rugged Sierra Nevada range and the deserts of Nevada, hell-on-wheels towns were not a problem. Part of the reason was that the construction supervisor for the Central Pacific, James Strobridge, would not tolerate prostitutes, gamblers, whiskey, and the other vices that followed the Union Pacific. It was also due to a lack of available white laborers. The Central Pacific used many Chinese workers who worked hard and did not have much use for bad whiskey and bad women. Besides, much of their wages went to pay off the exorbitant fees on loans that they had contracted to travel to the United States. Many of them saved the rest of their money hoping to eventually return to their homeland, buy their own farms, and settle down.

## Saloon Art

Saloon owners and bartenders soon found that customers needed something to look at while drinking. As a result, the interior walls of saloons were usually decorated with a variety of ornaments and pictures, all of them intended to appeal to male tastes and make the men feel at home while they drank. Popular subjects for saloon art were stuffed animal heads with trophy horns or antlers, mounted birds and fish, pictures of contemporary sports figures, seafaring scenes, horse racing, and portraits of American presidents.

One of the most popular pictures found over bars was one of several variations of General George Armstrong Custer's defeat with the Seventh Cavalry at the Battle of the Little Bighorn in 1876. One very popular version was a huge lithograph by F. Otto Becker, based on Cassily Adam's painting of *Custer's Last Fight*. The lithograph was commissioned in 1896 by the Anheuser-Busch Brewing Association of St. Louis, Missouri, who distributed 150,000 copies to saloons around the country.

But by far the most widespread and popular type of saloon art in these male gathering places was the bar-room nude. Despite popular perception, however, these pictures were not lewd or obscene, but were intended to be artistic. Popular images were larger-than-life paintings in elaborate gold frames of standing or reclining nudes, usually gazing off into space. Most of these oversized pictures showed the Victorian ideal of the feminine nude figure, though discreetly draped in the right places, showing a large expanse of voluptuous bosom and beefy thigh. The Victorian male's tastes typically ran to plump feminine figures with large bosoms, tiny waists, and rather large hips. Contemporary men considered Victorian women to have ideal forms when they weighed 160 or 170 pounds in an age where women were typically only five foot three or four inches tall.

To lend an air of respectability, many of the nude paintings had a classical theme from the literary or art world, using subjects such as Diana, Venus, Psyche, or Cleopatra, that reflected the Victorian fascination with the Greek and Roman classical period. Popular scenes were *Diana in the Bath*, *Venus Surprised* (or conversely *Venus in the Bath* and *Diana Surprised* for variety), *The Bath of Psyche*, *Venus Dressing at the Bath*, *Venus Disrobing for the Bath*, and *Cleopatra at the Bath*. These paintings showed a well-endowed, semi-clad or nude young woman ready to take a bath, preparing for a nap, undressing for bed, or reclining on a couch, bed, or similar piece of furniture. The artists portrayed partial nudity, but with innocence and modesty, thus producing art for the Victorian viewer that was not considered to be pornographic, but placed these women on an imaginary pedestal, in harmony with the Victorian view of women. These paintings were often placed behind the bar so that a customer could discreetly ogle them while tipping back his glass.

## The Saloon Becomes a Target

As a town reached maturity, however, and took on an air of respectability, the earlier open attitude towards saloons usually changed. The same saloons that had served an important social and economic function in the early days of a town's development were looked down upon by married women and reformers, who tried to sweep saloons, dance halls, gambling dens, brothels, and similar places from the community.

By the end of the century, as the functions and activities in saloons were changing, the name "saloon" itself became associated with vice and drunkenness, and the institution of the saloon became the target of reformers and temperance crusaders. As saloons went into a downhill spiral and became increasingly seedier, they tended to be located in poorer working-class and immigrant neighborhoods and red-light districts, areas of town that were often associated with high crime rates.

Saloons sprang up everywhere. The prime location for the owner was on a busy street corner where the building would be highly visible and could attract customers from two streets at the same time. Another prime location was near the entrance to a factory or other similar workplace where workers could drop in and cash their paychecks and have a drink on the way home.

To enthusiasts of the Temperance Movement, all these features of saloons were highly undesirable and needed to go. And admittedly most later saloons tended towards being low-class dives. Mabel Barbee Lee described her impression of the mining town of Cripple Creek when she first arrived there as a young girl with her mother. They arrived at a hotel on Myers Avenue (the red-light district) on the stagecoach at midnight during the boom days of gold mining in the 1890s. As Lee recalled, "The street was crowded with men and out of the uproar of yowling dogs and pistol shots we heard yells of 'Hello Sucker!' and 'Ah there, Yokels!' and 'Welcome, Tenderfeet!'"[13]

Logging towns such as Seattle and Portland, Oregon, also had their seedy skid rows, which were districts of cheap saloons and flophouses frequented by alcoholics. The name skid row originated in "skid road," which was a greased road or path down which logs were dragged to the sawmill by mules or oxen from where the trees were felled. Many logging towns grew up around a sawmill, often along the skid road to the mill, hence the term "skid road" came to refer to the brightly-lit section of town that was lined with saloons, gambling houses, dance-halls, and brothels. Eventually "skid road" was corrupted to become "skid row." This was an area of low-class saloons, where patrons were likely to spit on the stove, lie down on the floor, or collapse drunk in a corner. Some skid row saloons had a back room with no furniture where patrons too drunk to walk home could be laid out in rows on the floor to sleep it off until they were sober.

Due to the association of saloons with loose women, the Temperance Movement considered alcohol and prostitution to be two related evils. And, admittedly, reformers were correct when they claimed that a lack of family and the atmosphere of a stable community led to a lack of restraint in these matters in a working population that was generally dominated by young single males.

The atmosphere of noise and confusion that was associated with the saloon became offensive to reformers. Shouts, cries, screams, laughter, and curses from drunken revelers blended together and filled the air. Chestnut Street, in the boom town of Leadville, Colorado, boasted establishments such as the Keystone Saloon and the Theatre Comique. Here the atmosphere was so frenzied that customers on the main floor might find themselves being pelted by food and liquor bottles thrown by drunken patrons up in the balcony.

Eventually the name saloon came to be associated with vice, dirty patrons, filthy premises, and falling-over drunkenness. As an indication of how the general population looked on saloons, they were also known as watering troughs, bughouses, shebangs, cantinas, and gin mills. The inside atmosphere was made worse by the fact that there was a certain etiquette to drinking in the West. The drinker was expected to toss back his whiskey quickly, because nursing drinks was not considered to be the accepted practice for wetting one's whistle. In addition, being treated to a drink by a fellow-drinker meant that the recipient had to buy one in return, and all

This "Close the Saloons" poster appeared in 1918 when the final push by reformers and the anti-liquor lobby was underway to abolish drinking in the United States. Though many tactics were used with the intent of eventually banning alcohol, most of the efforts of reformers concentrated on the purported evils of the saloon and their goal of eliminating the perceived dual evils of drinking and prostitution (National Archives).

drinkers were expected to buy their fellow-drinkers a round from time to time. The practice of "treating" one another to drinks was of course, encouraged by the saloon-owner. Bartenders would even occasionally set up a free round to get the patrons started. They knew that the drinkers would then feel obligated to treat each other, thus substantially increasing the sales of whiskey. This practice promoted almost continuous guzzling and intoxication.

Author Mark Twain once commented that "Sometimes too much drink is barely enough." Drinking was so commonplace in the West that how much alcohol was too much was relative and was a matter of opinion. In most towns of the Old West, "drunk and disorderly" was the commonest crime that most law officers had to deal with. Heavy drinking was thought to be an expression of manliness and males were expected to assert their manhood by showing that they could drink to excess with the best of them.

Though saloons were often the center of social life in early communities during the settling of the West, they were not without opposition. However, because of the importance of the social and economic aspects of saloons, the temperance movement did not make much progress in the West until near the end of the 1800s, when settlement of much of the West was shifting from a population of predominantly young single working men to older men with wives and families.

Though the liquor and women of easy virtue found in the saloons were popular with many of the single men of the West, such as cowboys, railroad workers, miners, fishermen, and loggers, they were not always accepted by respectable women, and temperance workers soon banded together to try and save the men from themselves, lumping alcohol and prostitution together as two interrelated evils. Reformers felt that the lack of family and community provided an atmosphere that led to a lack of restraint in a population dominated by young single males.

Moral reformers used Prohibition as part of their attempts to suppress anything that was perceived as contributing to immorality. For example, histories were collected by social workers from fallen girls whose ruin was summed up in the concept, "I had a few drinks, then I don't remember what happened next." In another tactic, Horace Greeley's *New York Tribune* warned mothers against the sinister dangers of their daughters eating "...ice cream drugged with passion-exciting vanilla."[14] In hindsight, these fears, however, seem a little simplistic, and it was easy and popular to blame liquor for the natural urges of young single people.

Another aspect of the saloons in the West that was considered to be a bad influence was the violence that was associated with them. Though reports of violence in cattle towns has been greatly exaggerated, occasional violence certainly erupted from the saloons, most of it resulting from drink. The saloons, gambling dens, and brothels of the cattle towns were overrun with young men who were adventuresome, aggressive, and thought themselves to be tough, a combination that led to frequent barroom brawls and drunken shootouts. A newspaper reporter visiting Ellsworth, Kansas, in 1872 wrote this description of an incident he saw. "Last Saturday evening about seven o'clock as I was walking down the street from supper, I heard three shots fired and saw a man rush out of a saloon and up the street with a six-shooter in each hand, he ran about half a block and fell, but immediately got up and went into another saloon; shortly after he entered two more shots were fired."[15]

Moral reformers claimed that saloons were associated with disorder, fights, violence, assaults, homicides, gambling, prostitution, and other crimes, though their reports of saloon crime were probably exaggerated by the machinery of propaganda. Criminal rings for fencing stolen goods and con games were prevalent. Other, more minor, disruptions were shooting at the ceiling, loud singing, and generally disturbing the peace. This was pretty much true around the West.

These aspects of the saloon were seen as threatening the family, and being contrary to the Victorian values of self-discipline, upright behavior, sexual restraint, community stability, and a stable home. On the contrary, the saloon was seen as a symbol of permissiveness, self-indulgence, and loose women who served to tempt young men, husbands, and fathers into immoral ways.

By the end of the century, as the function of the saloon had changed from a social meeting place into a place for heavy drinking and associating with prostitutes, the name "saloon" was associated with vice and drunkenness, and the institution of the saloon was the target of reformers and temperance crusaders. The reformers' obvious solution was to eliminate the saloon and restore the old values.

What started out with social concerns about the harmful effects of whiskey on the working man in the 1850s and the drive to close the traditional old-time saloons festered through the last half of the century, culminating in the early part of the twentieth century with National Prohibition.

# 2

# The Pathway to Prohibition

THOUGH THE WORD PROHIBITION is traditionally linked to the time period between 1920 and 1933 when the saloons were closed and alcoholic drinks could not be legally obtained in the United States, attempts to ban liquor had a history that preceded it by almost 200 years.

## Early Experiments with Prohibition

During the 1660s Massachusetts passed legislation that closed taverns on the Sabbath. However, a provision was included that the "faint and sick" could be served medicinal liquor at any time of any day, with the result that alcoholics who craved a drink on Sundays often felt a sudden attack of faintness and sickness overcoming them.[1]

Serious attempts to limit drinking were made as far back as the 1700s, but resentment among the masses was stronger than the authorities' ability to regulate the use of alcohol, so these efforts were generally abandoned. In 1733, the governor of Georgia, Gen. James Edward Oglethorpe, alarmed by what he saw as the excessive use of brandy and rum, made the first attempt to enforce total prohibition when he told colonists that the manufacture and importation of "ardent spirits" would not be permitted. His reasoning was that because many of the colony's inhabitants came from English debtors prison, cutting off temptation by cutting off liquor would help them make a fresh start in the new world.

Idealistic though he may have been, Oglethorpe's good intentions backfired. The settlers paid no attention to the ban that said they couldn't purchase alcohol and instead they started to make their own rum from molasses. Stills to make moonshine were set up in hidden places all over the colony to produce local liquor. In addition, rumrunners transported rum and brandy from South Carolina in boats that were unloaded by armed bootleggers who sold the alcohol in local towns and villages. Drinking places that were the equivalent of the later speakeasy sprang up in private homes, in the backs of stores, and in small buildings on the edges of settlements. Because almost everyone was breaking the law and there was no police force to enforce Oglethorpe's announcement, he finally repealed his proclamation. Thus this first attempt at prohibition in America was a failure.[2]

The British colony in Georgia experimented again with prohibition from 1735 to 1742. Due to the perceived poor condition of the colony, the British Parliament passed an Act in 1734, that went into effect in 1735, prohibiting the importation of rum and brandy into Georgia. Deprived of their sources of legal and illegal spirits, the settlers again settled down to devote themselves to making their own liquor. As a result, drunkenness increased and the colonists did indeed start to neglect the upkeep of the colony.

Though Colonial Americans, regardless of gender, age, class, or geographical region, drank large amounts of beer, wine, brandy, gin, and corn whiskey, their favorite distilled spirit was rum. As with later National Prohibition in the 1920s, the officials of the Georgia colony were unable to stem the flow of liquor. In addition, accusations were made that some of the local authorities were making a profit from the illegal liquor. So in 1742 the trustees of the colony reversed direction, abandoned prohibition, permitted the importation of spirits, and instituted licensing for taverns. Rumrunners, bootleggers, and speakeasies disappeared, and the colony began to prosper under the rum trade.

By the mid–1700s some of the dominant religious groups in the other new colonies started to discipline their members for drunkenness. No particular lasting action resulted from this, however, and many church members continued to drink.[3] By 1763 rum was pouring from 159 commercial distilleries in New England alone. In 1792 there were 2,579 registered distilleries in the United States.[4]

After the Revolutionary War (1775 to 1783), moral watchdogs among the elite promoted the idea that in order to be successful in life, the common masses needed to have self-discipline and restraint in their drinking habits. The concept of enjoying too much pleasure was not acceptable to reformers, so the idea of temperance seemed perfect for the cause. National groups, such as the Society for the Promotion of Morals and the Society for the Suppression of Intemperance, sprang into existence, along with various temperance groups at the local level.

The excessive use of whiskey was equated by reformers as being associated with idleness, lying, and fraud. It was also connected with swearing, quarreling, fighting, obscenity, and loose morals. And indeed it was true that even in moderate quantities, whiskey lowered a drinker's sense of good judgment, concentration, and insight, and made many drinkers excitable, impulsive, argumentative, and belligerent.

As a result of heavy drinking, the incidence of alcoholism among men was high. The more severe cases included hallucinations, delusions, and the visible tremors of *delirium tremens*. Known also as "the DTs," the "jimjams," "the rams," "the jitters," and "the horrors," the DTs manifested itself in trembling hands and legs, sweating, and hallucinations. The victim imagined that snakes or spiders were crawling all over him and he shook constantly as he tried to fight them off. Not as visible, but still major elements of the medical side of alcoholism, was the internal damage of cirrhosis of the liver, kidney deterioration, and the dulling of mental capacity.

In the early 1800s further concerns were raised about increasing levels of consumption of drink, along with fears that the United States was becoming a nation of drunkards. Certainly, excessive use of alcohol was bad for the drinker's health and well-being. Its abuse affected personal relationships and family life, and reflected poorly on the drunkard's social standing. As a result, alcohol became the subject of contention. On one side were the "wets," who enjoyed drinking. On the other were the "drys," who constantly sought to prohibit drinking and ban all alcohol.

The initial American Temperance Movement was directed primarily against distilled spirits, and not against beer and wine. The effects of distilled spirits were considered to be intemperance, vice, and disease, and liquor was blamed as the cause for "puking, tremors, and death," along with idleness, swearing, murder, and obscenity. To some extent this was true. Consumption of liquor had increased through the 1700s and, by the 1820s, liquor was so freely available that it was less expensive than tea.[5] This excessive drinking in turn led to a developing awareness of the problems of drunkenness. Moderate drinking was acceptable, but outright drunkenness was not. One punishment was that an unrepentant drunk might be locked in the local stocks and pelted with horse manure.[6]

The initial meaning of "temperance" was to practice moderation in the quantity of drink and self-restraint in drinking. But the initial intent and goals of the Temperance Movement soon underwent change and the movement started to promote the total prohibition of alcohol. During the 1820s and 1830s evangelical preachers vehemently condemned sin, much of which was considered to be drinking or that which occurred as a result of drinking. "Temperance" became "Prohibition." For example, the local temperance society at Laingsburg, Michigan, originally required a pledge that members would agree to only moderate drinking. In 1826 a new pledge calling for total abstinence was forced on the group by those who were in favor of no drinking at all.

Prohibitionists were of the opinion that any alcohol was detrimental to mental health and good physical condition, and felt that completely outlawing the manufacture and consumption of alcohol would improve American society. The American Temperance Society (ATS), for example, founded in 1826, was mainly responsible for the first Temperance Movement and served as a model for many later groups. By 1835 the ATS had reached 1.5 million members. By 1836, the ATS had changed its definition of temperance to total abstinence.[7]

Though heavy drinking was an acceptable form of recreation for the male segment of the population, heavy drinking among women was not considered to be acceptable and carried a social stigma. Women who drank were suspect and unfairly targeted by that portion of the population obsessed with the morals of others. A tract from the National Temperance Society stated that moderate drinking "is a mighty strengthener of lawless desire in man, and a great weakener of the resisting power of women."[8]

The early 1830s were a time of expansion of temperance groups that were working towards the outright prohibition of alcohol. Members "took the pledge," swearing to abstain from alcohol. The members were characterized on the membership lists as O.P. or Old Pledge, or T for total abstinence. In time this notation spread.[9] Drys, who numbered about 1.5 million in 1830, wrote the letter "T" for total abstinence next to their names on the membership rolls of temperance societies, thus creating their name of "teetotaler."[10]

By the mid–1800s, temperance groups were rapidly trying to move America along a pathway towards virtue through abstinence for everybody and many more anti-drink groups sprang up. In less than fifty years the view of whiskey was transformed from a healthy drink into an invention of the devil and the alleged cause of every known disease. By 1850, the Sons of Temperance had enrolled 230,000 members. As a result of the efforts of temperance groups like this, by 1855 thirteen states and territories had banned the sale and manufacture of alcohol.

A bill forbidding the sales of all liquors was passed in Georgia in 1846. However it was so weakened by amendments that the end result was that wholesalers and importers could continue to operate as long as they sold no less than twenty-eight gallons of alcohol in each transaction. The rationale was that it would be financially and physically burdensome if a casual buyer had to purchase and carry away all this liquor at one time. Thus this law attempted to restrict the sale of alcohol rather than prohibit it. Meanwhile, medicinal and industrial alcohol continued to be sold.[11]

In 1846 the legislature of Maine passed statewide prohibitory laws after a businessman from Portland, Maine, and his wife collected 40,000 signatures on a petition to create an *Act for the Suppression of Drinking*

*Houses and Tippling Shops.*[12] Liquor sellers, however, soon found various ways to circumvent the law. Bootleggers sold individual drinks from a flask carried in the tops of their boots, and liquor was smuggled into town in cases of crockery, dry goods, and other lawful merchandise.

One method of obtaining a drink was that the potential drinker paid a fee for admission to an empty room. Inset into one wall was a small partition on a wheel that revolved. When the wheel was rotated, a glass of rum appeared that had been poured by unseen hands in the room behind. Another method to circumvent the Maine prohibition law was for a saloon to sell a pickle, a slice of cheese, or a soda cracker at an inflated price. The purchase was then accompanied by a free drink. This met the letter of the law because only the actual sale of alcohol was prohibited. Another ingenious scheme to provide liquor involved setting up a display tent where the drinker paid an admission fee to see a pig or some other common farm animal, and then received a drink as part of the admission price.[13]

Between 1851 and 1865, several states declared alcoholic beverages to be illegal. Minnesota, Rhode Island, Massachusetts, and Vermont passed prohibition laws in 1852; Michigan in 1853; Connecticut in 1854; Indiana, Delaware, Iowa, Nebraska, Pennsylvania, New York, and New Hampshire in 1855. In Wisconsin, New Jersey, North Carolina, and Illinois, similar legislation lost by very narrow margins. These victories were a high point for the Temperance Movement, however, and for the next twenty-five years forward progress declined as no other states adopted prohibition.[14]

Not everyone was in favor of prohibition, though, and popular resentment started to change anti-alcohol opinions. As a result, every state except Maine repealed or drastically modified its prohibition laws. Maine re-enacted prohibition in 1858. By then New York, New Jersey, Delaware, the New England states, and several other states had followed Maine.[15] Interestingly—as many of these state laws were found to be unconstitutional, were repealed, or were simply ignored—the overall consumption of alcohol jumped by 63 percent.[16]

Prohibition supporters tried to pass amendments to state constitutions to ban alcohol, rather than creating statutory laws. The reason was that statutory laws could be repealed by the legislature fairly easily, whereas state constitutional amendments were more difficult to repeal and were therefore more likely to remain in force. Statutory law could be changed by succeeding legislatures, depending on the political climate at the time. The statutory law in Massachusetts is a good example. It was enacted in 1852, repealed in 1868, re-enacted in 1869, amended in 1871, further amended in 1872, re-enacted in 1873, and again repealed in 1875. Kansas, on the other hand, adopted a constitutional prohibition amendment in 1880 that prohibited all forms of alcohol for the next sixty-seven years.

SAID PROHIBITION MAINE TO PROHIBITION GEORGIA:
"HERE'S LOOKING AT YOU."

*Puck* magazine poked fun at early prohibition efforts with this satirical cover from 1907 by cartoonist Louis Glackens. These are Prohibition Maine and Prohibition Georgia, with Maine holding a bottle of cold tea and Georgia, a bottle of orange phosphate, a tangy soft drink of the late 1870s. Both have their pockets filled with other half-hidden bottles (Library of Congress).

## The Temperance Cause Grows

When the American Civil War started, many temperance leaders and churches temporarily lost interest in the issues of temperance and moved their efforts to the abolition movement.[17] Though the activities of the temperance groups slowed during the 1860s, the prohibition movement rebounded with renewed energy during the 1870s and 1880s after women became involved on a large scale. As one example, The Sons and Daughters of Temperance was organized in Virginia City, Nevada, in 1863 and met every Monday evening.

The Prohibition Party of the United States was founded in 1869 to promote temperance. Supporters of temperance were known as "white ribboners," because they wore white ribbons to show their loyalty to the Temperance Movement. As one example of the increased interest in prohibition, the residents of Leadville, Colorado, obviously considered their town to have such a drinking problem during the 1870s that they founded the Blue Ribbon Society, the Leadville Temperance Club, the Praying Orchestra, and the Anti-Treat Society.

Many women were attracted to the Temperance Movement because it was linked to the early beginnings of the movement towards women's rights. The original Temperance Movement gradually embraced other social reforms, such as child labor, women's suffrage, and the abolition of slavery.

## The Woman's Christian Temperance Union (WCTU)

Between the Civil War and the turn of the century, various organizations promoted voluntary abstinence from drink. The Midwest was the home of the largest concentration of prohibition supporters.

One of the leading groups that crusaded against saloons was the Woman's Christian Temperance Union (WCTU), which was organized in Cleveland in 1874 as an attempt to bring Protestant churches into the fight to impose prohibition. Within a decade there were branches and meeting rooms of the WCTU in virtually every city and town in the United States.

The individual who worked hardest to move the group forward was Frances Elizabeth Willard. Willard was elected corresponding secretary at the first meeting in 1874 and was elected president in 1879. She held the position until her death in 1898. Under her leadership the WCTU became the most powerful temperance organization in the world. It became a vast anti-liquor propaganda machine and was only surpassed by the later Anti-Saloon League.

During the 1880s, Willard was one of America's best-known women. She lectured extensively, spending much of her time on a grueling schedule of speaking engagements. She somehow also found the time to write books and pamphlets that expounded on the purported evils of alcohol. Due to Willard's efforts, the WCTU rapidly gained in popularity during the 1880s, and by 1890 membership had grown from 27,000 to an estimated 150,000 members in 7,000 branches.[18] By the 1920s the organization was the largest women's organization in the United States.

Some of the WCTU's efforts were unfortunately misguided. In the beginning, the WCTU saw drink as a cause of poverty, but by the late 1880s they began to see drink as the result of poverty rather than the cause. As part of their campaign to promote temperance, the WCTU published various inflammatory pamphlets, such as one that loosely claimed that alcohol was a poison. Many of their publications on the "evils of alcohol" were based more on propaganda than factual information.

Much of the image of the drunkard was, in fact, thinly-veiled propaganda. Temperance supporters loved to promote the sordid image of a drinker's downward spiral into the depths of booze and alcoholic degradation. They loved the concept of the drunken wife-beater, but not that of the hard-working man having a couple of beers for relaxation after a long day's work. The temperance cause wanted drinkers to be roaring drunks and disgusting alcoholics. And indeed, much of the popularity of the Temperance Movement was due to the lurid appeal of the scandalous nature of this propaganda image. Tales of moral wrong-doing added into the mix were often invented, frequently exaggerated, and widely circulated.

The temperance cause received support from various sources. One was anti-alcohol political cartoons in magazines and newspapers of the time. Typical cartoon strips started by showing a well-dressed person sipping a drink. As the cartoon panels progressed, the man became a drunk, a thief, a wife-beater, and maybe all three. By the last of the panels he was depicted as a hopeless alcoholic.

Temperance songs were popular, with people singing the lyrics to ballads such as "Drink Nothing, Boys, But Water," "Father, Bring Home Your Money Tonight," and the "Lament of the Widowed Inebriate." In 1866, songwriter Mrs. Susan Parkhurst wrote a cheerful-sounding song titled "Father's a Drunkard and Mother is Dead." In 1870 she added the heart-rending lament "The Drunkard's Child," in which a child complains to her mother that she is ignored because she is poor and her father drinks.

Temperance promoters frequently traveled the lecture circuit, though the tone of the meetings was often more like vaudeville antics with an actor doing dramatic impersonations, including that of a drunkard suffering the agonies and hallucinations of *delirium tremens*. Audiences loved it.

Under Willard's leadership the direction of the WCTU eventually shifted and the organization lost its focus. Under the guise of the temperance crusade, women added other causes including political lobbying and the vote for women. Willard's added causes promoted women's suffrage, allied the WCTU with political groups and labor unions, and supported Christian Socialism. Among other dislikes, Willard opposed gambling, plural marriage, prostitution, cruelty to animals, and tobacco.[19] The WCTU also became involved in the reform of inmates of jails and asylums, and the rescue of "fallen women." When the WCTU started to support issues that were only remotely connected to drink, such as government control of the railroads, women's rights, a wealth tax, equal pay for women, the anti-tobacco movement, the anti-corset supporters, kindergartens, vegetarianism, and the abolition of lynching, they lost their direction as the primary temperance organization.[20]

## The Anti-Saloon League (ASL)

By the end of the century, temperance groups were pushing efforts towards governmental prohibition of the manufacture and sale of intoxicating beverages through local options and state laws. The primary temperance group that accelerated the process was the Anti-Saloon League. The Anti-Saloon League was formed as a state organization on May 24, 1893, by temperance crusader and Congregational minister Howard Hyde Russell and representatives of the Methodist, Baptist, Congregational, and Presbyterian churches, who met in Oberlin, Ohio.[21] The Anti-Saloon League became a national organization in 1895 and worked to put political power behind the Temperance Movement. To do this, the organization produced and endorsed anti-alcohol candidates who supported its cause and sought to achieve its mission. The Anti-Saloon League was the most efficient of the temperance groups, and became the prime mover of the temperance cause.

Compared to the WCTU, the Anti-Saloon League was single-minded, was not affiliated with any political party, and did not endorse any particular religion. The ASL was purely a political action group made up of influential businessmen. It grew to be the most-successful single-issue organization in American history, because it targeted only the saloon. The League was very active, with a membership that expanded into the millions. Its stated objective was to clean up "drunkenness, gambling, and fornication." In actual practice, their campaign went after drinking, assuming that control of the saloons would lead to control or abolishment of the other two associated problems. The ASL developed the theme that the root of all evil was in drink and that the banning of alcohol would usher in a time of peace, happiness, and universal prosperity.[22]

The ASL clearly understood the power and influence of the printed word and published temperance literature of all kinds. In 1909 the League established its own publishing house and printing plant, turning out a variety of magazines, books, leaflets, tracts, pamphlets, and folders. By 1912 the League had turned out forty tons of material, equivalent to approximately 250 million book pages. The ASL aimed to make the word "saloon" a nasty word in the English language and have it officially banned from the nation's vocabulary. And they were only one part of the anti-liquor propaganda machine that was flooding the country.[23]

The Anti-Saloon League was successfully aligned with the church in the fight against alcohol and called itself "the church in action against the saloon." Wayne B. Wheeler, who had been recruited by Howard Russell to be a district manager for the ASL before going on to become a lawyer and the ASL's general counsel, enlisted the support of America's fundamentalist churches and conservative small-town America. Wheeler was so dedicated to his temperance work that author J.C. Furnas has aptly referred to him as the "Scourge of The Saloon."[24] Wheeler realized that if organized religion could be mobilized in the fight to advance the Temperance Movement, the fanaticism that is often part of the religious temperament could carry them to victory. The League therefore coordinated and centralized the work of the anti-liquor evangelical denominations and temperance organizations and pushed them into politics.[25] Both the clergy and abstainers believed that people needed to be protected against all the forces that undermined their self-control, thus temperance reform came under the umbrella of the evangelical churches.

As general counsel for the Anti-Saloon League, Wayne Bidwell Wheeler, at his desk in 1920, was the most effective campaigner for the passage of the Eighteenth Amendment and was the behind-the-scenes author of the Volstead Act (Library of Congress).

Other attacks on liquor came from the theater, in the form of successful temperance plays such as *The Drunkard; or, The Fallen*

*Saved* and the highly influential temperance play *Ten Nights in a Bar-room*. Both of these plays were strongly supported by the Woman's Christian Temperance Union and the Anti-Saloon League, and they continued to be presented at temperance meetings and in medicine shows until well after the turn of the century.

The aims and efforts of the WCTU became fragmented and supported a variety of causes. The Anti-Saloon League, on the other hand, did not support any other causes or issues, only the abolition of saloons.[26] The Anti-Saloon League worked within the existing system to limit the consumption of alcohol through tactics such as licensing drinking establishments. Their motto was "The Saloon Must Go!" And admittedly, by the time they were a dominant force to be reckoned with, most saloons were not very elegant establishments.

## *The Evangelists*

The medical effects of alcohol on the human body and a drinking individual's economic downfall were not strong religious points for evangelical preachers, so the emphasis on alcohol was transferred to the soul. Liquor became an offense against God. Drunkenness was equated with damnation and a lack of salvation. Intemperance was attacked from the pulpit, particularly by the Methodist and Congregational churches. Fiery fundamentalist preachers threatened drinkers with debility, despair, and eternal damnation. Interestingly, the Baptists were not totally convinced and did not join in. Likewise the early Puritans were heavy drinkers and did not denounce alcohol.[27]

Then as now, sinister generalizations were used to further the cause. A circuit-riding Methodist preacher named James B. Finlay darkly stated without hesitation, "I never knew a man who was in the habit of drinking regularly that did not become a drunkard." This was echoed by Congressman Gerrit Smith from New York who said, "I would that no person were able to drink intoxicating liquors without immediately becoming a drunkard."[28]

An allied widespread Victorian concept was that men were constant infernos of lust that would be exacerbated by liquor and that women had to be protected by self-appointed moral authorities from these dreadful desires brought on by drink. Orson S. Fowler, one of the leading promoters of phrenology, said, "A man or women, be they ever so moral or virtuous, when under the influence of intoxicating drinks, *is of easy virtue*. Before the *first* advantage can be taken of a virtuous woman, she must be partially *intoxicated*, and the advantage can be taken of almost any woman thus stimulated."[29]

The supporters of Prohibition predicted that life would be better without saloons, and banning alcohol would create clean living, family harmony, less crime, and economic prosperity. This message resonated with many people as the 1910s were a time of political and social upheaval and the new deadly horrors of World War I ("The War to End All Wars") with its dreadful new ways of conducting warfare with poison gas and machine guns. Thousands of Americans longed for a return to an older, simpler time when the world seemed to be a safer and more stable place, and morals had been better.[30]

## Liquor and Taxes

The desire by the Temperance Movement to close the saloons put many government officials on the horns of a dilemma. The problem was that liquor provided a large amount of federal and local revenue, and the question was how to make up that potential loss if banning alcohol were to succeed.

The first tax on distilled alcohol was the Excise Act of 1791, known as the "whiskey tax," that was enacted to raise revenue without which the United States would not have been able to maintain an army. The tax was repealed by President Thomas Jefferson in 1802, but a new alcohol tax was imposed in 1814 by James Madison to pay for the war of 1812. This tax was repealed in 1817.

In 1862 President Abraham Lincoln brought back a federal tax on liquor with the Internal Revenue Act, which included a tax on whiskey, to help raise money to pay for the Civil War (1861–1865).[31] This legislation levied a tax of $1 a barrel on beer and 20 cents a gallon on liquor. The tax on beer was doubled in 1864.[32] Up to 25 percent of government revenue came from the liquor trade. During the American Civil War, all the states that had enacted Prohibition, except Maine, repealed their laws because the federal government in the north needed the tax revenues on alcoholic beverages to finance their fight against the south.

By the time the Civil War ended, this tax had become an important source of revenue for the government and this time it was not repealed, but continued for years afterwards. For the next thirty years the tax provided at least 20 percent of federal revenue. In some years, this rose to more than 40 percent. The tax was later doubled to pay for the Spanish-American War. Foreshadowing what would happen again in the future, the temperance crusades of the early 1870s were estimated to have forced 25,000 to 30,000 saloons and 750 breweries out of business throughout the country. As a result, collection of liquor-related taxes by the federal government decreased by nearly $300,000 in Indiana and Ohio alone.[33] The tax also spurred the moonshine business, which was tax-free, because some individuals simply did not want to pay taxes.

By 1910 the federal government was collecting more than $200 million from alcohol taxes. That was 71 percent of the internal revenue and more than 30 percent of total federal revenue.[34] Thus one thorny problem for the supporters of the prohibition movement that was hard to dispute was the valid argument that prohibition of alcohol would mean a serious loss of revenue, as whiskey taxes formed a large part of the government budget. Various government agencies wanted and needed the taxes that came in from saloons and liquor.

Because the shutdown of the alcohol industry would create a serious loss of tax revenue, the solution was to create an income tax to make up for the deficit. This idea had been suggested and supported by the WCTU as early as 1883, therefore the ASL pushed hard for income tax legislation.[35] The concept received the support of Congress, and the Sixteenth Amendment to the Constitution of the United States to create an income tax was ratified on February 3, 1913. With continued funding now assured, legislators who favored prohibition could move ahead with plans for a ban on alcohol.

## The Road to Perdition

By the end of the 1800s, the number of saloons had grown. Indeed, in many towns city blocks in the commercial areas frequently contained multiple saloons, with perhaps one on each corner of a block and two on each side in the middle. Many saloons operated in connection with dance halls, gambling joints, and houses of prostitution. In 1906 the 16,000 inhabitants of Rhyolite, Nevada, were served by forty-five saloons, but only two churches.

As the name "saloon" continued to be associated with vice and drunkenness, the institution of the saloon was the prime target of reformers and temperance crusaders. The Rev. Joseph Cook, who founded St. Mark's Episcopal Church in Cheyenne, Wyoming, said of the seventy saloons in town in 1868, "The wickedness is unimaginable and appalling.... Almost every other house is a drinking saloon, gambling house, restaurant, or bawdy."[36]

Not all saloons were ghastly dens of vice, but they were generally located in the part of town that contained brothels, dance halls, billiard parlors, gambling halls, and opium dens. Thus in the eyes of reformers saloons were lumped together with the rest of them. And nobody could dispute the fact that saloons were associated with sidewalks slippery with beer, unpleasant smells, drunks lurching in and out of the doors, loafers sitting on the sidewalk, and objectionable sounds of cursing and fighting coming from the inside. Respectable women went well out of their way to avoid such places.

The levels of drinking continued to be quite amazing. As early as November of 1864, obviously expecting a hard winter, a wagon train pulled into Denver with a load of 1,600 barrels of whiskey and 2,700 cases of champagne.[37] One liquor wholesaler in Tombstone kept a steady inventory of several hundred barrels of whiskey to ward off any alcoholic emergencies.

A change came when the more recent residents of a town, who had brought their wives and children with them, became concerned with the quality of life in their new home town. Saloons, dance halls, and houses of prostitution did not fit the family man's perception of a decent place to live. Social reformers claimed that saloons were hotbeds of disorder, violence, assaults, homicides, gambling, prostitution, and other crimes. These aspects of the saloon were seen as threatening the family, and being contrary to the Victorian values of self-discipline, upright behavior, sexual restraint, community stability, and a stable home. Due to the close association of saloons with women of dubious reputations, the Temperance Movement considered alcohol and prostitution to be two interrelated evils. Thus Victorian moralists stepped up their efforts to close the saloons in order to protect the inherent values of home and church. The saloon was seen as a symbol of all that served to tempt young men, husbands, and fathers into immoral ways.

The reformers' proposed solution was to eliminate the saloon and restore the old values. Crusaders claimed that the elimination of liquor would make America into a more moral country, with peace, prosperity, and order for everyone. Progressives firmly believed that the elimination of alcohol would also eliminate poverty, crime, immorality, and even insanity, which they blamed on liquor.[38]

Temperance crusaders held meetings during which audiences listened to fervent anti-whiskey speeches. Reformers used every tactic of persuasion and appealed to a person's sense of pity, shame, and protection of the family home. They praised the noble working man who brought home his paycheck, as opposed to the drunkard who cashed his check in the saloon. Then, worked up to an almost religious frenzy by these fiery speakers and anti-liquor songs, the entire group marched to the nearest saloon carrying temperance banners and singing temperance hymns. When they reached the saloon, they sang more hymns and knelt on the boardwalk outside the saloon to pray.

Prohibitionists were so focused on the horrors of drink that they were convinced that any kind of indulgence in alcohol led to problem-drinking and alcoholism. They did not distinguish between moderate drinking and drunkenness. Temperance supporters deliberately focused on the confirmed alcoholic and the self-destructive drinker who had been ruined by alcohol, and insisted on total abstinence.

With overstated hyperbole, the editor of the *Daily Miner's Register* in Central City, Colorado, described the habitual drunkard in this way: "They are the excrescence of society, and like the fungus which fastening itself upon the trunk of a living, thriving tree, must be speedily removed else they will communicate decay and rottenness to every thing with which they come into contact."[39]

Perversely, in the world of the temperance crusader, the moderate drinker was unpopular because he did not fit with the popular drunken image that they wished to promote. The Temperance Movement wanted saloons to be dark, sordid places, full of passed-out drunks. For their purposes, a disagreeable and bestial drunkard with *delirium tremens* who spent all the family money on drink, who constantly threw up in the gutter outside the saloon on his way home, then went home and beat his wife, was a far more popular image than a casual social drinker. The well-dressed businessman having a single relaxing glass of beer or whiskey in a well-lit respectable drinking place after a hard day's work before going home was of no use to their cause. They wanted the obvious disgusting drunk.

The moderate drinker, in reality, was more likely to be a family man who stopped in at the saloon after work and had a social drink or two with his friends in a quiet corner, then went home to his family and children in a relaxed and mildly intoxicated mood. The moderate drinker was a nuisance because he could have a drink and not beat his wife and wreck his home, and end up in a drunkard's grave. With logic that must have been hard to follow even then, the Rev. Eli Meech of Rhode Island concluded that the respectable, moderate drinker did far more than anybody else "to perpetuate the evil of intemperance." With even odder logic, Thomas Grimké of Charleston, South Carolina, said that "Temperate drinkers are the parents of all the drunkards who dishonor and afflict our country."[40] Those moderate drinkers who could take a drink or leave it were a nuisance and had to be persuaded to stop.

Typical of the anti-saloon literature of the time was the book *Inebriety: Its Source, Prevention, and Cure* by Charles Palmer. The books starts with a section titled "Morbid Conditions and Perverted Sensations," which includes mysterious statements such as, "The majority of drinkers are not diseased; there is no inherited diathesis or cachexia responsive to narcotic excitement."[41] Later pages list the ghastly characteristics of different types

HAS SHE A FAIR CHANCE ?

"Our religion demands that every child should have a fair chance for citizenship in the coming Kingdom. Our patriotism demands a saloonless country and a stainless flag."---P. A. Baker, General Superintendent Anti-Saloon League of America.

SERIES G. No. 94.

THE AMERICAN ISSUE PUBLISHING CO.,
Westerville, Ohio.

Titled "The Overshadowing Curse," this type of intimidating propaganda poster was widely used by the Anti-Saloon League to further its prohibition cause. A hairy, evil-looking, threatening hand, with fingernails like talons, is poised menacingly over a child (Library of Congress).

of drinkers that followed the pathway to intemperance. The following is Palmer's stereotypical description of one type of drunkard:

> "The Brutal Criminal Inebriate of Our Cities—In the foreground we have the blackguard drunkard of our streets, big of limb, broad of chest, low of brow, and black of visage; born of the gutters; the braggart and bully of his less offensive neighbors, evil triumph in his eyes; with strong assumption of physical power, but cowardly by instinct; thief and murderer by inherent qualities, and only needing an accident to make either or both; at times politic with the lowest form of animal cunning; the woman-bruiser by nature and nurture; his language as polluted as his mind, which reverences nothing but the brute force which overcomes him; always the concentrated living spawn of the accumulating growth of generations of depravity."[42]

Anti-saloon fever reached its zenith with the turn-of-the-century hatchet-brandishing crusades of Carry Nation, born Carry Amelia Moore in Kentucky in 1846. She came from a curious family. Her mother thought herself to be Queen Victoria, and she had an aunt who believed that she was a weather-vane. Carry herself experienced visions and strange dreams. Though she was fanatically anti-liquor, she also had other targets. She believed in sex education, opposed wife-beating, and championed equal rights for women. On the other hand, she unleashed some of her strongest verbal abuse against tobacco, immodest fashions, kissing, corsets, and fraternal societies.

Her first husband was a heavy drinker and a cigarette smoker. Her second husband, David Nation, received a savage beating at the hands of drunken saloon patrons at the Red Hot Bar in Richmond, Texas, in 1889, and this incident was partly responsible for her anti-liquor fervor. Starting her ax-wielding "hatchetation" career at the age of fifty-four, she campaigned vigorously against "Demon Rum" across the plains of Kansas, trying to save men from the evils of liquor. Almost six feet tall, weighing 175 pounds, and with a formidable appearance, Carry would stride into a saloon in a Kansas town at the head of her crusading ladies and start in on the bottles, windows, mirrors, and pictures of bar-room nudes with her hatchet, destroying whatever she could reach. These tactics became too extreme for many temperance supporters and even the WCTU felt that they could not endorse her actions, which tended to be more sensational than effective.

Kansas, where she crusaded, was a good example of what happened when liquor was prohibited. In 1879 the voters of Kansas passed a constitutional amendment to make the manufacture and sale of intoxicating beverages illegal, except for medical, scientific, and mechanical purposes. Though the law was upheld in 1883 by the State Supreme Court, it was more observed in its breach than its observance. Every Kansas town had its saloons, in many large towns operating openly. In others they operated as a speakeasy, with a front room that was a restaurant or other legitimate business, and a rear room that had bartenders serving liquor. Many drugstores in Kansas had a counter that held barrels of whiskey and beer. A prescription was not often required, but if so one was readily available from most physicians.

## The Drys Move Towards Success

By the late 1800s the temperance cause had enough momentum that it moved from the state level to the national level. In 1876 representative Henry Blair of Vermont introduced an amendment to the United States Constitution that outlawed the nationwide sale, manufacture, or importation of alcohol, except for medicinal and industrial uses.[43] However, amendments to the Constitution require a two-thirds majority in both houses of Congress, plus ratification by three-fourths of the states. Blair's proposed legislation never made it out of committee. Later, as a senator from Vermont, he tried again in 1887 and introduced prohibition legislation that was defeated in 1889 in the Senate by a vote of 33 to 13.[44] Another proposed amendment to prohibit all alcohol was introduced by Senator Plumb of Kansas in 1880, but it remained buried in committee.

Some temperance efforts succeeded, and actually proceeded with amazing speed as a few states voted to become "dry" before National Prohibition passed into law. Kansas, for example, passed a constitutional amendment prohibiting the sale of intoxicants in 1879. It was ratified in November 1880 and became law on March 10, 1881. It was intended to control excessive drinking in end-of-track cattle towns, but was difficult to enforce. The effort proved to be ineffective and illegal drinking behind closed doors started almost immediately.

Though Kansas officially went dry, drinking habits could not be changed by legislation, and Kansans continued to drink in prodigious quantities. In 1900 Kiowa, Kansas, had a population of about 800. To serve the town were a dozen saloons, several drugstores where liquor could be openly purchased, and many bootleggers who peddled their wares with disregard for the law. Reportedly one bootlegger went from door-to-door twice a week, like an itinerant salesman, selling bottles of whiskey from a gunny sack slung over his shoulder.[45] "Medicinal" alcohol, in the form of whiskey, wine, and beer, was freely available by perfectly legal prescription for colds, cramps, biliousness, colic, and the chills, as well as "nervousness" and "general debility."

The Wilson Act of 1890, which was upheld by the Supreme Court in 1898, affirmed the right of a dry state to impose its law on liquor arriving from outside its boundaries. It did not, however, prohibit the shipment of liquor into dry states for personal consumption. As a result, a vast mail-order business in bottled beer and hard liquor sprang up to allow drinkers in prohibition states to order all the liquor they wanted. Door-to-door salesmen from wet states, along with direct advertising, solicited orders from customers in dry states and companies either set up warehouses in the state to fulfill the orders immediately or shipped the liquor direct to the consumer via express and freight companies who acted as agents. Wholesalers in wet states also were sources for local bootleggers and speakeasies in dry states.

Mail-order liquor houses proposed all sorts of incentives to create business. One obviously macho-oriented one offered an interesting-sounding special package deal of "a quart of whiskey, a box of cigars, and a revolver."[46]

Under the category of be careful what you wish for, the temperance laws that emerged sometimes had unexpected consequences. In 1895 Senator John Raines from New York crafted legislation that became known as the Raines Law. This legislation allowed hotels with at least ten bedrooms to serve drinks on Sundays to guests who ordered meals. Because maintaining business on Sundays was important for liquor sales, many saloon owners added ten small bedrooms to their establishments in order to qualify as a hotel. As a result, Brooklyn's number of "hotels" jumped rapidly from 13 to over 2,000. To put these empty rooms to use and make money, the saloon owners typically rented them out to prostitutes as cribs. Thus the unintended result of the legislation was to increase prostitution in New York City.

Another expected result was the so-called "Raines sandwich," which was never eaten but which dutifully appeared in front of each drinker as his "meal." This sandwich was often just dried-out cheese-and-bread. Drinks were always paid for with cash, but the sandwich was supplied on credit and it never had to be eaten or paid for. It was usually re-cycled for the next drinker.[47]

A similar travesty took place in New Mexico where a drink could only be ordered with a meal. In this case, the "meal" was a hot dog. After the "meal" was over, the hot dog was returned to the bartender, who dutifully washed it off and served it to the next customer.[48]

## The Right to Vote

The prohibition of alcohol was linked to the companion progressive effort of women's right to vote. The first political entity that allowed women to vote and hold public office was Wyoming Territory, which passed the appropriate legislation in 1869. This legislation may actually not have been as forward thinking on the part of the Wyoming lawmakers as it at first appears. Legislators may have hoped that giving women the right to vote would attract more females to settle in the territory, because there were hardly any women in Wyoming at the time and the territorial population was only about 9,000. Interestingly, the Wyoming Territorial Government apparently had second thoughts about what they had done and in 1871 voted to repeal the bill. The attempted repeal failed by one vote.

By 1896, only three additional Western states, Colorado, Idaho, and Utah, had given women the right to vote. It was not until 1920, and the passage of the Nineteenth Amendment to the Constitution of the United States, that women universally gained the legal right to vote.

In the states where women were allowed to use the ballot box, state laws that prohibited saloons were quickly enacted by popular vote. Before 1919, these states were Wyoming, Colorado, Utah, Idaho, Washington, California, Kansas, Oregon, Arizona, Montana, Nevada, and New York. All but California and New York adopted state laws banning saloons. Thus an unintended consequence of the women's vote was that the West and the South forced National Prohibition on the wet cities of the Northeast and upper Midwest, first by local option and then by statewide vote.[49] Typically urban populations opposed Prohibition, whereas small towns and rural voters were in favor of it.

In 1907 Georgia and Oklahoma passed dry laws. Constitutional amendments in Mississippi and North Carolina passed in 1908, and in Tennessee in 1909. West Virginia followed in 1912.[50]

By 1913 the wets had not gained the power to determine who would be elected, but the drys had. The Anti-Saloon League, the Prohibition Party, and WCTU and other temperance groups had so much political power that they could determine who would be elected. As a consequence the drys organized vigorous campaigns to elect men who would pledge to vote in favor of a National Prohibition amendment.

The Webb-Kenyon Bill that prohibited the interstate transportation of alcohol into dry states was passed over President Taft's veto in 1913. At the end of 1914 the drys in the House of Representatives attempted a trial run at legislation to create Prohibition in order to see what the wets would do, even though they felt it would not pass. The vote was close, but it was defeated at 197 to 190, and did not have the two-thirds majority required to be passed. The drys decided to hold off until 1917 to try again.

By the time the United States entered World War I on April 6, 1917, prohibition legislation had passed in 26 of the 48 states. Though California was not one of them, most California counties were dry or partially-dry.[51]

Liquor was banned from naval vessels and navy bases during World War I, and the availability of liquor was limited around naval bases and munitions plants.[52]

## The Eighteenth Amendment and the Volstead Act

The Temperance Movement was finally able to force the passage of legislation in 1917 that led to National Prohibition. By this time, local and federal government officials knew that if they wanted to be re-elected they had better vote for the Eighteenth Amendment.

The new law stipulated that Prohibition would start one year after ratification of the amendment. Mississippi was the first state to ratify the amendment on January 8, 1918. The thirty-sixth state was Nebraska on January 16, 1919. Rural Protestant America forced Prohibition on urban industrial Americans, who consisted mostly of a mixture of races, religions, and ethnic backgrounds.

During World War I the Food Administration prohibited the use of grain in the production of beer.[53] When World War I ended in November of 1918, the government extended the law because the Eighteenth Amendment was well on the way to being ratified. On November 21, 1918, ten days after the signing of the Armistice, Congress passed the temporary War Prohibition Act (also called War Time Prohibition), attached as a rider to the 1918 Agricultural Bill by California Congressman Charles H. Randall.[54] This wartime prohibition prohibited distilleries from making beverage alcohol in order to save grain for the war effort. Congress went back and forth on wartime prohibition and finally passed the legislation in 1918. This legislation prohibited the manufacture of beer and wine, and the sales of all liquor in 1919.[55]

The legislation for National Prohibition passed on December 18, 1917, and was ratified on January 16, 1919. Prohibition was set to be effective on January 16, 1920. However, by December 1918, twenty-seven states had already voted themselves dry and had imposed prohibition.[56] When ratification of the Eighteenth Amendment was complete in 1919 and National Prohibition was close at hand, thirty-three of the forty-eight states were already dry.

The Eighteenth Amendment had three main provisions. One prohibited the sale, manufacture, and transportation of unauthorized "intoxicating spirits." Curiously, the Eighteenth Amendment did not ban the purchase or possession of alcohol, but it made buying liquor legally very difficult. After January 16, 1920, individuals could not sell, make, or transport intoxicating beverages, but the law did not cover purchasing or possessing liquor, and owning a case of whiskey was not illegal. While it was illegal to possess liquor that was purchased unlawfully, drinking it was legal. The ramifications were all rather confusing. The full text of the Eighteenth Amendment is contained in Appendix 1.

Drinkers with enough foresight and money could lay in a stock of liquor, could keep it, and could keep on drinking it. The writers of the Prohibition bill decided that mere consumption of alcohol in one's home would not be illegal.[57] Before Prohibition became effective, thousands of individuals purchased whatever liquor they could and stored it in basements and home wine cellars. Businessmen and the rich knew the value of liquor, and wealthy individuals with the foresight and money to stock up ordered cases of liquor to store in their wine cellars or basements. Rich people who had the money to invest in stocks of liquor and owned residences large enough to store it took advantage of the time before implementation of the law to buy and store as much as they wished, some of which they might not even consume for years.

The second provision of the amendment was that Congress and the states had the concurrent power to enforce the Eighteenth Amendment by appropriate legislation. The third was that the amendment had to be ratified within seven years. As it turned out, to the surprise of the wet supporters, the amendment was ratified with unprecedented speed by thirty-six states in less than fourteen months. Eventually only two states, Connecticut and Rhode Island did not ratify the amendment.

The specific legislation required for the implementation and enforcement of the Eighteenth Amendment and Prohibition were spelled out in the National Prohibition Act, popularly known as the Volstead Act, which was sponsored by Republican Representative Andrew John Volstead from Minnesota, who was chairman of the House Judiciary Committee. In reality it was essentially drafted by Wayne Wheeler of the Anti-Saloon League.[58]

Congress passed the Volstead Act in October of 1919. It was initially vetoed by President Woodrow Wilson, but his veto was overridden by Congress on October 27, 1919, by the necessary two-thirds margin. And so it became illegal to manufacture, transport, sell, or possess (but not to purchase or consume) alcohol in the United States after January of 1920.

The author of the Volstead Act had two concerns. One was to not appear to be regulating personal behavior. The right to continue to possess and consume alcohol was based on the fact that prohibitionists did not wish to be seen as trying to regulate individual behavior and private personal conduct. They understood that trying to regulate an American citizen's personal behavior would be offensive and seen as interfering with individual rights, and would therefore hurt their cause. Their other concern was not to be seen as regulating the marketplace. Just as individual consumption was protected as a right, so too were the efforts of private enterprise and businesses.

Punishments for violations of the Volstead Act included closure of the premises where liquor was sold, fines of not less than $100 or more than $1,000, imprisonment for not less than thirty day or more than one year, and confiscation of property, such as houses, boats, and cars used in liquor transactions.[59]

As a concession to industries in California and New England, sacramental wines were exempted, as was medicinal alcohol prescribed by a physician. The Volstead Act allowed each family to make 200 gallons of wine or "non-intoxicating" cider and fruit juice for use at home.

The complexity of the Volstead Act created enormous administrative and legal problems. It was intended to codify the best features of various existing state prohibition laws, but instead it became a mixture of complicated and contradictory cross-references and unusual modifications of ordinary legal procedures.

One of the first difficulties of the new law was how to define the nebulous term of "intoxicating." The term was finally defined as anything containing more than 0.5 percent alcohol. Ironically and confusingly, however, this limit included the natural fermentation that took place in some foods, such as sauerkraut, which contained fermented cabbage and could contain small amounts of alcohol, or in German chocolate cake. In a move to remove any Germanic connotations during the war with Germany, sauerkraut was renamed "liberty cabbage." Similarly, "hamburger" became "liberty steak."

An exception to the Volstead Act was cider and other fruit juices that generated some alcohol through the natural process of fermentation. Home fermentation of hard apple cider that could contain as much as 6 to 7 percent alcohol was still considered to be acceptable.

Businesses could continue to manufacture and sell industrial alcohol to companies who made paint, antifreeze, and other similar legitimate chemical enterprises, as long as the alcohol was made unfit for human consumption. Churches could still serve sacramental wine, but it had to be produced by specially licensed wineries for that purpose alone.

Reformers saw Prohibition as an instrument of social improvement and a way to help the poor and needy to help themselves. The drys associated alcohol with urbanization, violence, laziness, and corruption, and persuaded themselves that sober men would be better American citizens. Miscreants would stop beating their wives, hold down jobs, go to church (preferably a Protestant one), and save their money. This new sober society would be patriotic, stable, pious, and prosperous.[60]

This vision was a grave miscalculation, and rebellion against the new law was immediate by individuals who felt that their government was being oppressive, tyrannical, despotic, and unrealistic. Bootleggers quickly planned to make and sell illegal liquor and drinkers prepared to consume it.

Prior to Prohibition even becoming effective, multiple thefts occurred, some of them from guarded warehouses. In one theft, sixty-one barrels of fine quality bourbon disappeared from a government warehouse in Bardstown, Kentucky, under what were considered to be mysterious circumstances.[61] Within an hour of the Volstead Act going into effect, six armed bandits wearing masks ambushed a railroad crew, locked them up, and stole two freight cars of medicinal whiskey from a train in Chicago.[62] The first recorded arrest under the new law occurred two hours after Prohibition started when federal agents seized two truckloads of whiskey leaving a warehouse in Peoria, Illinois, stolen by the officials of the distillery that made it.[63]

With that, what became called "The Noble Experiment" had begun.

## 3

# The Real Thing?
# Or Do-It-Yourself?

PERVERSELY, WITH THE ONSET of Prohibition, the demand for alcohol rose sharply. At the same time grain and corn prices fell with a depressed economy and farmers realized they could make more money by turning corn into whiskey. And so they did.

Making whiskey had always been a tradition of economic necessity for rural Americans. Early colonists in isolated farmhouses or settlements had to make their own alcohol if they wanted a drink, and some farmers made extra money on the side by distilling their excess grain into whiskey and selling it. Rye was one of the first grains to be used for distilling by European settlers, and rye whiskey was the liquor of choice in the East after the American Revolution.[1]

Farmers harvested their corn in late summer and made whiskey in the autumn. This benefited farmers economically in several ways. Farmers were typically rich in land, but poor in cash, so they used whiskey as a cash substitute and liquor became a type of currency. In early times the government even accepted whiskey as payment for taxes.[2]

The origin of fermented beverages is lost in antiquity, but archeological evidence shows that wine and beer were consumed in the Stone Age, and some vessels for grinding grain found in Israel have been dated to be as old as 13,000 years. The origin of wine also dates back for thousands of years.[3]

The word "alcohol" was derived from the Arabic *al kohl*. *Al* is the equivalent of "the" and *kohl* was originally the name for powdered antimony sulfide that was used as eye makeup for women. The combination referred to the extraction of antimony from the mineral stibnite, and thus the reduction of this naturally-occurring material to its "essence" or "spirit." The change of meaning to apply to distilled spirits occurred with later European usage as the distillation process produced the "essence" or intrinsic heart of a fermented drink, or alcohol.

Alcoholic beverage drinks are classified under three very general categories: beer, wine, and liquor (distilled spirits). Beer and wine are fermented beverages produced from sugar or starch-containing plant materials. Spirits, also known as hard liquor, are produced by the process of distilling this fermented material in order to raise the percentage of alcohol present. The typical alcohol content of beer is 3 to 6 percent, wine is 10 to 12 percent, and whiskey is 40 percent. The amount of alcohol in a particular type of alcoholic beverage depends on the type of material used to provide the sugar that is being fermented, the strain of yeast used for fermentation, and the temperature of the process. By contrast, the Volstead Act defined intoxicating liquor as any beverage containing more than 0.5 percent alcohol. Even vanilla extract had a higher alcohol content than that as it was legally required to contain at least 35 percent alcohol.

## Fermentation

"Drinking" and "alcohol" refers to ethyl alcohol (ethanol), the type of alcohol that is commonly drunk for pleasure as a fermented intoxicating beverage. Fermentation is the process by which yeast produces alcohol from plant material that contains sugar, such as molasses, or from any similar substance that can be chemically broken down into sugar, such as the starch present in various grains. In the wild, this can occur as a natural process in which various species of wild yeasts and bacteria convert fruit sugars into alcohol. Fruit that is overripe or rotten contains a much higher alcohol content than fruit that is merely ripe.

The number of plants that can be, and have been, used to produce drinking alcohol is very large. Practically all grains, fruits, berries, and vegetables can be fermented and, at one time or another throughout history, almost all have been.

During the fermentation process, yeast turns the starch contained in rye, barley, corn, or wheat into sugar. The yeast then eats the sugar, in turn producing ethyl alcohol and carbon dioxide gas as byproducts. Chemically speaking, the resulting ethanol is part of a family of organic chemicals that consist of carbon atoms connected to hydrogen atoms and one hydroxyl (-OH) group, the specific type of alcohol depends on the number of carbon atoms in the backbone of its chemical formula. Ethanol is a relatively simple alcohol, with a chemical formula of $C_2H_5OH$. Each molecule contains two carbon atoms linked together as its backbone and the five hydrogen atoms and single hydroxyl group attached to its sides and end.

Different types of sugar may be used as a base for fermentation, such as glucose, fructose (fruit sugar), galactose (milk sugar), or sucrose (cane sugar). Glucose and fructose are monosaccharides or simple sugars. Sucrose (table sugar) is a disaccharide and is chemically more complex than monosaccharides. Yeast ferments the molecules of sugar present into two molecules of ethyl alcohol and two of carbon dioxide gas.

Yeasts are classified as fungus and there are more than 1,500 different species found in nature. Like all fungi, yeasts lack chlorophyll and cannot manufacture their own food. The type of yeast commonly used for fermentation is *Saccharomyces cerevisiae*, which is a type of microscopic fungus that feeds on the sugar and produces alcohol as a by-product. This is the same yeast that has been used for thousands of years for baking bread and for fermenting alcoholic beverages. Preparing bread produces a little alcohol that adds to the taste; however, most of this alcohol evaporates during the baking process. The carbon dioxide gas produced causes the dough to rise. The type of yeast used for baking is classified broadly as "brewer's yeast."

Appendix 2 summarizes the sources of the commonest types of fermented beverages and the percentage of alcohol contained in each.

## Beer

Beer is the most popular alcoholic beverage in the world. In the late 1860s, many Germans immigrated to the United States and brought with them their taste for lager beer. *"Lager bier"* in German literally means "stored beer," because in the German method the beer was aged by being stored in a warehouse for several months after it was brewed.

The brewing industry in the United States expanded rapidly in the late 1880s and, by 1890, beer was the largest-selling alcoholic beverage in the country. Working in a brewery was a popular job because employees in many breweries were allowed to drink as much beer as they could manage, a benefit that was not viewed with amusement by temperance workers.

Beer was brewed through the action of brewer's yeast (*Saccharomyces cerevisiae*) on barley or other cereal grains, with hops (the ripe dried cones from the hop plant) added for flavor to give the characteristic beer taste.

To brew beer, barley was soaked in water to make the grain germinate to release the enzymes needed to convert the starch present into sugar. The resulting material was then dried in a kiln to stop the germination process and reduce the moisture content. The process of soaking, germinating, and drying produced a material called malt. Different roasting times and temperatures in the kiln produced different colors of malt from the same grain. The darker the malt, the darker the beer.

The primary grain used for brewing beer was barley, but rye, wheat, and rice were also used. The malting process contained three parts: steeping, where barley or other grains were placed in a vat and hot water was added to allow the grain to germinate and sprout; germination, which took place over a period of several days of soaking; and kilning, where germinating malt was dried under high temperature to produce the final "malt." The malt was then ground up or "cracked" by milling. The next step was to add hot water for "mashing," and corn, rye, or sorghum might be added. This step converted the starch released into sugar that could be fermented. The resulting liquid, called wort, was rich in sugar. Brewer's yeast was added, and the mixture was allowed to ferment.

The beer stopped fermenting, or "working," when either all the available sugar was used up or when the alcohol content rose to a level that killed the yeast. Most beers brewed in the West contained 3 to 6 percent alcohol, but some beers contained up to 10 percent alcohol by volume. Brewer's yeast used for fermenting beer could tolerate an alcohol content of up to 5 to 6 percent before the yeast died. The carbon dioxide gas that resulted as a side product produced the carbonation in beer.

Though yeast was nearly always added to the sugar solution to induce fermentation, it was not essential to add it to start the process. It was possible to manufacture a crude beer by chewing some fruit and then spitting it into a container. Spontaneous fermentation of the saliva and the plant sugar produced a low-grade alcohol, a practice carried on by some primitive native Indian cultures in South America.

## Wine

Although many yeasts can induce fermentation, various species of *Saccharomyces* were generally used for beer and wine because they were comparatively efficient at alcohol production and could tolerate higher levels of ethanol than can most yeasts. The specific yeast *Saccharomyces cerevisiae* has been widely used for fermentation of wine for thousands of years. Though wine could be fermented naturally through the action of wild yeast that was present on the surface of ripe grapes, commercial fermentation of wine used a strain of cultured yeast that could tolerate a higher percentage of alcohol, up to 12 to 15 percent, than brewer's yeast. This produced more reliable and uniform fermentation.

Most wine was produced from grapes, though other sources of material as diverse as apples, cherries, plums, pears, and dandelions have been used. The flavor of a particular wine comes from the type of grape (or other material). As part of the preparation process, the grapes have to be crushed. To make white wine, the pulp and skins of the crushed grapes were removed before fermentation. When making red wine, the grape skins, pulp, and juice were all fermented together.

When the concentration of alcohol in wine rose to between 10 percent and 15 percent (typically about 12 percent with an upper limit of 18%), the yeast started to be inhibited by the alcohol it produced and died off, thus halting further production of alcohol. Ironically then, the yeast's own success in producing alcohol killed it off and placed a natural ceiling on the strength of the alcohol in wine. Champagne (and sparkling wine) was supplemented with additional carbon dioxide to achieve a bubbly appearance.

## Distilled Spirits

After fermentation, the alcohol content of the resulting material contained anywhere from 5 percent to 16 percent alcohol. In order to raise the alcohol content to the 40 percent contained in most liquors, such as bourbon and vodka, it was necessary to distill the fermented product. Drinkers soon found that by concentrating the alcohol in their beverages through distillation they could induce a faster and stronger feeling of intoxication. Alcoholic beverages produced by fermentation and then distillation were called "spirits." Whiskey, for example, was distilled from a fermented mixture of grain to produce a high alcohol content. As another example, the high alcoholic content of brandy was produced by distilling wine.

Distilled spirits were initially produced for medicinal use before drinking them expanded to recreational use. The origin of distilling and distilled spirits is lost somewhere in ancient history, but the distillation of alcohol is known to have been used in China, Japan, and India as long ago as several thousand years. Modern distilling techniques probably appeared during the Middle Ages.

Some of the first historical records of distillation and fermentation are described in the making of perfumes in Babylon and Mesopotamia. After distillation and concentration, the resulting alcohol was flavored with various herbs and spices, including sage, lavender, angelica, ginger, cinnamon, and nutmeg. The distillation process spread to Europe, where monks fermented and distilled fruit and grain to make alcohol for use in religious services. Ireland and Scotland performed the distillation of alcohol during the eleventh and thirteenth centuries, and the Scots became the leaders in the production of high-quality whiskey in the late 1400s. When Scottish and Irish emigrants left their homelands and migrated to America, they brought with them the knowledge of how to make good whiskey.

Rum, which was popular among early colonial Americans, was derived from molasses. Rum is thought to have originated on plantations in the West Indies sometime during the sixteenth century. Rum started with a type of beer that was naturally fermented by yeast spores settling on discarded liquid cane juice and left-over molasses from sugar mills. The first regular importation of rum into the northeast United States began around 1670 as a result of trading by New Englanders with Newfoundland.

A popular drink from Holland in colonial days was gin, which received its characteristic flavor from the addition of berries from the juniper tree to the raw alcohol. The original name for gin was *geneva*, from the French word *genièvre* for the juniper berry or juniper tree. Dutch gin was drunk extensively by fighting men of the time, hence the expression "Dutch courage" for one who obtains his bravado from drink. Less formally, *geneva* was nicknamed "strip-and-go-naked" and "blue ruin."[4]

Scotch whiskey was distilled from barley malt. Bourbon was made from corn, rum from sugarcane or the left-over material from making molasses, brandy from distilled wine, tequila from the *agave* cactus, and vodka from potatoes. In the Midwest corn and other grains were commonly used.

Like beer, the primary raw materials used as the basis for many spirits are the cereal grains. Whiskey, for example, is made from several cereal grains, including wheat, rye, oats, and barley. Bourbon began with mash that had a 51 to 79 percent corn base, with other grains being barley, wheat, or rye. Because of its common origin in barley, whiskey was also referred to in colonial days as "barley water" or "John Barleycorn." Some of these early spirits were so strong and raw that Colonial Americans called alcohol produced by distillation "ardent spirits," with the adjective "ardent" meaning "burning" or "on fire."

What most people refer to as "alcohol" is not the chemist's version of pure ethanol, but is a mixture of ethyl alcohol with substances added during processing to create the flavor and color of the particular alcoholic drink. The flavor and color of Scotch whiskey, for example, results from adding peat and "aging" the resulting alcohol in barrels that were previously used to store sherry.

Kentucky bourbon is alcohol made from corn mash that is distilled and also aged in oak barrels to create its characteristic flavor. The name bourbon started appearing around 1820 in Kentucky, probably named after Bourbon County (though nobody is sure) to distinguish Kentucky bourbon whiskey from rye whiskey made in Maryland. Bourbon was previously called "Kentucky" or "Western" whiskey. Over time, all corn-based whiskey became generically called bourbon.

In Colorado and other parts of the Southwest where sugar beets were an important crop, bootleggers made a fiery alcoholic drink called

Sugar Moon from beet sugar. This potent product was said to be quite raw and very strong. It was also said to produce a bad hangover by those who apparently knew from experience.[5]

After fermentation in the whiskey-making process, the alcohol content of the resulting mash was about 15 percent or, put another way, the water content was about 85 percent. The rest of the mash was a series of different compounds called "congeners," which gave whiskey most of its body and flavor. These compounds were removed if the mash was distilled to 95 percent alcohol or higher. On the other hand, vodka is almost pure alcohol, so the premium vodkas are essentially colorless, odorless, and almost tasteless.

Historically, alcohol has been designated by "proof," which is a measure of the alcohol content. The "proof" of spirits is twice the alcohol content, thus 80 proof is 40 percent alcohol by volume. Most spirits today, such as whiskey, gin, and vodka, are 80 proof.

The term "proof" originated in the eighteenth century when British sailors were paid partially with 100 proof rum. To ensure that the rum was not diluted with water, it was "proofed" by pouring it onto gunpowder and setting the mixture on fire. If the gunpowder did not flare up and produce a steady blue flame, it was presumed that there was too much water in the rum and it was considered "under proof." In the United States, for simplicity 100 proof is 50 percent alcohol content. In England, 100 proof is 57.1 percent alcohol, because that is the percentage at which alcohol burns steadily.

All whiskey as it comes from the still is essentially colorless. Distillation produces more alcohol and less water. The process relies on the fact that the boiling point of alcohol occurs at a lower temperature than that of water. The boiling point of alcohol is 173°F at sea level, while water boils at 212°F. Thus, when an alcohol and water mixture is heated, the alcohol starts to evaporate at 173°F, while the water remains in the liquid state.

In making brandy, for example, a closed container of wine is heated at a low enough temperature that the alcohol in it boils off, but the water does not. The resulting alcohol vapor is passed through what is called a condenser that cools the vapor and converts it (condenses it) back to a liquid again, and the resulting spirits are collected. In this way much of the water is removed from the original wine and the resulting liquid becomes concentrated to 40 percent to 50 percent ethanol.

One of the most important parts of the process of making whiskey is aging the alcohol. Neutral spirits are distilled from grain at greater than 190 proof. All body and flavor are lacking. At room temperature, this pure ethanol is a colorless, clear liquid with a rather unpleasant and very raw taste. Pure alcohol has to be diluted with water or it will burn the throat when drunk. Dilution with water even makes pure alcohol taste better. Without any aging, the alcohol is raw and colorless and not much in demand for drinking. Absolute alcohol is distilled to 200 proof and is supposedly 100 percent alcohol, but it actually contains about 1 percent water.

Whiskey is distilled to 160 proof or less, and then is stored in charred oak barrels for varying periods of time. The alcohol absorbs color and taste from the charred wood. The burned inside surface of the barrel adds color to the whiskey, and at the same time removes many impurities and mellows it, resulting in a smooth taste. This process makes quality liquor out of the raw distillate. Conversely, though, if whiskey remains too long in the oak barrels, it often acquires a bitter taste. The usual aging period is from four to eight years. About 3 percent of the alcohol evaporates during the aging process, an amount that is known in the industry as the "angel's share."

The designation of various types of whiskey is strictly controlled and depends on the raw grain that is fermented. Rye whiskey must contain at least 51 percent rye as a starting material. Bourbon must contain at least 51 percent corn. The most common type of whiskey, however, is blended whiskey, which consists of at least 20 percent by volume of 100-proof straight whiskey, combined with whiskey or neutral spirits made from other grains. A blending agent is also added, often consisting of sherry or prune juice, but which cannot be more than 2.5 percent of the total volume.[6]

## Legal and Illegal Alcohol

Even though the manufacture of beverage alcohol was banned during Prohibition, a large amount of alcohol was still manufactured and distributed legally. During the Prohibition era an estimated 100 million gallons of alcohol a year were legally manufactured by licensed distilleries.[7]

When the manufacture and sale of beverage alcohol was banned, three types of alcohol could still be manufactured legally, though all were intended for limited use. The first exception was that alcohol could still be produced for specialized beverage purposes, such as wine used for sacramental purposes. Alcohol was also allowed for the production of preparations for human consumption, such as pharmaceuticals, candy, spices, and food extracts. The second exception was beverage alcohol prescribed by physicians for medicinal use. The third was alcohol manufactured for chemical and scientific uses.

Legally-manufactured alcohol was stored in government warehouses under one of three classifications: pure, specially denatured, or completely

**The quantities of illegal alcohol handled by a bootlegger could be huge, as shown by this warehouse full of cases of confiscated liquor. This photograph is thought to be from 1921 (Library of Congress).**

denatured. Alcohol was withdrawn from these warehouses by manufacturers for legal purposes under a permit issued by the Prohibition Bureau.

Pure ethanol was used for human consumption. Much of the alcohol produced legally, however, was processed through denaturing plants where it was made unfit for human consumption by adding various chemicals, most of which were poisonous. Specially denatured alcohol was used by industrial chemical producers in cosmetics, insecticides, soap, photographic supplies, and human external remedies. Completely denatured alcohol went for various chemical uses and its sale was unrestricted. The principal use for this type of alcohol was for antifreeze for car radiators, and for paints and varnishes.

Coincidentally, Prohibition occurred a time when the American chemical industry was increasing in size and this growth was encouraged by the government. In 1906 one million gallons of industrial alcohol was manufactured. By 1910 this figure had risen to a little less than seven million gallons. By 1930, almost ten years after the start of Prohibition, this figure had grown to almost thirty million gallons. Where much of this went was anybody's guess. The government did not keep track of the production or supply of industrial alcohol, so nobody knew the legitimate alcohol requirements of the chemical industry and what portion might have been diverted for use in illegal alcoholic consumption.[8]

One fallacy of the system was that a permit to manufacture legal alcohol for industrial purposes could be obtained relatively easily, and then the final product diverted to illegal use, namely drinking. Many chemical companies were founded without any product or the intention of manufacturing anything. These were shell companies and false partnerships used to hide business dealings in illicit alcohol.

A key provision in the law that benefited bootleggers was that the Prohibition Bureau did not have the legal authority to investigate transactions other than the original purchase of the alcohol. Thus a manufacturer "sold" legal alcohol to its fake shell company, who then supposedly used it to manufacture some nebulous product, such as paint or cosmetics, but in reality often diverted it to bootleg whiskey. Prohibition agents did not have the legal authority to investigate further than the original sales invoice from the alcohol manufacturer, and was thus unable to track purchases further.

## Medicinal Whiskey

One of the exceptions in the Volstead Act allowed for the legal distribution of alcohol for medicinal purposes. Not every state allowed alcohol for medical use and its distribution was forbidden in twelve states.[9]

Legal whiskey could be purchased by obtaining a doctor's prescription for medicinal alcohol and going to a local drugstore to fill it. During the 1920s millions of gallons of alcohol were doled out to customers across pharmacy counters, distributed in one-pint bottles that were labeled as "medicinal whiskey."

Whiskey had long been used as a cure for many different medical ailments. Whiskey was prescribed for everything from sore throats and digestive problems to dog bites and snakebites, as well as for nervous tension and various other mental illnesses. During the nineteenth century, alcohol in the form of whiskey was popularly prescribed to treat many common diseases, such as influenza, malaria, childbirth fever, typhoid, typhus, cholera, and diabetes. Whiskey was considered to be the standard cure for those with wasting diseases in order to build up their strength. Whiskey was also used as an anesthetic during surgical operations and as an antiseptic to clean and sterilize wounds. Medicinal whiskey was known by the impressive Latin medical name of *Spiritus frumenti*, which literally meant "Spirits of Grain." Medicinal brandy was known by the similar magnificent title of *Spiritus vini gallici* (Spirits of French wine).

In 1917, just before the start of Prohibition, the American Medical Association (AMA) stated the prevailing medical view that the use of alcohol as a medicine had no scientific value and that its use should be discouraged. Only two years later, the AMA restated its position on alcohol and declared its use to be a treatment method for nearly thirty illnesses.

Physicians were allowed to write up to a hundred prescriptions per month on government-issued watermarked forms that were individually numbered. A patient was allowed to obtain a prescription for one pint of whiskey or other liquor every ten days. Refills were prohibited, but multiple prescriptions were not. A typical prescription read "Whiskey: take one tablespoon three times a day" or "Whiskey as directed." One physician prescribed his medicinal alcohol with the directions: "Take three ounces every hour as a stimulant until stimulated."

To fill prescriptions, druggists used grain alcohol, which they obtained from government-controlled warehouses in five-gallon cans that contained 180 proof alcohol. Most of this was diluted with an equal amount of distilled water to create 90 proof (45% alcohol) liquor. Some medicinal alcohol was made into a more appealing drink by adding flavoring such as oil of orange or oil of juniper, or whatever other flavor the druggist felt would be popular with his customers.

Beer was also prescribed for medical use. In 1926 the average amount of beer prescribed by physicians for a wide variety of ailments was 2.5 gallons.[10]

When prohibition began, stocks of whiskey were stored in warehouses for later bottling as medicinal whiskey. During the first six months of Prohibition, approximately 15,000 physicians in Chicago applied to obtain licenses to dispense prescriptions.[11] Another 57,000 pharmacists applied for licenses to fill those prescriptions. The cost was typically $3 to purchase a prescription from a physician, and then another $3 to have it filled at a pharmacy, which produced a good income for the drugstore owner ($3 had about the same buying power as $43 in 2021).

During the first six years of prohibition, the Prohibition Bureau issued permits for medicinal whiskey to an average of 63,000 physicians every year. By 1929, the number of permits had risen to more than 100,000 a year. Physicians wrote approximately eleven million prescriptions a year. As well as legitimate prescriptions issued by legitimate physicians, many forms were forged or were counterfeit, and many had been stolen from doctor's offices or had been purchased from an illegal dealer.

Dentists were licensed to issue prescriptions the same as physicians and so, curiously, were veterinarians.[12] Prescriptions were soon consuming a million gallons of medicinal alcohol a year.[13] In 1921 the owners of drugstores withdrew over eight million gallons of medicinal whiskey from federal warehouses.[14] Business was so good in California that one block of Santa Monica Boulevard in Los Angeles was able to support three competing drugstores.

As whiskey was available legally from government-controlled warehouses to lawfully fill prescriptions, one easy unlawful technique to obtain some of this whiskey was to simply forge a series of liquor prescriptions. The resulting alcohol was shipped to different cities, then sold on the black market. Another illegal technique used in many major cities was for a bootlegger to set up his own bogus wholesale drug company. The bootlegger obtained a permit to withdraw medicinal whiskey from a legitimate warehouse, and then sold it to willing customers.

Another illegal method used was with "whiskey certificates" that allowed the holder to sell alcohol legally on the medicinal market. Whiskey certificates were distributed by officials in each state, and allowed alcohol to be taken out of bonded warehouses. Such certificates could be purchased from crooked Prohibition agents or on the black market. Another method was that they could be forged or faked. In this way certificates could be obtained to purchase and re-sell medicinal whiskey. Certificates varied in price from under $1 to $4 a gallon. If the official was really corrupt, he might add a fee on each case of liquor at whatever price he felt he could get away with. This could amount to up to $20 a case in additional illegal payments. He might also put the certificates out to bid to the highest bidder, then pocket whatever additional money he could extort.

## Patent Medicines

Closely linked to medicinal alcohol were patent medicines, which had always been popular for their high alcohol content, but which became even more popular during Prohibition. The use of patent medicines started to flourish in the 1870s and peaked in the 1880s, but their popularity continued until about the 1930s. Some of these medicines are still sold in modified form today.

Patent medicines, also sometimes called "proprietary medicines," were a series of alcohol-based tonics and potions that were concocted by various manufacturers, often based on their own ideas of healing, and were mostly without any curative powers. Patent medicines at that time were not regulated under any governmental supervision and were freely available from any drugstore, from traveling medicine show salesmen, or directly from the manufacturer through the mail.

The name "patent medicine" originated in Europe. In England, royal patents were granted for proprietary medicinal concoctions, hence the name "patent medicine" was used to describe them. American patent medicines were not "patented" in the same sense that inventions were patented by registering them with the U.S. Patent Office. Instead, they were proprietary drugs with secret formulas. If American "patent" medicines were patented through the Patent Office in the same way as inventions, the manufacturer would have been required to disclose the formula as part of the patent application. Then this information would become common knowledge for competing manufacturers to copy. Another factor was that it would have been difficult to patent these medicines in the ordinary sense, because their formulas were frequently changed by the manufacturers whenever they saw fit.

These medicines were essentially tinctures, which were medicinal ingredients in a base of ethyl alcohol. The active substances were often vegetable ingredients derived from various roots that were dissolved in the alcohol. Though these remedies were not classified as medicinal alcohol, they often contained as much alcohol as alcoholic beverages and people purchased and drank them for their high alcohol content. The percentage of alcohol of various patent medicines is given in Appendix 3.

Pharmacists had been selling alcohol-based patent medicines for decades for use in the treatment of a variety of ailments, including diabetes, cancer, upset stomach, and asthma. The commonest use was for general "debility" or some other such obscure term. The brand of whiskey sold as Old Grand-Dad claimed vaguely in its advertising that it was "Unexcelled for Medicinal Purposes," and was useful specifically for sick, blind, and lame patients.[15]

The alcoholic addictive properties of these medicines were well-known. As far back as 1836, physicians Gardner and Aylworth had commented, "They [alcohol-based tinctures] are excellent for administering a great variety of medicinal agents, but in some cases there may be an objection to them in consequence of the spirits they contain."[16] One popular contemporary manual of household medical advice warned, "Though a convenient form of preserving some medicines ... the use of them [the alcohol in them] frequently induces habits of intemperance."[17] Colden's Liquid Beef Tonic, for example, contained 26 percent alcohol and had the impudence in its advertising to recommend its use for treatment of the alcohol habit.

The high alcohol content of many patent medicines made them ideal for consumption by desperate drunks. During Prohibition, some saloons sold Dr. J. Hostetter's Celebrated Stomach Bitters by the drink.[18] As far back as 1878 the Internal Revenue Service was aware that Hostetter's was being sold in saloons in Sitka, Alaska, as an alcoholic beverage. On that basis they decided that these drinks should be taxed as though they were liquor. Seeing the obvious connection to drinking, on February 28, 1921, two carloads of patent medicine that contained 55 percent alcohol were seized by government inspectors in Chicago.[19]

The sale of patent medicines was primarily fueled by women, who tended to be the medical provider of the typical family. One of the most popular patent medicines was Lydia Pinkham's Vegetable Compound, which contained 21 percent alcohol. The tonic, developed in 1873 by housewife Mrs. Lydia Pinkham of Lynn, Massachusetts, as an herbal remedy, was recommended for pneumonia, tuberculosis, appendicitis, and advertised as the "only positive cure and legitimate remedy for the peculiar weaknesses and ailments of women."

Drinking by women, certainly in saloons, was not accepted by contemporary society, so women tended to seek their alcoholic pleasure in private at home. Many women kept a bottle of whiskey hidden among the kitchen supplies and could discreetly take a drink or two in private if they felt the need for pain relief at "that time of the month."

Patent medicines with their high alcohol content made even this subterfuge unnecessary. Many patent medicines proclaimed themselves to be a "female remedy." Thus women who subscribed to temperance principles could swear that a drop of liquor had never passed their lips while they were happily ingesting a several spoonfuls a day of an alcohol-laced patent medicine and still believing that they never touched drink. One clue to the contents of many of these "medicines" was that the name "bitters" was used as a generic term for medicinal alcohol with herbs dissolved in it. Luther's Temperance Bitters, which contained 17 percent alcohol, would seem to be somewhat hypocritically named.

An unusual use for one of these patent medicines was as a primitive temperature gauge in Dawson in the Yukon Territory of Canada during the great Klondike gold rush of the late 1890s. Conventional thermometers had a lower limit below which they were not useful. So, in cases of extreme cold, a bottle of Dr. Perry Davis' Celebrated Painkiller was placed in the window of a prospector's cabin. If the high-alcohol-content patent medicine froze, then the men knew that the temperature was at least -72°F. And indeed it was important for safety reasons to know this, as brutally-cold dangerous temperatures as low as -80°F were recorded near Dawson during the winters of 1897 and 1898.

## Moonshiners and Bootleggers

Within days of the enactment of Prohibition, illegal stills were set up around the country, and a new underground industry manufacturing illegal liquor appeared. Booklets of recipes for making brandy and whis-key were available in many stores for a dollar. The basic steps to make liquor were simple, using a process that had hardly been modified in the thousand years since it first began in Scotland and Ireland. All that was needed was a simple container for the mash, a still for boiling the alco-hol, and a copper condenser to cool the vapor and collect the resulting liquid. Supplies were grain, yeast, and water, and perhaps some addi-tional sugar. It has been humorously said that some ingenious residents of Scotland could make whiskey with only corn, water, a fire, a kettle, and a wet towel to condense the evaporated alcohol back to a liquid. When the towel was soaked with condensed ethanol, it was wrung out to recover the alcohol.[20]

The source of sugar as a basis for alcohol might vary, depending on the part of the country where the distiller lived. In Arkansas, molasses was frequently used, because sugar cane was freely available. In Colorado, sugar beets were often used in the eastern part of the state as they were widespread as an agricultural crop as a source of sugar.

The addition of various substances turned distilled pure alcohol into various types of bogus "liquor." The raw alcohol could be cut with some water, then caramel added to make "whiskey." The mixture was then bot-tled, a bogus label attached, counterfeit revenue stamps attached, and the bottle was ready to go to a speakeasy.

Another technique used was to extend the volume of real whiskey. A pint of authentic contraband whiskey was mixed with grain alcohol, some additional coloring and flavoring was added, and magically one pint of authentic whiskey had been expanded into five of the counterfeit stuff.

Some stills were run by individuals and were as small as a one-gallon capacity. Some operations used large stills that could produce as much as 1,000 gallons a day, making whiskey on a commercial scale both to ensure a steady supply and to make a sizeable profit. Large permanent installa-tions might be built with brick furnaces for heating the mash, and large storage sheds to store the barley or corn, and any additional sugar.

Moonshine was typically made from barley, corn, or rye that was kept warm and moist for six or eight days until it germinated. Then it was ground up and added to a vat of water and allowed to turn sour, a pro-cess that took six to eight days. The resulting brew was called "sour mash." Then a few yeast cakes were added, along with about five pounds of sugar for every fifty gallons of liquid. The mixture was heated in a still to make the alcohol evaporate. The vapor was directed through a coil that cooled it, often by placing the coil in a nearby creek bed or a barrel of cold water to lower the temperature. This condensed the alcohol vapor back into liq-uid alcohol. The resulting clear liquid was between 140 and 160 proof,

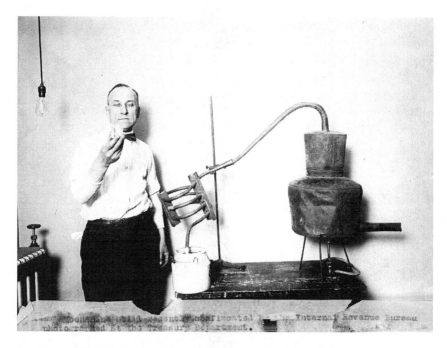

On the small end of the scale, this home-made still confiscated by Prohibition agents used only a single Bunsen burner (at the right) under the cooker for heat, and a small copper coil on the left for condensing the alcohol fumes. The government agent is looking at a glass of something presumably distilled from this primitive apparatus (Library of Congress).

depending on how many times it was run through the still. A fifty-gallon barrel of mash might produce four to six gallons of alcohol.[21]

The first distillation run through small stills did not result in pure alcohol. The fermented mash contained between 5 and 10 percent alcohol. After the first run through the still, the result was 30 to 40 percent alcohol. If it was run through a second time, the percentage of alcohol rose to about 60 to 70 percent. A third run through the still resulted in almost pure alcohol. The three XXX's caricatured on whiskey jugs indicated that the product had been run through a still three times and was almost pure alcohol. The pure distillate emerged as a clear liquid, then different ingredients, such as iodine, bark, charcoal, or tobacco, were added to make the final product look like authentic aged liquor.

Moonshining, also nicknamed "alky cooking," quickly became part of criminal activities. In some big cities organized crime provided a still and the raw materials to individuals. These small stills, which were primitive but effective, were set up by bootleggers in houses and apartments, with the liquor being collected on a regular basis. Several arrangements might be used. Sometimes small operators split the profit with the gang they worked for, sometimes the operator worked for straight wages, and sometimes individuals were simply told they had to make alcohol under the threat of violence.[22]

Bootleggers set up stills everywhere. In the mountains, on farms, and in buildings in small towns. Moonshine stills appeared in houses, cellars, barns, abandoned buildings, caves, pits in the ground, and anywhere that an enterprising moonshiner could set up in business. The equipment required was a boiler to cook the mash and a condenser to cool and collect the alcohol vapor. A still might be hidden in a pit under a barn, in a chicken coop, in an underground room such as a storm cellar, or even in the family home.

According to the Prohibition Bureau, 696,933 illegal stills were seized between 1921 and 1925. And it was estimated that for the number of stills that were discovered and seized, there were probably many more that were never discovered. Estimates were that as high as 90 percent of the operating stills were never found.

One of the unintended consequences of making illegal booze were that common items became the unlikely targets of theft. For example, metal garbage cans were often stolen from private houses, as they could be used to make a cheap boiler for a still. Another unlikely target of theft were the heavy iron grates that were placed over municipal storm sewers. A metal grate could be placed over an open fire as a support for a still (somewhat in the manner of a barbecue grill), perhaps even one made out of a garbage can that had also been stolen.

Making home brew was common in many households. The common stereotype was that gin was sometimes fermented in bathtubs. The accompanying joke was that this type of gin was only aged for a maximum of six days, as the tub was needed for the family bath time on Saturday nights.

One of the shortcomings of the Volstead Act was that applications for warrants to seize liquor and stills had to show proof that the liquor was for sale. Even if an individual had large amounts of liquor at home, no matter how it was obtained or what its intended use, Prohibition agents had to show evidence that a commercial transaction was involved. This avoided the issue of home manufacturing, both for personal use and as part of the cottage industry of distilling liquor that was organized as part of large criminal enterprises.

Large cities typically had a still or two in every block. One problem faced by all these moonshiners was how to dispose of the left-over fermented mash. In some cities the prevalence of stills caused a problem for municipal services as the residues of distilling, such as prune pits, potato peelings, and left-over mash and grain, were simply dumped into local sewers to dispose of them. This often clogged the underground pipes.

This photograph shows the Detroit police inspecting an illegal hidden underground brewery; examples like this of Prohibition agents confiscating and destroying illegal breweries and distilleries were common all over the country. This particular instance is interesting due to the size of the tanks and pumping equipment, worthy of professional-scale manufacturing levels (National Archives).

Another problem for the moonshiner was that the telltale smell of the mash and smoke coming from a still might give away a moonshine operation. Good revenue agents didn't always need to see a still to find it. They could often smell the distinctive yeasty odor of fermenting mash on a breeze in the early morning, perhaps with a slight added smell of alcohol vapor. Experienced agents could smell yeast from up to 300 feet away. Thus it was important to hide the used mash out of sight of any Prohibition agents and particularly outside of the range where anyone could smell it. One method used by moonshiners was to dump the remains in a local lake or reservoir. Anecdotal stories tell of ducks feeding on the leftover mash and weaving around the water in a drunken frenzy.

The leftover pulp from the mash was also used to feed farm animals at a low cost. It was often fed to pigs, cattle, mules, and donkeys, though the remnants contained enough alcohol that they often became drunk.

Farmers reported very happy-looking cattle staggering around in their fields. Similarly, some bootleggers who raised chickens fed them the left-over mash, resulting in obvious drunkenness in their chickens and other farm animals.

In 1921 a farmer named Dolores Martinez in Wagon Mound, New Mexico, heard a rumor that a Prohibition agent was coming to search his farm. He wasn't sure how to dispose of the mash he was cooking, so he dumped it into a nearby pig trough. The pigs happily ate it. By the time agent John Beaver arrived, the pigs were staggering around in a highly ine-briated state. Martinez' excuse was that he was testing a new type of pig feed. The agent, however, wasn't amused or taken in by the story and the case went to the grand jury anyway.[23]

Dumping leftover mash in local forests was also common, with simi-lar effect on the local population of mule deer and other wild animals. One ingenious hunter deliberately spread mash out for the local quail. Suppos-edly they became so drunk that they could not fly and made for easy hunt-ing. There was a story of one rancher who dumped his used mash into the ranch reservoir, and unexpectedly created some very tipsy birds. His bonus was that the experience made for good duck hunting.

## Near Beer

The Volstead Act outlawed beer, but permitted the manufacture of "cereal beverage" or near beer. One of the popular brands of non-alcoholic beers in the 1920s was called Bevo, made by Pabst Blue Ribbon.[24]

The alcohol content of near beer was required by the Volstead Act to be less than 0.5 percent. As part of the process to make near beer, it was necessary to first make real beer. This contained from 3 percent to 8 percent alcohol. The excess alcohol was then extracted until the level left in the remaining "beer" was less than the legal limit of 0.5 percent. The alcohol that was removed was supposed to be sent to government ware-houses for denaturing for industrial purposes but, as would expected, a large amount of it ended up in the hands of bootleggers. Sometimes this diversion was done deliberately by the brewery or it was done as a sideline career by dishonest employees.

Because near beer contained less than 0.5 percent alcohol, the taste and the resulting lack of intoxication was not very appealing to most beer-drinkers, so the beverage was not popular and sales were disappoint-ing. As an alternative, in most parts of the country ingredients for making beer at home were sold openly. Suppliers advertised "make your own beer at home" for only 20 cents a gallon.

One step in the manufacturing process of beer produced wort. The beer-making process could be stopped at this step before adding yeast. Wort had no alcohol in it, thus it was legal to own and could be purchased from many shops with a package of yeast to complete the fermentation process. This subterfuge helped brewers to circumvent the law and stay in business.

This easy method to make beer was to purchase wort, add a cake of yeast, and let the mixture ferment. When fermentation was complete, the yeast was filtered out and the resulting brew was beer. The customer was supposed to take the brewing process to only the 0.5 percent legal limit but, of course, most didn't.

Most cities had shops that sold all the ingredients for making beer, including malt, hops, wort, and yeast, along with bottles, caps, capping machines, and all the other supplies necessary to brew at home. Most grocery stores routinely sold cans of malt syrup, claiming that it was a foodstuff, which was completely legal. The national production of malt syrup by 1927 was estimated at nearly 880 million pounds, which would account for about 6.5 billion pints of beer. In 1929 the Prohibition Bureau estimated that almost 700 million gallons of beer were produced at home.[25]

## Making Whiskey

Even though some moonshiners could turn out a quality product that was safe to drink, what was labeled "whiskey" was not always the legitimate product. Genuine whiskey was made from malt, which was grain (usually corn or barley) that had been moistened, allowed to sprout, and then dried. When fermentation was complete, the liquid was distilled and the resulting alcohol stored in tanks or cisterns. Most whiskey was bottled at 85 to 100 proof. The legal minimum of alcohol in order that it could properly be called whiskey was 80 proof though, under the law, the proof could be as high as 110.[26]

Bogus whiskey, however, might have been manufactured in the back room of a speakeasy or had been supplied by any one of a number of people who made their own. Sometimes a dubious mixture started in a barrel in the cellar, and then somehow found its way into fancy bottles at the bar upstairs. Bootleg whiskey could easily be made by starting with a fifty-gallon keg of raw alcohol, then diluting and spicing it up by adding various chemicals and flavoring materials until the result could fool inexperienced drinkers.

The flavor and color of legitimate whiskey came from storing it in wooden barrels that were charred on the inside. Legitimate distillers used barrels that had been previously used to age sherry. Moonshiners used oak barrels that had been used to store and transport a variety of goods, such as salted meat or vinegar, and re-used them for whiskey. It was a common practice to fill these old barrels with straw and set it on fire to clean and char the inside.

Rather than aging the alcohol in charred barrels to create the legitimate flavoring and coloring of whiskey, tobacco, tea, strychnine, soap, red pepper, prune juice, gunpowder, tree bark, and creosote were often added to give raw alcohol the general appearance of whiskey, along with an appropriate amount of kick.

Various other types of liquor could be counterfeited by mixing different additives to simulate the taste of gin, or whatever was desired. Gin, for example, could be a mixture of raw alcohol, water, glycerin, and juniper oil. Juniper oil for flavoring gin was imported primarily from Austria and Italy. After the start of Prohibition the importation of juniper oil skyrocketed to 9,000 pints in 1920. This is an interesting number, as juniper oil did not have uses other than flavoring gin and, even then, one ounce of oil was sufficient to flavor several gallons of the final product.[27]

Many colorful names were applied to illegal liquor, such as coffin varnish, corpse reviver, jig juice, nose paint, phlegm-cutter, tangle-leg, tonsil varnish, bathtub gin, bootleg whiskey, and home brew. Bootleg whiskey that was distilled by a tribe of Alaskan Indians known as the Hoochinoo was called "hootch," a name that became a generic slang name for any type of crude alcohol.

Like the thrifty Scotsman, liquor could be distilled from mash using only a kettle on a low flame with a towel draped over the spout to condense the evaporated alcohol fumes back to liquid. This, however, was an unreliable method and the resulting liquid also contained dangerous and disgusting-tasting products of distillation that a moonshiner would discard.

Perversely, as soon as the saloon was outlawed and liquor became illegal, it seemed like everybody wanted it. Books and magazine articles that described how to perform fermentation and the distillation process to produce alcohol could be found in most city libraries. The Department of Agriculture published a series of bulletins between 1906 and 1910 on how to make alcohol from many varieties of produce, including grain, sugar beets, and potato peelings. Apparently with one hand not knowing what the other was doing, these pamphlets continued to be distributed long after the Eighteenth Amendment was in effect.

Stores sold perfectly legal hops, yeast, grains, corn syrup, malt syrup, fermenting pots, copper tubing, and all the other supplies that were needed for brewing and distilling at home. Small portable stills were also available for purchase for about $6, though they were sold with the understanding that they were not to be used for distilling hard liquor.

A bootlegger's still might be as simple as a tin washtub filled with mash that was propped up on bricks, with a fire lit underneath. The tub was covered with a horse-blanket to catch the fumes of alcohol that were driven off by the heat. The blanket was occasionally run through a clothes wringer and the resulting alcoholic liquid was bottled as "whiskey."

A more typical distilling operation consisted of five 50-gallon barrels, a dozen 5-gallon oak kegs, a huge copper kettle, and fifteen feet or so of copper tubing for the condenser. This set-up could be used to rapidly process a thousand pounds of fruit or corn, and an equal amount of sugar. Raisins might also be used as they fermented quickly and easily, and produced a high yield of alcohol.[28]

Bubbles of carbon dioxide gas rose out of the mash as a by-product of fermentation as the yeast turned the sugar into alcohol. The moonshiner knew that fermentation was complete when the bubbles became smaller and appeared less often, and the surface froth dissipated. At this point the mash was ready to go into the still. As the mash heated, it was stirred slowly so that none would scorch on the bottom. A simple still could be made from a copper coffeepot with copper tubing coming out of it in the form of a coil. The coil was placed in a barrel of cold water to cool and condense the alcohol fumes and the resulting liquid was collected.

The first few ounces of liquid out of the still was called the "foreshot," and contained some undesirable and poisonous chemical byproducts of fermentation, such as wood alcohol, acetone, and various aldehydes. The best alcohol was what distillers called the "heart," or the middle 75 percent of the liquid. This was good drinkable whiskey. The last bit of liquid was called the "aftershot" or "the tails." This consisted of further nasty chemicals, such as fusel oil, that vaporized after most of the alcohol had boiled off. Fusel oil was an oily poisonous liquid with a pungent smell that remained in the alcohol when the alcohol had been insufficiently distilled. It was generally a mixture of undesirable complex by-products, such as amyl, butyl, and propyl alcohols. This noxious liquid was also discarded by knowledgeable bootleggers as it would contaminate the whiskey. Slight traces of fusel oil remaining in the liquor was what produced the headache that accompanied a hangover.

Whiskey, even bootleg whiskey, needed to be at least 40 percent alcohol (80 proof) to be acceptable to most drinkers. When using a simple still, the alcohol often had to be run through a second or even a third time to raise the alcohol content. The more complex industrial stills could achieve the desired high alcohol level the first time through. The result was a clear, but raw, alcohol.

To produce the distinctive caramel color and taste of legitimate whiskey, the alcohol was aged in charred oak barrels for several years. Moonshiners usually skipped this step. Waiting for whiskey to age tied up their inventory when they could be selling it. Aging also made the entire moonshining operation riskier, as it was difficult to physically move barrels of whiskey while it was aging, which increased the risk of being caught by Prohibition agents.

Bootleggers often sold their product out of the back of their cars. In order to make extra profit at the expense of the customer, some bootleggers were known to sell what was called a "short pint." This consisted of only eleven to thirteen ounces of liquor, instead of the usual sixteen ounces. A short half-pint, also called a "mickey," consisted of only six to seven ounces instead of a full eight ounces.[29]

Distilling out in the woods and backcountry was usually carried out over a fire fueled by wood. In order to prevent detection of the resulting smoke, the manufacture of illegal alcohol was carried out in secluded areas. Prohibition agents learned to watch for wisps of smoke rising into the air in these remote areas. This was often a sign of an active still heated with a wood fire. Experienced moonshiners eventually learned to heat their stills with stoves that used white gasoline or propane to fuel the burners instead of wood fires, in order to avoid any tell-tale plumes of smoke. One well-known name for gasoline-fed stoves was Ozark burners. As well as tipping off lawmen and Prohibition agents, the same smoke might tip off undesired competitors to the fact that a still was operating in the area and there might be ripe pickings for hijacking.

Another tip-off for revenue agents was the purchase of large amounts of copper sheeting or copper tubing, which might be used as part of an illegal still. To avoid detection, purchasers of these items might claim that they were making boilers for cattle feed, or making gutters, or lining coffins, or some other subterfuge.

Moonshiners were all in favor of anything that was a shortcut and led to faster production and sale of their product. Sometime plain sugar was used for the mash instead of corn, because sugar would ferment quicker than corn and would yield more of the final product. As a countermove and one way to trace illegal stills, one technique used by Prohibition agents to detect bootlegging was to investigate which local stores sold large amounts of sugar and yeast. Agents made sugar suppliers show them the records of large sugar sales and give them the names of the recipients of the sugar.

Sugar sales were significant. The production of corn sugar went from 152 million pounds in 1921 to 960 million pounds in 1929. Similarly, during one four-year period, the sales of Fleischmann's Yeast rose from 64,000 packages to 189,000 packages.[30]

Moonshine in the back country and mountains was traditionally sold in ceramic pint and gallon jugs. Stoppers might be as simple as round pieces of wood forced into the neck of the jug or, in a pinch, an old corn cob could be wedged into the spout (left front) (author's collection).

Finished moonshine was usually stored away from the still in a separate location in order to hide it from revenue agents. One technique was to store the finished alcohol in culverts or in winter in snowbanks. If this cache was discovered by agents, they did not know to whom it belonged so they could not arrest anyone and all they could do was to destroy it.

Favorite jugs for storing moonshine were ceramic, cylindrical with a dome-shaped top, with a loop handle on the side. One enterprising individual who used these jugs stored them in post holes and then placed posts on top. Customers could judge the amount of inventory of liquor he currently had available by looking at the height of the fence posts.

## The Hazards of Moonshining

Moonshining was not without some danger to the moonshiner. Rather than making their own, some gangs set up roadblocks and hijacked cars and trucks transporting liquor. Sometimes they simply shot the drivers and grabbed the liquor. Warehouse robbery was also not uncommon.

The danger was so real and the profits so great that the larger operations mounted armed guards with shotguns or submachine guns twenty-four hours a day to protect their supplies of liquor.

In some instances thieves entered bonded warehouses and siphoned off some of the whiskey stored there, replacing it with water. One amusing story concerns a group of thieves who broke into a storage area and successfully siphoned off some whiskey. What they did not realize was that they had escaped with only whiskey-flavored water. Two years earlier another gang had siphoned off the real whiskey and topped up the containers with water to hide the theft.

As well as creating a product that might be dangerous to the consumer's health, moonshiners also faced various dangers on the job. One of them was that operating a still was inherently dangerous. Liquid alcohol was highly flammable and dangerous to handle, particularly for inexperienced distillers. There was also a real danger that if the still was not properly maintained and operated, any escaping alcohol vapor would catch on fire. If the copper boiler or condenser somehow developed a leak or wasn't constructed very carefully, vaporized alcohol accumulated in the air if adequate ventilation was not provided, to a point where the vapor reached a dangerous concentration. The volatile fumes could then easily ignite, and the resulting explosion could literally blow up a building, along with the bootleggers.

One example of the unforeseen dangers of bootlegging was that of Bertie "Birdie" Brown, a young black woman from Missouri who lived by herself on a homestead in Montana in the Lewistown area during the 1920s. Locals described her homemade whiskey as the "best in the country." In May of 1933 just before Prohibition ended, she was cooking a batch of illegal alcohol and at the same time was dry cleaning some clothes with gasoline, which was a common practice in those days. The cooker ignited the gasoline fumes and the still exploded in her face. She died a few hours later from the burns she received.

# 4

# Beware of What You Drink

BANNING LIQUOR DURING PROHIBITION predictably led to an increase in illegal alcohol. One of the associated unintended consequences was the dangers of bad booze on the health of the drinking public. Almost all bootleg alcohol was potentially dangerous and much of it was downright poisonous. The problem was the noxious and hazardous ingredients that were often contained in this so-called liquor.

The most popular drink during Prohibition was whiskey, or at least something that was named whiskey, though typically raw alcohol or neutral spirits was the base used in the production of bootleg whiskey, brandy, gin, rum, liqueurs, and other popular drinks. With no controls on who made the alcohol or how it was made, much of the moonshine and "bathtub gin" type of liquor was extremely dangerous to drink.

The underlying motive, of course, was profit. A gallon of moonshine could be produced for about 50 cents to 70 cents a gallon. This was sold by bootleggers to speakeasies for about $6 a gallon or to the consumer for anywhere from $12 to $60, depending on the supply and demand, or whatever the bootlegger thought he could get away with. In Kentucky in 1923 moonshine typically sold to the consumer for $16 a gallon. An attractive profit indeed.

Brand-name liquor that was smuggled into the country by rumrunners was the legitimate product from distilleries in Canada or other places overseas. If the liquor had not been tampered with, it was safe to drink. But much of the product sold as "fine old whiskey" was not. Somewhere between the distillery and the customer, the desire to make some additional profit resulted in the product being tampered with, diluted, or counterfeited in various ways. Even if the bottle had a label and seals that looked genuine, that was not always the case.

A case of legitimate whiskey sold for from $80 to $100; however, much of the authentic good whiskey that was available went into making counterfeit booze instead of being directly sold to the customer. Real liquor was blended with raw alcohol and additives in a process appropriately called "cutting." In the western part of the country, most of the adulteration was performed in major West Coast cities, such as San Francisco and Los Angeles, in large, well-equipped cutting plants that were outfitted with mixing vats, fake labels, bogus bottles, and counterfeit revenue stamps in order to turn out a believable facsimile of a name-brand liquor.

One easy method of making fake booze was that genuine distillery whiskey from a name-brand company might simply be diluted with water to make it go further, and then a little tea or tobacco juice added to bring the resulting liquid back to an approximation of its original color. This simple practice extended the number of servings and could yield drinks at the bar of three or four times the original quantity of alcohol, hence raising the profits for the saloon or speakeasy owner.

Another technique was to dilute the real whiskey with bootleg alcohol. All that was needed to accomplish this was several large drums of ethyl alcohol and a few cases of real whiskey. Operators at the cutting plant poured the whiskey into a large vat and added enough water to dilute it to the desired amount. Then enough raw alcohol was added to bring up the proof to any level that the bootlegger thought would be acceptable to the customer. Typically this was between 85 and 100 proof. Then some burnt sugar, caramel, or prune juice was added to give enough color to make the mixture look like aged whiskey, and perhaps some oil of rye or oil of bourbon was added to enhance the flavor of the result.

Other manufacturing techniques for these "overnight whiskies" used no real liquor at all. Bogus whiskey was made by starting with raw ethyl alcohol that had just been distilled and diluted, then adding various substances to flavor and color it until it was transformed into a reasonable approximation of whiskey and the result could fool inexperienced drinkers. Potentially dangerous chemicals were added to counterfeit booze to "improve" the flavor, to give it some kick, or to stretch the amount of bootleg alcohol to make it go further.

Grain alcohol was cut with water, then flavored with juniper and sugar to make gin, or with caramel and brown sugar for whiskey, then the results bottled as Canadian Club, Gordon's Gin, White Satin, or one of the other well-known liquor brands. Over one two-year period, prohibition agents in Minnesota confiscated 350,000 gallons of alleged rye, bourbon, and scotch, and less than three gallons of that total was real liquor from a genuine distillery. Numbers like this were thought to be representative of the illegal liquor produced in other states.

Moonshiners used chewing tobacco, caramel coloring, or creosote to achieve their idea of the correct color of whiskey. Some of the other not-so-pleasant additives used to give raw alcohol the general appearance of whiskey were tea, coffee, red pepper, prune juice, gunpowder, and tree bark. In addition, burnt sugar, molasses, sagebrush, black bone meal, or dried peaches might be added to give color and flavor. Barrels used for storing counterfeit whiskey often contained three or four plugs of tobacco nailed to the bottom to give the "whiskey" its color and flavor as it "aged." Some bootleggers were even known to add a few rusty nails to their brew to give it an approximation of the correct color.[1]

One stomach-turning story from San Pedro, California, related how a thirsty player in a pool hall wanted a bottle of liquor. One of the men went out to contact a bootlegger and came back a few minutes later with another man who had a bottle of clear alcohol. The pool player said that he did not want clear alcohol, but wanted aged whiskey. The bootlegger left saying he would be back shortly with the kind the player wanted. The bootlegger came back a few minutes later with a bottle of amber-colored alcohol and the pool player was happy. His fellow pool players didn't say anything at the time, but had a good chuckle among themselves later. What they knew was that the bootlegger had gone outside and simply dribbled some of the juice from the tobacco he was chewing into the bottle until the color looked about right. Then he came right back in to a happy customer.[2]

Nobody really knew exactly how much illegal liquor flowed into the country during Prohibition or how much was manufactured in moonshine stills. Estimates of the amounts of illegal booze that have been made were estimates and wild guesses, and were often inflated figures used to justify further governmental control and funding. And, in addition, nobody really knew how much medicinal or industrial alcohol was swilling around the country. The only fact that can be stated with any certainty is that if someone wanted a drink they could obtain it almost anywhere very quickly with relative ease.

The safest liquor was that smuggled into the country from foreign shores, such as Britain or Bermuda, or across the border from a legitimate distillery in Canada. But just because the liquor came in a bottle with a recognizable shape and with an authentic-looking label on it didn't mean that it was a legitimate product. Counterfeit bottles, even those of proprietary design, were freely available to moonshiners and so were reproductions of labels that sported the brands and names of legitimate distilleries. These labels might be pasted onto bottles of alcohol that had been made at an illegal still and often contained dangerous ingredients. The bottom line was that it was very important to know where liquor came from and if it was safe to drink.

## Moonshining and Bootlegging

Before Prohibition, liquor held in warehouses was whiskey manufactured by legitimate distillers. By 1922, these supplies of legitimate authentic whiskey were mostly exhausted, much of it the target of theft by bootleggers. Two outcomes resulted. One was that bootleggers started hijacking industrial alcohol, which was in plentiful supply. Their plan was to re-distill it or otherwise process it and make it into saleable alcohol for consumption in speakeasies. The other outcome was that they started making and distilling their own alcohol.

The manufacture of home-made whiskey in America came from a long tradition of distilling spirits in Europe. Distilling whiskey for home use during colonial times was not illegal and was performed on thousands of farms. Even George Washington had a still for producing alcohol on his Mount Vernon farm.[3] And such a firm temperance supporter as leading physician Dr. Benjamin Rush in the late 1700s suggested improving cider by boiling apple juice to half its bulk before fermenting it and then storing it for two years in a cask. This must have made a powerful drink.[4]

It was not until 1862 that making whiskey without a federal license (which was in reality part of the tax to help pay for the Civil War) became a federal offence. Distilling whiskey illegally continued to be popular, however, and bootleggers avoided paying taxes on their product. As dubious alcohol of doubtful heritage was lower in cost than the legitimate product, it was popular for purchase by individuals who wanted to save money and by unscrupulous saloon owners who wanted to make an additional profit at their bar.

In the United States, moonshine whiskey had been continuously produced since the 1700s, commonly in the region of the Appalachian Mountains and in the South. Distillation to produce whiskey mostly used corn as a base, but apples and peaches were also used. Moonshining became a popular cottage industry among farmers when corn prices dropped so low that the market for corn became unprofitable.

Moonshine liquor had many nicknames. It was variously called mountain dew, hooch, rotgut, happy Sally, stump whiskey, white mule, farm whiskey, home brew, Kentucky mule, white lightning, and many other names. The name "lightning" was used in 1858 in San Francisco for any strong, raw liquor, but the name was generally reserved to describe the powerful headache-inducing liquors that were made on the western frontier, such as the raw and powerful Taos Lightning made in New Mexico starting in the 1820s. The term lived on in the 1920s name of "white lightning." Bourbon whiskey was also sometimes called "red liquor," because of its reddish color, though it was also similarly called "redeye," "red ink," and "red disturbance."

The illegally-distilled alcohol itself was called "moonshine." The names "moonshiner" and "bootlegger" were often used interchangeably but, strictly speaking, the moonshiner was the manufacturer of the illicit alcohol, whereas the bootlegger was the individual who transported and sold it.[5] During the Revolutionary War, bootleggers were also called "blockade runners" because they shipped their illegal liquor through and around coastal blockades.

Making moonshine liquor was simple. One formula called for a barrel of water filled with corn, a gallon of barley malt, a pound of yeast, and sixty to eighty pounds of sugar. This was the mash. The mash usually fermented in three to four days if the mixture was kept warm. When fermentation was complete, the mixture became a type of beer called "corn beer" or "distiller's beer." The spores of wild yeast that occurred naturally in the air would start the fermentation process, but colder temperatures and the absence of sugar and yeast lengthened the process to two or more weeks. Adding commercial yeast made the process faster and more reliable. The mixture had to be stirred frequently during this stage, so moonshiners often slept out near their cooking pots in the open or in tents. Even today decayed mattress springs may often be found near the sites of old stills.

The fermented result was distilled in a home-made still to concentrate the alcohol, which was collected as a clear liquid. Forty gallons of mash produced six to seven gallons of 90 proof whiskey. To speed up the process and produce product at a lower cost, alcohol might be made from corn

The term bootlegging is said to have come from the historical practice of smuggling illicit liquor hidden in the tops of boots. In 1922 this prohibition-era woman demonstrates the art of hiding a bottle of alcohol in the top of one of her Russian boots, a style of calf- or knee-length boots that were popular in the 1920s. This type had the reputation of being worn by women who frequented saloons and speakeasies. Note that the swastika on the floor was an ancient religious icon and an American Indian spiritual symbol long before it was used by the Nazis. It was used in America as a symbol of good luck until the 1930s (Library of Congress).

sugar. Ten pounds of sugar could be used to produce a gallon of 100 proof alcohol.

If the beer was heated in a kettle to about 180°F several times, the resulting vapor collected was 99 percent (198 proof) alcohol. This concentration was so strong that it was harmful to drink, so water or something else had to be added to cut the strength and create drinkable bootleg "booze." Most moonshiners used water to dilute the alcohol, but some unscrupulous moonshiners were known to use wood alcohol, turpentine, or ammonia.

Commercial whiskey had a golden or amber color due to storage and aging in oak barrels. When bootleg corn alcohol was fresh from the still it was clear and colorless like water, which gave it the name of "white lightning" or "white mule."

Some iodine might be added for customers who wanted a little more spicy flavoring in the taste of their whiskey. Iodine was added to create a burning sensation in the stomach that some drinkers believed was essential for good liquor. In this way, many customers thought that this whiskey was good strong stuff because it burned the throat going down. Unfortunately, iodine was also a poison, a strong antiseptic that burned and stained the skin. An antiseptic tincture of iodine contained about 7 percent iodine in alcohol. The medical dose of iodine was a few drops, but some bootleggers added as much as two ounces to a quart of liquor (around 6 percent). Other unscrupulous bootleggers occasionally used embalming fluid (formaldehyde) to produce an even greater burning effect. As a result, various homemade alcohols packed a powerful jolt, leading to the variety of colorful names that were attached to them. The unplanned result was that some unfortunates died from drinking them.

## The Bead on Whiskey

Whiskey of good quality was supposed to have a good bead, which was the layer of unbroken bubbles that formed at the surface when the liquor was shaken. Many buyers thought that genuine undiluted whiskey should have a good bead, and used it as a gauge to estimate the strength of the alcohol. One fallacy of bootleg booze was that inspection of the bead in a bottle of liquor was an indicator of the alcohol content, and liquor "experts" felt that they were able to determine the strength of the liquor by studying its bead. Supposedly the longer the bead was present, the lower the proof. Large bubbles that disappeared quickly indicated a high alcohol content, while smaller bubbles that disappeared slowly indicated a lower alcohol content. Real experts knew that half of a true bead would stay in the liquor and half would float on top.

To produce a good bead on counterfeit liquor, a little soap was often added to the mixture. Some moonshiners added cooking oil (called by them "beading oil") or lye to poor quality whiskey to make it seem that the product had a high proof. Others added a touch of glycerin, fusel oil, or sulfuric acid to produce a reasonable-looking bead.

Another unreliable test was sometimes used to determine the quality of moonshine. The purchaser poured a small quantity of bootleg liquor into a spoon and lit it with a match. The folk legend was that if the alcohol was safe to drink, it burned with a blue flame. If it was contaminated, it burned with a yellow flame and was thus unsafe to drink. The extension of this test was that if the liquor burned with a reddish flame, it was contaminated with lead, showing that the liquor had perhaps been distilled in an old automobile radiator or galvanized washtub.

## Dangerous Additives

The art of making fake alcoholic drinks was well-known long before Prohibition bootleggers revived it. In the early 1700s London vintners made a type of Bordeaux from sloes (a small blue-black plum-like fruit) and champagne from apples. Neutral spirits were colored with caramel, flavored with various adulterants, and diluted with water to 20 percent alcohol by volume to make "sherry."[6] "Jersey champagne" was a drink made from turnips, brandy, and honey.

Some of the substances used to doctor wines were sugar of lead (lead acetate), opium, henbane (deadly nightshade), arsenic, and vitriol (sulfuric acid). One retired Philadelphia merchant assured the local temperance society that the nutty flavor of his Madeira wine was produced by dissolving cockroaches in it.

Do-it-yourself manuals recommended the use of logwood (a source of red vegetable dye), cayenne pepper, caramel, and assorted herbs to stretch a single bottle of sherry into several. There was no Food and Drug Administration to protect the consumer and wine customers who were experts were few.

The practice of adding noxious chemicals to liquor was certainly not new. On June 6, 1857, one of the leading national newsmagazines of the time, *Frank Leslie's Illustrated Newspaper*, reported that the Ohio legislature had recently banned the use of strychnine in manufacturing liquor.

Moonshiners had a variety of ways to make their own versions of "whiskey." Though the recipes for some of the "overnight" whiskeys sound bizarre when reading their ingredients, they could cause serious harm to the unwary recipient. These potent brews frequently resulted in alcohol poisoning or other chemical side-effects. Drinkers who did not know the source of the liquor they were drinking faced some very real health risks in what they drank. Jackass brandy, made from distilling wine, for example, could be so strong that it caused internal bleeding.

The typical number of people who died each year from rotgut booze has been estimated at 1,565. In 1923 government reports showed that 2,467 deaths occurred from drinking bad liquor, a figure that was up 30 percent from 1922.[7] Twenty occurred in California, 400 in New York, and 200 in Illinois. In 1923 Philadelphia reported 307 deaths from contaminated alcohol and Chicago reported 163.[8] The total numbers are uncertain, but perhaps as many as 50,000 drinkers died from drinking contaminated alcohol during Prohibition. Regardless of the specific numbers, the total was a tragically high amount.

Dubious chemical ingredients, such as tartaric acid, sulfuric acid, ammonia, strychnine, turpentine, or creosote, might find their way into the brew to give it a little bite. One recipe for making "fine Irish whiskey" involved a barrel of raw alcohol with a half-pint of creosote added to counterfeit the smoky flavor of Scotch.[9] Creosote, also called dead oil or pitch oil, was a poisonous oily liquid distilled from coal tar. It was used as a wood preservative and disinfectant. It also contained acridine, which was used as an insecticide. Creosote could also be added to cheap wine to make a similar product.

Another common additive was antifreeze made from methanol that was drained from automobile radiators. Bootleggers claimed that the rust that was often in it added to the flavor.[10]

Other dangerous additives were after-shave, soft soap, camphor, mouthwash, hair tonic, paint thinner, and denatured alcohol. A particularly dangerous additive was bichloride of mercury, a highly corrosive form of mercury that was used to treat syphilis and preserve biological specimens. Some bootleggers added oil of coriander and other flavorings to produce a pungent odor thought to be associated with good liquor.

One formula for "whiskey" combined a barrel of raw alcohol with two ounces of strychnine to give the drinker a jolt, half-a-pound of red pepper to give the drink some spice, five bars of soap to produce a good bead, and three plugs of tobacco to add a whiskey-like color. The only step remaining was to age the mixture for a few hours.

Though these additives may sound humorous now, the side-effects of drinking them could cause serious harm to the unwary recipient. Thousands of drinkers died after ingesting bootleg booze, either directly or later from kidney damage or other medical problems brought on by improperly-produced alcohol.

Another recipe for home-made whiskey started with a mixture of a gallon of raw alcohol and three gallons of water, with a pound of tea or tobacco added to give the mixture the right color, and some ginger and

Just because booze was supplied in a fancy bottle didn't mean that it was of high quality. Counterfeit bottles with the distinctive shapes of brand-name liquors, bottle corks with the correct trademark, bogus labels, and fake revenue stamps that looked like the real thing were freely available to criminals who wanted to pass off inferior home-made alcohol as quality liquor to fool an unsuspecting purchaser (author's collection).

a handful of red peppers to give it a tangy taste. One variation of this all-purpose drink was to add a quart of blackstrap molasses to the mixture and call the resulting concoction rum. Counterfeit rum could also be made by mixing four gallons of neutral spirits, one gallon of real Jamaica rum, a half-ounce of sulfuric acid, four ounces of ethyl acetate (a sweet-smelling solvent used in glues, nail polish remover, and perfumes), and eight ounces of burnt sugar for coloring.[11] So-called yack yack bourbon, made in Chicago, contained burnt sugar and iodine. Soda Pop Moon, made in Philadelphia, was manufactured from rubbing alcohol, which was used commercially as a disinfectant and in gasoline. Rubbing alcohol was also known as "rub-a-dub" by the confirmed drinkers who swilled it down.

Other beverages might be counterfeited in a similar manner. Bogus wine might consist of watered-down alcohol with some appropriate coloring and flavoring, such as cherries or prunes. Counterfeit brandy could be made from a half-barrel of alcohol with enough grape juice, burnt sugar, sulfuric acid, and tobacco added to provide color and flavoring. Some so-called brandies were produced by simply adding some raw alcohol to grape juice.

An approximation of gin could be made by mixing five gallons of raw alcohol with five gallons of water (or more or less depending on the desired strength of the liquor and the profit motive) and adding glycerin and oil of juniper. Juniper berries for flavoring could be obtained at no cost from trees grown in the garden, a nearby park, or in the mountains.

Counterfeit Scotch could be made by adding caramel coloring, prune juice, or creosote to raw alcohol. Scotch of even lower quality could be made by adding some burnt sugar to raw alcohol to create color and flavoring. One moonshiner's recipe for Scotch specified four gallons of neutral spirits, one gallon of water, five drops of creosote, and a quarter of a pint of burnt sugar. An approximation of the flavor of Scotch or bourbon could be produced by adding wood shavings, chips of oak bark, or burnt redwood sticks to alcohol, or storing it in barrels that had been burned and charred inside to contribute to the flavor. This made the liquor slightly reddish and approximated the color of bourbon, as well as adding a taste that made it appear as if the liquor had been aged in wooden barrels. This trick might increase the sales price, as the resulting liquor could be advertised as genuine "aged in wood." To age bourbon in this manner, however, took additional labor and time that most moonshiners were not willing to invest.

People wanted to believe that the liquor they were drinking was the real thing, so an ancillary business developed to produce barrels, kegs, and bottles of every size and description, including the distinctive containers used for famous brands of liquor. It was possible to purchase whatever was needed, such as whiskey cases that looked like those of famous distillers.

Moonshiners often tried to obtain empty bottles from customers for re-use. Discarded bottles were also scavenged from trash dumps. Bootleggers would then refill these bottle with bogus liquor and add fancy counterfeit labels.

Some crafty bootleggers also developed methods to drain high-quality liquor out of original distillery bottles without disturbing the original seals, and then refilled them with bootleg liquor. One method was to make a tiny hole in the bottom of the glass bottle with a red-hot wire, remove the genuine liquor and replace it with their own bootleg booze, and then re-seal the hole in the bottle with a glass rod melted over a hot flame. The motive as usual was additional profit. The original high-quality liquor in the bottle might be worth $24, whereas the bogus booze they put back in the bottle might be worth only $4, but the purchaser paid the $24. The general drinking public was willing to pay a premium for what they thought was high-quality liquor.

Another trick used to add to the illusion was that the labels used on the bottles might be soaked in sea water before being glued on, in order to make them look like the whiskey had been thrown overboard during a Coast Guard chase and then rescued and sold. That added an appearance of authenticity to the origin of the bottles and raised the sales price.[12]

## Fusel Oil

One of the nasty chemicals that ended up in bootleg whiskey was fusel oil. Fusel oil, a clear liquid slippery substance, was one of the poisonous by-products of distilling that was normally carefully removed from finished whiskey by legitimate distillers. It was a toxic product of fermentation that was thought to trigger severe mental disturbances such as paranoia, hallucinations, sexual depravity, murderous impulses, or even insanity.[13]

Fusel oil was the chemical that gave drinkers a hangover and was present to some degree in all alcohol, but was removed as much as possible by the best distillers. Fusel oil (also called primary or normal isoamyl alcohol, or grain oil) was used commercially as a solvent for oils, resins, and varnishes, and also in the vulcanization of rubber.[14]

If the distillation of moonshine alcohol was not properly performed, the result could contain a high concentration of fusel oil or wood alcohol, both of which were poisonous. Competent moonshiners used charcoal to remove the fusel oil.[15] Amateur moonshiners filtered the alcohol through French bread, because the bread supposedly absorbed the oil. Perversely, a small amount of fusel oil was sometimes added back to bootleg alcohol by unscrupulous moonshiners to create additional flavoring.

## Other Dangers

Moonshine could be dangerous simply because of poor manufacturing conditions and a lack of quality control in the production environment. Other dangers were that the final product might contain an unknown and variable alcohol content, harmful contaminants such as lead from a poorly constructed still, or poisonous chemicals deliberately added to increase the "kick" of the liquor.

Some moonshiners deliberately add harmful substances, such as manure, embalming fluid, bleach, rubbing alcohol, acetaldehyde, or paint thinner to increase the kick in the drink. In other instances, heavy metal contaminants might be present in high amounts, consisting primarily of lead, but also arsenic, zinc, and copper.

Moonshiners were not always as knowledgeable as they should have been in making a still. The best material for constructing a still was copper sheeting and condenser tubing in order to prevent lead from leaching to the alcohol from galvanized construction material. However, this still looks like it has soldered seams, which could eventually leach lead into the alcohol and give the drinker lead poisoning (author's collection).

A serious problem was a high content of lead in some illegal alcohol because home-made condensers were often made from old automobile radiators that contained lead solder that leached out into the alcohol. Some stills were constructed so cheaply that solder from their seams similarly leached lead into the alcohol and made it poisonous. Galvanized tubs and five-gallon metal cans were notorious for leaching lead into the alcohol mixture and causing lead poisoning. Lead toxicity affected the circulatory system by inhibiting the production of hemoglobin, the major component of red blood cells that carries oxygen. It also produced kidney failure and neurological damage. Accumulated lead could be stored in the body for thirty years or more.

During the 1920s, one unknowing Denver automobile mechanic made a still by combining a galvanized gas tank from an old car with a piece of gas pipe whose end was covered by towels. The tank was used as the cooker and the pipe as a condenser, and the towels caught and collected the dripping alcohol. Along with poisonous by-products.

Obviously there was no government inspection or control of bootleg distilling conditions, so they might be highly unsanitary. Tubs and cooking vats were seldom cleaned. Impure water might be used, perhaps from a nearly creek or spring containing dead animals and insects, or water contaminated by various chemical substances. There are reports of Prohibition agents finding moonshine vats that contained dead rats, rabbits, and cats that had inadvertently fallen into the container and couldn't get out again. To top it off, the moonshiners themselves were often unsanitary, dirty people who worked and produced their questionable alcohol in dirty surroundings.

## Denatured Alcohol

Ironically, the largest source of illegal liquor was legal spirits. The total production of legally-distilled alcohol rose from 187 million gallons in 1912 to 203 million gallons in 1926. Most of this increase was a result of the greatly expanded demand for industrial alcohol, which sold for about 20 cents a gallon.

During the 1910s and 1920s the American chemical industry experienced unprecedented growth. Between 1920 and 1925 the manufacture of legal industrial alcohol doubled, and then doubled again between 1925 and 1930. Alcohol was legitimately required for a wide variety of industrial purposes, including the manufacturing of dyes, paints, varnishes, cosmetics, explosives, anesthetics, photographic film, cleaning products, gasoline, disinfectants, perfume, after-shave, tobacco, and for scientific research. The author and enforcers of the Volstead Act had to be careful that the new legislation did not ruin this major growing segment of American industry. Manufacturers of synthetic textiles, for example, were large users of ethanol. One plant that manufactured a textile product called Rayon used 2 million gallons of industrial alcohol each year.

To meet the various needs of the chemical industry, the Prohibition Bureau allowed the distillation of ethanol, but required that the manufacturer add a denaturing chemical to render the alcohol unfit for human beverage purposes. Denatured alcohol was ethanol mixed with substances such as wood alcohol, sulfuric acid, benzene, ether, hydrochloric acid, pyridine, aniline, or iodine to make it unsuitable for human consumption, but still allowed it to be used for industrial purposes.

Other denaturing agents were lavender, soft soap, oil of wintergreen, oil of peppermint, tobacco, carbolic acid, mercuric chloride, menthol crystals, acetone, camphor, and other unpleasant ingredients, depending on the final intended use. Carbolic acid, also called phenol, was a powerful disinfectant, but was highly corrosive. Mercuric chloride, also known as corrosive sublimate, was also a disinfectant, but was highly toxic and destroyed human internal organs. These substances were so deadly that they were frequently used by prostitutes in the Old West to commit suicide. These women did not really understand what they were doing because though both chemicals produced an eventual death, it was preceded by lingering agony.

There were seventy-six different chemicals that were approved for the denaturing process, various ones being used for the specialized denaturing requirements of different industries. These additives were used to give the alcohol a terrible taste and smell to discourage people from drinking it.

Products such as automobile antifreeze and varnishes were required to be completely denatured. Completely denatured alcohol might contain benzene, ether, pyridine, kerosene, gasoline, mercuric acid, formaldehyde, bichloride of mercury, or wood alcohol. Other alcohol was only partially denatured because the denaturing chemicals would not allow the alcohol to be used for its intended purpose.

The single most significant factor in the expanded production of denatured alcohol was the spectacular growth of the automobile industry. In 1919, there were 7.5 million passenger cars and trucks registered in the United States. By 1926, this had grown to 22 million. Ninety percent of the cars were originally open to the elements and therefore not suitable for driving in cold weather or at night. By 1926, 70 percent of cars were enclosed, which increased the use of driving in cold weather. Antifreeze suddenly became essential to protect the engine from freezing and, as a result, three-quarters of the total output of completely denatured alcohol went for manufacturing antifreeze. Predictably, antifreeze started to be stolen from the radiators of automobiles.

Two options were open to the criminal who wanted to use denatured alcohol to provide his customers with a drinkable product. The first was to attempt to recover the original ethanol from partially denatured alcohol using an expert chemist with the appropriate equipment. Millions of gallons of industrial alcohol were stolen and re-distilled, then sold by bootleggers to speakeasies. From a technical standpoint, the distillation process took skill to perform, with usually two or three passes through the still to remove all the chemical impurities.

The other option was to steal or divert some of the alcohol intended for industrial use to bootleggers via an unscrupulous manufacturer or his employees directly after the distillation stage and before denaturing. This could be done by as simple a method as altering the consignment documents and shipping the product straight to a bootlegger. Alcohol could also be diverted by altering the labels on the container itself before or even during shipping. This was not necessarily performed on a small-scale. Shipments might be as large as fifty barrels, which made the entire process quite profitable. In 1925, about 10 million gallons of the 87 million gallons of ethanol that were legally distilled nationally could not be accounted for. They were probably diverted to bootleggers and went into some form of illegal drinking alcohol.

The option of direct stealing was, of course, the preferred choice as the pure alcohol could be cut and flavored by the bootlegger to make "whiskey" and then sold very quickly. Re-distilling and removing the denaturing chemical, on the other hand, could be time-consuming and complicated, resulting in a higher possibility of being caught by federal agents before the alcohol was finally re-processed and moved out.

The other drawback to re-distilling the alcohol to remove the denaturant was that the process required special skills and, if not done correctly, resulted in much of the denaturant being left in the alcohol with the resulting potential for poisoning the ultimate consumer. Unfortunately, in a majority of cases, this was not of great concern to the bootlegger, who figured that someone purchasing an illegal product and drinking it probably deserved what they got. They merely added enough flavoring to disguise any undesirable chemical smell or taste, and passed the rotgut booze straight on to the speakeasies. This horrible stuff was called with some reason by slang terms such as "undertaker's highballs" and "graveyard gin."[16]

In 1927 in New York, 480,000 gallons of liquor were seized by Prohibition agents. Government chemists analyzed the seized alcohol and found that 99 percent of the liquor still contained some of the denaturing chemical.[17] Liquor seized from fifty-five of the city's speakeasies contained traces of wood alcohol. These figures were not unusual. The problem appeared to be more prevalent in areas further from the coast, because these areas were less likely to have imported legitimate liquor and relied mostly on bootleg booze.

## Wood Alcohol

A common additive used for denaturing ethanol was methyl alcohol (methanol), which was poisonous if drunk and could cause nerve damage, blindness, and death. Methanol was a colorless liquid with a faint aroma.

Methyl alcohol was also known as wood alcohol and wood spirits, because this particular alcohol was at one time made by burning wood in a process known as "dry distillation of wood" or "pyrolysis." It could also be manufactured from methane, which is found in natural gas, and is produced industrially by chemically combining carbon monoxide with hydrogen. Methanol was very volatile and has been used as a fuel for rockets.

Methanol was widely used in the manufacture of plastics, paints, varnishes, and adhesives. It was also used as an industrial solvent, and as a component of antifreeze for automobile radiators. Methanol was also used in windshield washer fluid, carburetor cleaner, fuel additives, windshield de-icer, paint thinner, various cleaning products, canned heat, and fire starter fluid. Confirmed alcoholics drank them all.

Because wood alcohol could not be removed by any simple chemical treatment, Prohibition bureaucrats assumed that nobody would drink it. However, bootlegging gangs thought they could use their own chemists to extract the original alcohol.

Some denaturants were easy to remove, but wood alcohol was among the chemicals that were very difficult to remove. Wood alcohol was chemically closely related to ethyl alcohol (beverage alcohol), with a boiling point that was only slightly lower. Wood alcohol boiled at 149°F while ethanol boiled at 173°F. The process of re-distillation to extract the ethanol required an expert chemist to be performed safely, and most bootleggers were not experts.

Most bootleggers attempted to re-distill the mixture of methanol and ethanol by simply boiling it in a still. Heating and re-distilling the denatured product removed some of the wood alcohol that did indeed evaporate off, but dangerous amounts of it remained and contaminated the resulting product. Bootleggers left it to the workers at the cutting plant to disguise any bad taste with various flavorings. If methanol was still present in the ethanol, however, the drink was deadly. The resulting rotgut booze poisoned thousands of speakeasy customers.

Among its other properties, methanol was a poison that attacked the nervous system. Symptoms of poisoning included nausea, vomiting, severe headaches, abdominal pain, and a blue tinge to the skin. The victim became delirious, went into convulsions, and then into a coma. The respiratory system became paralyzed and the victim died. Poisoning from drinking wood alcohol was not new. One Army report, for example, mentioned two sergeants from the Eight Cavalry in South Dakota who accidentally drank wood alcohol and died as a result.[18] Even in small amounts, methanol attacked the nerve cells of the retina at the back of the eye and the victim became partially or totally blind.

Bootleggers were able to reduce the content of wood alcohol used for denaturing ethyl alcohol fairly easily from about 5 percent to 1 percent. Then if the alcohol was cut with an equal amount of water to lower the proof to 100, and coloring and flavoring ingredients added to make the alcohol resemble liquor, the resulting wood alcohol content was lowered to about 0.5 percent, which the bootlegger considered to be acceptable. In reality, a wood alcohol content this low was still considered to be dangerous to the nervous system, and the toxicity was cumulative.

In 1927 the Prohibition Bureau realized that trying to stop people from drinking reclaimed alcohol was not working, so the government ordered manufacturers of industrial alcohol to double the amount of wood alcohol they added. They also mandated the addition of kerosene and pyridine to make it taste worse and make the methanol nearly impossible to remove. The cold-hearted attitude was that drinkers got what they deserved if they continued to drink illegal alcohol. This attitude created an outcry of public opinion and started to raise political opposition to Prohibition.

The alcohol that inexperienced bootleggers produced could contain methanol, propyl alcohol, butyl alcohol, or other complex alcohols that were poisonous. Propyl alcohol, also known as propanol, was not suitable for beverage purposes. Propanol was used as a solvent for plastics and was used in cosmetics, such as shampoo, hair spray, after-shave, and mouthwash. Isopropyl alcohol, or rubbing alcohol, which has a slightly different chemical structure, was used as a paint thinner and in antifreeze. In a 70 percent concentration, it was used as an antiseptic and as a soothing liniment for rubbing and massaging the skin. Ethylene alcohol (ethanediol or ethylene glycol) was used as an antifreeze for automobile radiators, as a de-icing fluid, and in manufacturing plastics. None of these alcohols were suitable for drinking and consuming them led to serious toxic side-effects, such as blindness, kidney damage, and death.

## Jamaica Ginger

One of the most dangerous liquor substitutes of the Roaring Twenties was Jamaica Ginger, a substance that when ingested could cause paralysis and untimely death. Popularly known simply as "jake," this was a late nineteenth century patent medicine that contained 82 percent ethyl alcohol. Because of its high alcohol content it was classified as a medicine. Jamaica Ginger was used medicinally, often mixed with a little warm water and sugar, for headaches, stomach-aches, upper respiratory infections, menstrual troubles, winter chills, and intestinal upsets. It was sold by prescription in two-ounce bottles costing 30 cents to 50 cents.

The high alcohol content also made Jamaica Ginger attractive to drinkers who were looking for something cheap to drink. Even for serious drinkers, though, the medicine was too strong to be drunk undiluted, so it was usually mixed with ginger ale or a similar fountain drink to improve the taste. The taste was also improved by following a swig of Jamaica Ginger with a milkshake. For a while a popular women's drink was "hot ginger," a highly alcoholic drink of hot water mixed with Jamaica Ginger.

The original formula contained bitter-tasting ginger oils, but manufacturers later added other ingredients, such as molasses and castor oil, in an effort to save on manufacturing costs. One of the substitute ingredients tried was tri-ortho-cresyl phosphate, an odorless and tasteless substance that was used as a plasticizer in lacquers and paints, celluloid film, and explosives. At the time, the chemical, also known as Lindol, was thought by the manufacturer to be non-toxic. It was later determined to be a highly toxic substance that caused severe damage to the nervous system of humans, and especially to those nerves located in the spinal cord. The nasty drink therefore resulted in blindness, paralysis, and death. It also caused impotence in men.

Even small quantities of Jamaica Ginger nearly always caused a terrible form of partial paralysis that became known as "jake leg." After only two or three weeks of drinking jake, it caused paralysis of the drinkers' hands and feet, and left their legs flopping out of control when they walked. Drinkers lost control of their fingers and the muscles of the feet were affected so that the toes pointed downwards. This affliction resulted in a peculiar way of walking that became called the "jake dance" or the "jake step." Unfortunately sufferers were looked upon as comical figures and were cruelly called "jake trotters" and were described as having "jake feet." Unfeeling song-writers turned out ballads with such titles as "Jake Walk Papa," "Jake Liquor Blues," and the "Jake Walk Blues."

In 1930 the Prohibition Bureau estimated that there were about 15,000 victims paralyzed by jake, but the number of victims may have been as high as 30,000 to 50,000. Some eventually regained partial use of their hands and feet, but most did not recover completely.[19] There was no cure, even though a variety of quack practitioners tried a variety of unorthodox treatments.

Drinking Jamaica Ginger for its alcohol content was not a new practice. The original patent medicine was available until 1921 without a prescription and could be purchased over the counter by anyone. The "medicine" was sometimes drunk by soldiers of the frontier army in the 1870s and 1880s for lack of anything else to get drunk on. After the Battle of the Little Bighorn in June of 1876, there were reports of the survivors who were ferried out on the steamer *Far West* drinking whiskey and Jamaica Ginger, seeking alcoholic escape from the effects of the battle.[20]

## Other Strange Drinks

With the desire of some people to find anything alcoholic to drink, many strange and ingenious brews were washed down drinkers' gullets.

Confirmed alcoholics sometimes drank cosmetic preparations, such as after-shave lotion, hair tonic, rubbing alcohol, mouthwash, perfume, and toilet water.[21] One brand of after-shave contained 76 percent alcohol. Another popular brand contained drinkable ethyl alcohol instead of the usual toxic isopropyl alcohol and methanol.[22] Drinking eau-de-cologne was another cause of methanol poisoning.

Lemon extract was a legal product in spite of its high alcohol content. Hard-core drinkers poured the liquid into a depression chipped into a block of ice. The lemon syrup quickly solidified and hardened, then the remaining alcohol could be poured off and drunk. Some farmhands drank lemon extract neat, without all the bother of what they considered to be lengthy preparation work.[23]

Sailors desperate for a drink drained the alcohol from ship's compasses or drank the 180-proof grain alcohol that was used to power Navy Mark 14 torpedo motors. They strained this through French bread to try to remove any poisonous products.[24]

Solidified alcohol or alcohol gel, also known as canned heat (one popular brand was Sterno), was filtered through bread, squeezed through cheesecloth, or strained through an old sock or handkerchief to try to produce drinkable alcohol. These methods of extracting the alcohol gave the fuel the slang name of "squeeze." The gel was deliberately colored pink by the manufacturer as a warning that it contained undrinkable methanol as well as alcohol, which also gave it the nickname of "pink lady."

The desire for an inebriated sensation from alcohol was so strong that some farm hands became so desperate that they drank what they could drain from the sludge at the bottom of silos that contained an accumulated liquid from years of fermenting rotted animal feed.[25]

For those who did not drink, but still wanted the desired sensation of being intoxicated, an unconventional doctor named Albert Abrams reported that his electronic diagnostic gadgets could duplicate the vibrational frequency of alcohol and produce an electronic state of drunkenness.[26] Dr. Albert Abrams was a professor of pathology at Cooper Medical College from 1893 to 1898 and was the author of several reputable medical textbooks. Over the next few years Abrams developed a system for sensing what he called the "electronic reactions" of disease and used radio waves to diagnose and cure illness. Every disease supposedly had a specific vibration rate that he could detect and measure with his machines. The disease could then be cured by transmitting back to the patient the same frequency as the illness, in order to neutralize the vibrations of the disease and restore equilibrium. He proposed that he could do the same with drunkenness. However, whether his electronic "high" worked or not has remained unrecorded.[27]

# 5

## From Saloons to Speakeasies

As well as being careful of what they drank, Prohibition liquor customers had to be wary of where they drank it.

Popular images of Prohibition include bathtub gin, hip flasks, raccoon coats, rolled silk stockings, short skirts, bobbed hair, cloche hats, and the speakeasy. Though many saloons remained in full operation during Prohibition, one of the primary places to buy a drink on a night out on the town was in clandestine speakeasies.

As the demand for liquor quickly increased, criminal entrepreneurs emerged to take advantage of the opportunity for financial gain by breaking the new law and filling public demand by opening illegal establishments to supply beer, wine, and liquor. Thus the traditional all-male saloon gave way to the speakeasy. It has been estimated that every legitimate saloon that was closed by Prohibition was replaced by half-a-dozen speakeasies.

The speakeasy was a place to obtain access to legitimate or bootleg alcohol in a (mostly) glamorous atmosphere. At speakeasies, illegal beverages such as whiskey and gin were often served in coffee cups, though "coffee" might be the code name for whiskey, and the gin was ordered as "tea."

The name "speakeasy" came from the expression "speak-softly shop," a nineteenth-century Irish underworld phrase used as far back as the 1820s to describe an illegal drinking place where voices were kept low to avoid attracting attention.[1] The term was freely adopted during Prohibition as the name for a place where thirsty individuals could buy a drink.

These establishments were often operated by organized crime. The association of speakeasies with illegal liquor and the criminal underworld transformed drinking into a fashionable and exciting pastime for the rich. Limousines and taxis lined up outside speakeasies, where elegantly-dressed men and women whispered passwords through peepholes or gave secret coded knocks on the door before being hurriedly ushered inside. Speakeasies often provided music and dancing to entertain drinkers, and the coming of the Jazz Age provided employment for hundreds of up-and-coming jazz musicians.

Speakeasies were also known as "blind pigs" or "blind tigers," which were mostly low-quality speakeasies that sold low-quality liquor. They received this peculiar name because one meaning of "blind" was "out-of-sight" or "hidden," and these establishments certainly tried to operate out of the sight of Prohibition agents. "Blind tiger" was a name that was used mostly in the eastern United States, and was an expression not much used on the West Coast. Blind pigs operated by the thousands and the locations of these speakeasies in most towns were a poorly kept secret. During Prohibition, the city of Detroit was estimated to have 20,000 of them.[2] Other slang expressions for a speakeasy were a "whoopee parlor" and a "gin joint." Drinking associations called "Volstead Clubs" also flourished.

To avoid detection by the police and Prohibition agents, speakeasies frequently opened and closed in different locations that moved around a lot, often in an attic or a basement, or in a large room behind a legitimate business. Usually they operated behind a heavily-fortified locked door with a small peephole or little trapdoor inset into it for the guard at the entryway to be able to identify a customer before opening the door. The potential customer knocked on the door. The peephole opened up and, if the guard knew him or her, they were allowed in. If the doorman didn't know the customer, he or she didn't get in. Another way to gain entry was by the use of a secret password. This identified that the customer knew someone who thought that he or she was acceptable for entry. Common speakeasy features were camouflaged doors and hidden drinking rooms behind false walls.

Though illegal, a speakeasy was a relatively harmless way to seek forbidden pleasure. Speakeasies offered watered-down booze and false glamour. Secrecy was part of the aura that surrounded them. There was a certain thrill in sneaking down a dark stairway, knocking on an unmarked door, and whispering a secret password to a hulking doorman or bodyguard through a trapdoor at the entrance. Under any other name, speakeasies might simply be the old saloons, or might masquerade as restaurants, night clubs, or bars. The atmosphere ranged from plush nightclubs with music and dancing, while others were places for serious drinking in seedy basements. Stimulated by the atmosphere of illegal drinking, prostitution and gambling also flourished in the speakeasies as in the previous saloons.

Though speakeasy liquor was alleged to be bourbon whiskey, its true heritage was often dubious, because the appearance and general taste of bourbon was easy to simulate for unsophisticated palates, particularly after the customer had already swilled down a few cheap drinks. The content of a whiskey bottle may have been anything and the liquor might well be home-made. Even the real thing, if it were available, might have been

Not only was liquor confiscated and the still it came from destroyed, but Prohibition agents and other law enforcement officials put saloons and speakeasies out of business. Typically the premises would be padlocked and posted with *Keep Out* signs, but this photograph shows a group of determined Prohibition agents destroying the entire bar (National Archives).

adulterated, watered down, or otherwise corrupted between the bootlegger, the speakeasy storeroom, and the customer's glass. This practice could extend the number of servings to three or four times the original quantity of alcohol and hence raised the profits for the speakeasy owner. "Champagne" might simply be apple cider saturated with carbon dioxide gas, but cost $25 a bottle.

Champagne was easy to sell to unsuspecting and undiscriminating customers. Some champagne was made from carbonated hard cider and sold in fake French bottles. This too had a precedent. Some drinkers were so unsophisticated that in Leadville and Denver, in Colorado, in 1879 during the boom days of the silver rush in Colorado, reportedly some of the more gullible drinkers became quite inebriated on a low-alcohol mixture of brown sugar, water, and yeast that was sold as "champagne cider" for $5 a quart.[3]

Mixed drinks and cocktails, even though they were not an invention of Prohibition, quickly came into fashion among drinkers because bootleg speakeasy liquor needed something sweet and highly-flavored to disguise its raw or questionable taste. A mixer of ginger ale or a small glass of orange juice that cost $1.50 to $2 at the customer's table was used to help disguise the taste of the bad alcohol. Alternately, ice and soda or plain water were supplied as a setup at a cost of from $1 to $2 and the customer added his own liquor.

Quinine water, originally developed in India as a drink to help combat the ever-present malaria, was also used as a mixer to disguise the taste of gin of dubious origin. In similar fashion, ginger ale was used as a mixer for liquor instead of soda water as the flavor tended to mask bad liquor. Coca-Cola was popular, both as a straight drink and as a mixer, both to make bad liquor taste palatable and by itself as a non-alcoholic drink. Orange juice was used as a popular mixer to make a cocktail named an "orange blossom," which was the forerunner of today's screwdriver (vodka and orange juice). Sugar, mint, lemon, and various fruit juices were also used to hide the taste of poor whiskey.

Because near beer was not popular precisely because it contained almost no alcohol, speakeasies that sold near beer often added a shot or two of alcohol to increase the alcoholic content. Depending on the particular bartender or speakeasy, the resulting drink might contain anywhere from 3 percent to a whopping 20 percent of alcohol. The result of this concoction was often the intended drunkenness, but it also came at the price of a nasty stomachache and later hangover.

Another upsetting consequence for the drinker was that beer in speakeasies was often sold in the green state, a condition that also resulted in upset stomachs and roaring headaches. "Green beer" was originally the name for beer that wasn't yet ready to be consumed. It was a name used by brewers for beer that was too young or "green" to be sold. Green beer was not yet fully fermented and contained a high percentage of the chemical acetaldehyde, which made the beer taste bad and resulted in a stupefied feeling and stomach upsets. Beer companies actually warned that "biliousness" (an older medical term for vague feelings of physical discomfort, such as tiredness, headache, constipation, and loss of appetite) could result from drinking green beer.

This type of green beer should be distinguished from the "green beer" drunk in large quantities every year on St. Patrick's Day. Irish green beer as the symbol of the holiday is produced by adding food coloring to beer. The development of this type of green beer is traditionally credited to Professor Thomas H. Curtin, a physician who made green beer for his clubhouse in New York around 1914. Interestingly, the food coloring used was blue, as blue coloring added to yellow beer made the resulting color green.

Liquor flowed freely inside speakeasies at $1.50 a drink for watered-down Scotch or $25 a bottle for champagne that might be nothing more than sparkling cider laced with bootleg alcohol. A drink in a fancy speakeasy might cost $4 a shot. Speakeasies particularly liked to sell beer because of the large profit involved. Half a keg of beer cost about $1 to manufacture, then the brewer sold it to the speakeasy for around $25 to $30. At 25 cents to 50 cents a glass at the bar, the original investment brought in about $75 to $125.

To add to their illicit image, speakeasies were often smoky and noisy, but projected an image of glamour. The better places catered to well-to-do customers with jazz bands and dance floors, and offered lavish floor shows with a line of flashy chorus girls dressed in skimpy costumes. The thrill of possibly being the object of a police raid was considered by some patrons to be part of the fun.

The upscale speakeasy became a glamorous image of Hollywood films and was popular with movie audiences. And indeed it reflected the reality of the time and showed a world that the common man was not a part of, but could vicariously enjoy through the images on the screen. The motion picture production code in existence at the time, however, dictated that actual drinking could not be shown on-screen. To maneuver around this limitation, movies instead showed actors doing everything except the actual drinking, such as pouring drinks, holding full drink glasses, and supposedly swilling down drinks with their backs to the camera.

A popular misconception is that the speakeasy, the bootlegger, and the moonshiner came into being with Prohibition, but in fact all of them had been in existence since early colonial times. Government records show that between 1876 and 1906 that more than 30,000 illicit stills were destroyed, while fifty-four government agents were killed by moonshiners or bootleggers, and ninety-four were wounded.[4]

The interior of a crowded bar at midnight on June 30, 1919, when wartime prohibition went into effect. Somber-looking patrons are trying to guzzle down one last drink before it was illegal to manufacture, sell, or transport alcohol (Library of Congress).

Likewise, systems inside speakeasies to warn of impending raids went back to at least the 1880s. One example was Dewire's Saloon in Cambridge, Massachusetts, that was eventually raided by the police. When they searched the unlicensed premises, they found that the bar was equipped with an electric bell to provide warning of a police raid. Dewire's main supply of liquor was then rapidly hidden in a cavity behind a large picture that swung into place to conceal it.[5]

One speakeasy had a mechanism activated by the bartender that dropped all the liquor bottles at the bar through a secret trapdoor, where they fell down a chute so that the glass bottles would break and the liquor would drain away, thus leaving no evidence of illegal alcohol for revenue agents.

## Seedy Clip-Joints

Not all speakeasies were respectable places and the 1920s saw a resurgence of the old so-called "clip-joints." These were shady places that were often recommended by a taxi driver or hotel bellboy who was in cahoots with the management. Once the customer was inside, he was approached by one of the hostesses who persuaded him to buy her a drink, or better yet several. The girls in these places drank ginger ale or tea, which looked like whiskey and for which the sucker paid whiskey prices of $1 to $2.

During the entire scripted process, the inebriated customer might be charged for drinks he had not ordered, for some he had already paid for, for bottles of booze and cigarettes for the hostesses, and maybe a large cover charge. If he was drunk enough he might have his pocket picked or his wallet stolen. If he tried to protest, he likely as not would be beaten up, have the rest of his money taken, and he would be unceremoniously thrown out into the street. If the customer was drunk to the point of passing out, he might simply be robbed and dragged out into the alley behind the building and left there.

Seedy dancehalls were another source of illegal liquor and drinking, and were designed to extract the maximum amount of money from the customer. Dancehalls were a familiar feature of Western logging and mining country where loggers and miners loved to drink and had the money to pay for it. Dances in these places were intentionally short, perhaps only a minute, then the customer and the girl retired to a booth where he was expected to buy her a drink, or two if she could talk him into it. Her drink, of course was tea watered to look like whiskey, at whiskey prices. Typical prices were 10 to 12 cents for the dance and 25 cents for a drink. In a typical arrangement, the girl received half of the total and the dancehall the other half. Some readers might remember the song by Richard Rodgers and Lorenz Hart made hugely popular by singer Ruth Etting in 1930 titled "Ten Cents a Dance," in which she lamented the way in which dancehall girls were treated.

Everything about this type of dancehall was geared towards extracting the maximum amount of money from the customer as quickly as possible. For example, customers couldn't just sit around in a booth and talk to a girl or listen to the music. They had to constantly buy drinks for the women and pay for a dance every time the music started and stopped. Sometimes the girl might excuse herself and leave, then another eager (or at least thirsty) one would take her place and the customer was expected to buy her a drink also. In this way customers spent a large amount of money on drinks. Thus a ten-cent dance might cost the unwary customer anywhere from $5 to $20 an hour to stay in these places.

Customers were also expected to periodically buy a drink for the house. If there ten people hanging around the bar, the man paid for ten drinks, plus one for him and one for his female companion, and maybe even one for the bartender (which was never drunk). In some

The **Prohibition Bureau tried many different tactics to track down illegal alcohol. This is a "hootch hound" in action. These dogs were trained to sniff out liquor, in this demonstration successfully finding a bottle in the supposedly-oblivious fisherman's back pocket (Library of Congress).**

establishments where treating the house was the rule, the bartender might discreetly press a buzzer and all the girls who were not with a customer would flock to the bar from everywhere whenever they heard the signal.

Another arrangement was that the customer had to bring his own alcohol, but he had to purchase a glass of juice. There was no alcohol in the juice. That was supplied by the customer. The customer didn't even have to drink the juice, but he had to buy it. And keep on buying it.

## And Even Seedier

Some drinking places were not even as fancy as these dancehalls. A more primitive arrangement was to simply set up a counter somewhere in a shed, maybe in an alley, with a 50-gallon barrel or a couple of boards on barrels for a bar, a single shot glass, and some liquor. If a customer wanted a drink, he came in and laid 50 cents down on the barrel. The man behind the "bar" filled the glass, the customer drank it down and left, and the next customer came in.

The method of operation in this type of place was to serve the customer a drink as fast as possible and have him gulp it right down and leave. There was no fancy sipping or tasting the liquor. And no conversation. The operator didn't want any evidence sitting around in case a Prohibition agent should suddenly burst in through the door and didn't want the customer wasting any time. To assist him in this, local police officers, who were generally poorly-paid, could get a free drink or other payoff for looking the other way.

To keep the process moving, liquor was often served out of a pitcher, as in this way it would pour faster than out of a bottle. Likewise, it could be poured faster down a nearby sink or drain if a Prohibition agent should appear. This was followed by a jug of water down the drain to flush away the evidence. But even this scheme was not foolproof. Both the barman and the agent had to be fast to dispose of the evidence or to grab it, depending on their goal. Agents were known to disassemble sink pipes in order to retrieve any traces of whiskey from the trap underneath the sink as evidence. To try to beat this tactic, barmen sometimes used straight pipes instead of the S-shaped section of pipe commonly used under a sink, so that the evidence would be carried away faster and not be caught in the drain trap under the sink.

One trick that was used to hide a source of liquor in a cheap drinking place was to install a tall thin-walled tank with liquor in it inside a wall, with the outlet tube running down to a valve disguised inside an electrical light switch or wall socket. A copper tube from the tank was fed down inside the hollow part of an electrical conduit to the switch or socket, which contained a spigot to access the alcohol.[6]

For those who didn't want to go out to a speakeasy, but simply wanted to drink, liquor was also freely available in many drug stores, grocery stores, cigar stores, ice cream parlors, soft drink parlors, soda fountains, the back rooms of barbershops, delivery agencies, athletic clubs, shoe shine parlors, paint stores, malt shops, fruit stands, vegetable markets, boarding houses, and a whole host of other establishments. Some of these used a real store as a front to fool Prohibition agents, then had an attached back room that was a speakeasy. All sorts of storefronts were used for disguise, including grocery and hardware stores. Among the more unusual establishments were luggage shops, laundries, and clothing stores that had a specially-equipped "fitting room" in the back that served liquor. Even an occasional funeral parlor was known to serve a drink or two in the back room.

For those who traveled and wanted to drink in peace in their rooms, bottles of liquor could also be supplied or arranged by most hotel bellhops, desk clerks and night clerks, as well as by taxi drivers, restaurant waiters, and others in similar service industries. Hotels might have arrangements to accept local deliveries. The customer called a saloon or some other place known to supply bootleg liquor and a nameless, faceless man would shortly deliver the gin, whiskey, beer, or wine that the customer had ordered.

# 6

# The Pacific Ocean

At the same time that major cities along the Pacific Coast became bootlegging centers, smuggling liquor was an active business on land and by air, and also by sea using high-powered motor boats. One of the pathways that fed illegal legitimate liquor into the western United States during prohibition was bringing it in by sea to the many small bays and inlets that were located along the Pacific Coast.

The general shoreline of the Pacific Coast along the states of Washington, Oregon, and California was 1,293 miles long, but that figure expanded to 7,863 miles when all the attached bays, inlets, islands, river mouths, and creeks were included. This created an opportunity for many locations for rum-runners to sneak booze to shore via the sea. California alone had 3,427 miles of shoreline to guard.[1]

Because manufacturing alcohol was legal in countries bordering the United States, distilleries and breweries in Canada, Mexico, and the Caribbean sold their products to visiting Americans or to rum-runners who smuggled foreign liquor illegally from Europe, Canada, and the Caribbean into the United States to sell on the black market.

One official estimate at the end of 1930 was that 46,040 cases of illegal liquor had entered the country via the sea coast between July 1929 and July 1930. This did not include 7,000 cases that arrived from Canada via the Strait of Georgia and Puget Sound. Even these figures were probably low as there was a constant stream of transport ships lying offshore with smaller boats ferrying cases of liquor ashore daily.

The term "rum-running" originally referred to bringing illegal rum ashore in the fishing communities of the northeastern parts of the United States when rum was a popular drink during the early days of attempts to ban alcohol. This practice continued during Prohibition. By late 1921 large freighters were lying off the Atlantic Coast discharging cargoes of illegal liquor onto smaller ships that carried them to shore. By 1930, estimates were that smuggling foreign-made liquor into the country was a $3 billion industry ($3 billion had the same buying power as $50 billion in 2021).

Americans preferred Scotch whiskey and bourbon to rum during Prohibition, so in reality more whiskey than rum was smuggled; however, the name "rum" continued to be used generically as a name for all intoxicating liquors. During Prohibition the name "bootlegger" was applied to anyone who transported illegal liquor, whereas "rum-runner" was applied generically to any smuggler who transported whiskey by sea.

Rum-running started on the East Coast. During the year's grace period before Prohibition went into effect, many American distillers sent large quantities of bourbon and rye to the West Indies for storage, intending to bring it back after Prohibition ended, which seemed to them to be inevitable. Thus large stocks of liquor were already stored in the Bahamas.

In addition, British liquor producers were constantly providing more. In 1917 the Bahamas imported about 50,000 quarts of liquor. Two years after Prohibition started the town of Nassau boomed and the liquor trade increased to 386,000 gallons (1,544,000 quarts). By 1923, the islands were bringing in about ten million quarts per year, though most was shipped right back out again.[2] Like the United States, the Bahamas saw an undesired accompanying increase in crime as bootleggers, buyers, liquor gangs, and sailors crowded into the islands following the liquor.

One scheme for obtaining legitimate liquor took advantage of the fact that ship's captains could obtain alcohol at various naval facilities if it was strictly for medicinal use. As part of the paperwork to withdraw alcohol for use on board ship from bonded U.S. Customs warehouses, the government required five copies of the application. An enterprising lady named Agnes Cress developed an ingenious scheme to use this to her advantage to extract some additional alcohol for sale. Her method was to have an extra copy of the application slipped into the stack of five copies. After the ship's master had filled out the form, she used the extra copy to withdraw

Hundreds of cases of legitimately-distilled legal whiskey were shipped and stored in the Bahamas before Prohibition started, and then later shipped by rum-runners back to the United States at a large profit. This cache of Maryland whiskey is stacked on a beach in the Bahamas, possibly on Bimini Island (Library of Congress).

additional liquor. Ingenious though she was, she and her three partners in crime were eventually caught.[3]

Stores of liquor for on-board boat and medicinal use, and liquor going to a foreign port could not be confiscated by the Coast Guard. Within the territorial waters of the United States, however, any supply of liquor on a ship was required to be locked up or otherwise secured.

## The Limits of the Law

To try to stop illegal liquor importation into the United States from Canada, the West Indies, and Great Britain, the United States and Great Britain agreed to a treaty in January of 1924 to prevent the importation of liquor.

The boundary between national and international waters was originally set at three marine miles from the low-water limit on shore (originally about as far as a land-based cannon could fire). As a result, big supply ships, called mother ships, smuggled large cargoes of liquor, but anchored and waited outside this limit while smaller boats ran the booze to shore. Liquor was ferried to shore in sailboats, fishing boats, skiffs, dinghies, rowboats, speedboats, and even private yachts.

Large mother ships brought substantial quantities of liquor to the West Coast, but stopped just outside the boundary of international waters. Mother ships and the larger smuggling motorboats might anchor twenty to forty miles off the coast in the Pacific Ocean. From them the liquor went to shore in dory boats, which might be up to sixteen feet in length and held up to forty cases of liquor. These were flat-bottomed rowboats with high sides, a sharp bow, and a sharp V-shaped transom that could cut easily through the surf near shore.

In some instances transfer launches were used to carry the merchandise to shore. They would anchor just outside the surf line and transfer the cases of liquor into dories to make the final run through the surf and land on the beaches. Once there the liquor was loaded into cars or trucks for a fast trip to distribution centers and cutting plants in Los Angeles, San Francisco, or Sacramento.

In an attempt to try and cut down on the large amount of illegal liquor that was coming in on these mother ships, the international boundary was amended from three miles to twelve miles. This did not affect the mother ships, but did have the effect of cutting out some of the smaller transport craft, because twelve miles from shore in a small boat became risky in high seas. But even this change did not have the desired results.

In the next attempt to curtail the flow of illegal booze, the international boundary was extended to "one hour's steaming time" from shore.[4]

This became somewhat complicated because if a rum-runner used a speed-boat to bring the liquor in to the beach, a one-hour traversing time from mother ship to the shore could make the distance of the international limit anywhere from twelve to twenty-five miles offshore, depending on the speed of the boat. As the international limit was pushed so far out, most of the smaller independents who used skiffs and small speedboats dropped out of the business.

The new limit, however, had its quirks. The defense of the captain of one boat caught thirty miles from shore was that he was actually more than one hour's steaming time from the coast. Not believing such a flimsy defense, the Coast Guard took the boat out for a trial run. When the boat was loaded with 500 cases of Scotch, they found that the engines were in such poor shape that the captain's claim was indeed true. The eventual finding was that the boat had indeed technically been in international waters when seized and was released without being impounded.[5]

## The Real McCoy

One of best-known rum runners on the East Coast during Prohibi-tion was a Florida yacht builder and boat captain named William "Bill" McCoy, who decided to become a rum-runner. McCoy was originally from upstate New York and went to Florida with his brother in 1898. When Pro-hibition started he was struggling with a small line of expensive pleasure boats and operating a sea-going freight business. He conducted his illegal liquor trade using a series of two-masted schooners. Among other boats, he owned an American-built fishing schooner named the *Arethusa* which, after being changed to British registry for protection from U.S. Coast Guard inspection, became his flagship rum-runner the *Tomoka*.[6]

McCoy started bringing liquor from Nassau in the Bahamas to the United States in 1921. He purchased genuine Scotch in Nassau and resold it in the United States at a large profit. He sailed from Nassau to just out-side the three-mile limit from New York where the authorities had no jurisdiction. Buyers came out to him. McCoy claimed to be the first one to smuggle liquor from St. Pierre et Miquelon, French islands off the coast of Newfoundland.

Unlike some of the other rum-runners who cut their whiskey with adulterants, McCoy never cut or watered down his liquor and sold only a top-quality product. He had the reputation of providing his customers with a quality product and dealing fairly with them.[7] McCoy often boasted that he handled nothing but the "real McCoy," an expression that became commonly used to describe the genuine article when describing quality liquor rather than an inferior substitute. Buyers could count on his product, and the expression "the real McCoy" became part of American slang for anything that was genuine as advertised and was strictly on the level.

Urban lore has it that Bill McCoy was the origin of the phrase; however, the expression "the real McCoy" was in use before Prohibition and appears to have been in use at the end of the 1800s.[8] It is more likely that the original phrase dated back to a prize fighter named Kid McCoy, who was world welterweight champion from 1898 to 1900. McCoy's advertisements stated that he himself would appear in his fights rather than substituting some other inferior fighter, thus the audience would see "the real McCoy." Although it is unlikely that Bill McCoy the smuggler invented the phrase, his name certainly became popularized because of it.

McCoy's smuggling career came to an end in 1924 when he was caught red-handed on the *Tomoka* by the Coast Guard, six miles off the coast of New Jersey. He pled guilty to smuggling and spent nine months in jail. Afterwards he settled in Miami and died in 1948.

## *The Western Rum-Runners*

At the same time that rum-running ships were appearing off the East Coast, similar but smaller smuggling operations were being conducted in the Gulf of Mexico and along the Pacific Coast as illegal liquor was ferried from Mexico, Baja California, and as far away as Tahiti and Europe. This practice extended all up and down the coast from Vancouver to San Diego, though the short stretch of coast between Santa Barbara on the north and San Diego on the south was an important area of operations for the Pacific rum-runners. The area from Ventura to San Pedro and Long Beach was known as "Rum Row." In the northern part of the state, Half Moon Bay, Moss Landing, and even Golden Gate Bay were popular landing spots.

One of the well-known bootleggers on the West Coast was a former police lieutenant from Seattle, Roy Olmstead, who ran a bootlegging business that provided good liquor at reasonable prices and used high-powered motor boats to smuggle liquor. Olmstead was a businessman who did some rum-running on the side, smuggling Canadian whiskey from a distillery in Victoria down to Seattle.[9] He eventually built a large organization that included trucks, boats, salesmen, clerks, and warehouses, and through which his trucks delivered 200 cases of Canadian liquor a day in the Puget Sound area. In 1922 he organized a convention of bootleggers that was run as a formal professional business meeting. Rum-runners from up and down the coast met to set quality standards for their products, to establish price guidelines, and (with some hypocrisy) to create code of ethics

Coast Guard cutter U.S.S. *Seneca* capturing a small rum-running boat on the high seas, rifles held at the ready by the crew. Most rum-runners were armed and pitched battles on ocean waters were not uncommon if they tried to outrun the Coast Guard or started firing at their pursuers (Library of Congress).

to govern their business behavior.[10] In 1924 Prohibition agents caught up with Olmstead and arrested him, thus ending his career as a rum-runner.

Large mother ships, some of which could carry as many as 50,000 cases of liquor at one time, commonly stationed themselves off Ensenada, Santo Tomas, or Guadalupe Island in Mexican waters. Two examples of these large ships were the *Federalship* and the *Quadra*, both of which usually carried 30,000 to 40,000 cases of alcohol. They obtained their supplies of liquor from Canada or Tahiti, then discharged it 1,000 to 2,000 cases at a time into smaller boats that either went directly to the California beaches or stayed off the coast to rendezvous with smaller fishing boats or speedboats which would take 200 to 500 cases to the shore at a time.[11]

Though most of the illegal liquor on the West Coast was transported from Canada, some rum-runners went as far as Nassau in the Bahamas to bring back smuggled liquor, as well as transporting supplies from Cuba and Bermuda. The larger rum-runners had their own buyers who went to the West Indies, charted their own ships, and loaded their own cargoes.

Rum-running on the West Coast was never conducted on as large a scale as that operated on the Atlantic Coast, because the western United States had a much lower population than the East Coast cities. In addition, the Pacific Coast was a long distance from the main sources of supply, as well as from the larger and more lucrative Eastern markets.

The northern part of the Pacific Coast received large quantities of liquor that were shipped down from Victoria and Vancouver in Canada. Much of the liquor came by sea, through the Strait of Juan de Fuca, to the northern part of the West Coast of the United States. Much of this smuggled liquor diverted and went to Seattle, but a portion of it also went further down the coast to Los Angeles.

California, from the Oregon border to northern Marin County, had about 300 miles of rugged coastline that was suitable for illicit smuggling. There were few commercial harbors, but the coast had plenty of small bays and miles of winding deserted roads that were far from the Coast Guard at sea and lurking Prohibition agents on land. This was an ideal situation for sailboats, motorboats, and rowboats with outboard motors to rendezvous with the larger mother ships, pick up their orders of liquor, and head back to the coast.

Landing places for these transfer boats typically consisted of small inlets and dog holes. A dog hole was the name for tiny, isolated bays with steep cliffs that were used by lumber companies. The wood cutters installed A-frame structures on the tops of the cliffs and used them to lower timber by cable to barges that took the wood to San Francisco or San Pedro, south of Los Angeles, by sea for processing. During Prohibition, smugglers used these same frames to lift cases of liquor from boats in the dog holes to the tops of the cliffs and then load them onto trucks for transport.[12]

The California Coast had many popular coves for unloading illicit liquor. One popular rum-running rendezvous point was Smugglers Cove, south of Anchor Bay in Mendocino County. The bay was formerly named St. Orres Cove, but was renamed Smugglers Cove after the whiskey being landed there. It was not a very large bay, but was deep enough for speedboats to enter and reach the beach.

Humboldt Bay, near Eureka, had a small entrance and a convenient road system nearby. Smugglers could even unload their cargoes directly on the pier if the Coast Guard was not in port, or directly onto the beach, where it was transferred to trucks that headed north to Eureka or south to San Francisco with supplies of illegal liquor.

Other popular and convenient unloading places along the California coast were at Pigeon Point, Mendocino, Eureka, Half Moon Bay, Point Reyes, and Bodega Bay in the north, and Santa Barbara, San Luis Obispo, and Catalina Island to the south. One added benefit for smugglers on the northern California Coast was that shipments could often be transferred to land under cover of the frequent coastal fogs found there. The cover of coastal fog could also be used by the bolder of the rum-runners to slip directly into San Francisco Bay through the Golden Gate.

One nickname for men who picked up the loads of liquor from mother ships from the beach and delivered them to bootleggers, cutting plants, and various customers in San Francisco and other big cities was "land sharks." In an attempt to present at least some limited subterfuge, these men often tied fishing poles on top of their cars so that they looked like fishermen out for the day. The ones who brought the liquor in from mother ships to the shore and the waiting land sharks sometimes called themselves "water sharks."[13]

Smuggled liquor was not always of very good quality, though it had a self-created reputation among consumers for being the best. Most rum-runners, being in an illegal and shady business to begin with, were not beyond a little more larceny to raise their profits whenever they could. Some mother ships owned by shady criminals brought cheap Cuban rum with them and mixed it with liquor and other ingredients to make bogus booze on board the ship before unloading.

In addition to being an entry point for illegal liquor, the coastal waters of the Pacific provided a convenient location to provide all kinds of other illegal marine-based products and services. Beyond the three-mile coastal limit west of any point between San Diego and Santa Barbara, floating crap games and almost any other type of illicit pleasure were available on specially outfitted ships. For the convenience of patrons, fast launches picked up and delivered customers from the ends of darkened fishing piers or from yachts anchored off the coast and delivered them to the pleasure ships. These large ships cruised around just outside United States territorial waters for the weekend and provided what were referred to as a "cruise to nowhere" or a "booze cruise." The ships provided luxury dining, entertainment, gambling, and of course drinking. This type of cruising around just for entertainment was the start of the luxury cruise ship industry.[14]

## The Coast Guard

The United States Coast Guard and the Customs Service both played roles in pursuing and confiscating illegal alcohol. The Coast Guard was overwhelmed as they could only maintain stations at a few strategic points. The Customs Service was not directly involved in enforcing prohibition activities, except when liquor was smuggled or the smuggling involved marine vessels. Unfortunately there were very few customs agents to watch the entire shoreline, thus they and the Coast Guard were unable to stop the flood of liquor from the sea. On the other hand, servicemen in the Coast Guard were not always all pure and sometimes sailors protected rum-running ships, and were even known to help bootleggers unload their cargo.[15]

Rum-runners came up with a variety of tactics to try to outwit the Coast Guard. Sometimes they faked an engine breakdown to divert the Coast Guard ships. Another method was to send additional boats as decoys, complete with empty boxes and liquor cases, to accompany the boat carrying the real illegal liquor. When the Coast Guard joined in pursuit, the liquor boat sped away, leaving the decoys to be stopped and searched. Sometimes pursuits were spectacular, complete with shooting and casualties on both sides. Coast Guard boats were equipped with 3-inch cannons, and did not hesitate to use them.

Rum-runners developed another ingenious way to try to outwit the Coast Guard. Most rum-runners had a network of spies who knew when Coast Guard boats were out at sea, which might extend for ten days at a time. The bolder ones would then use bays and commercial piers in ports without concern. Smugglers might also leak out false information about their route when they were sure the information would reach the enforcement authorities they were targeting. Then they would use a different route.

Another trick of the rum-runners was the use of a mechanism to rapidly dump a cargo of liquor overboard. If the Coast Guard came close to capturing a rum-runner, one of the crewmembers pulled an emergency lever that quickly dumped the cargo into the water. The load of alcohol, which was already wrapped in canvas, was dumped overboard with a small buoy attached to mark the location. Meanwhile, the rum-runner sped away from the Coast Guard ship. If the rum-runner was caught, there was no incriminating liquor left aboard, and the boat had to be released. The rum-runner then returned at his leisure to the place marked by the buoy and retrieved the liquor.

## Ships and Boats

Liquor was ferried from the mother ships to shore in fast speedboats. Popular power plants for these smaller rum-running ships were 400-horsepower Liberty engines that had been used to power American military aircraft during World War I. The powerful Liberty twelve-cylinder aircraft engines could be purchased as surplus from the federal government for as little as $100 each in an original crate.[16] Many rum-runner's boats were powered by three of these Liberty engines that

**Vast quantities of whiskey were smuggled to the West Coast of the United States by sea from Mexico, Canada, Tahiti, and even as far away as the Bahamas, literally by the barrel. Shown here are Prohibition agents inspecting barrels lashed to the deck of a rum-runner captured by the Coast Guard cutter U.S.S. *Seneca* in 1924 (Library of Congress).**

had been converted to marine use. Transfer boats of seventy-five-foot length powered by three Liberty engines could reach speeds of up to fifty knots and outrun most of the slower Coast Guard boats. A nautical mile is 6,076 feet, as opposed to a statute mile on land which is 5,280 feet. One knot is one nautical mile per hour or the equivalent of 1.15 statute miles per hour. Thus fifty knots is equivalent to almost fifty-eight miles per hour on land. Though considered to be a low cruising speed for an automobile on a freeway, this speed is somewhat alarming to those riding in a fast boat over choppy water. At such speeds, however, these fast boats were usually able to outrun the slower Coast Guard boats.

Other engines were also used. One smuggler's boat used 860-horsepower Packard aircraft engines. At a cost of $7,000 each, two were installed in a fifty-six-foot-long boat, which gave it a top speed of forty knots. Italian automaker Fiat made a similar engine that could be converted to marine use.

If the Coast Guard was able to capture one of these fast rum-running boats, it was often confiscated by the government then used by the Coast Guard to pursue other rum runners. One such boat was the *Diatome*, which was captured by the Coast Guard in 1931 after a running gun battle in which one of the crew members was killed by machine gun fire. After confiscation, the boast was renamed CG 827, and was based at the harbor in San Pedro, on the south side of Los Angeles.[17] Powered by three Liberty engines, its power plant boasted a whopping 1,200 horsepower. This allowed the boat to travel over water almost twice as fast as most conventional Coast Guard ships, making it ideal for chasing rum-runners.

On the other hand, in shallow water, small boats powered by small outboard motors were far more useful than the larger powerful boats because many of the coastal bays consisted of lowland estuaries and marshes that were very shallow. Small rum-running boats using outboard motors could be easily maneuvered in depths of only one to three feet of water. The depth of water was so shallow or the entrances so narrow at some small bays that Coast Guard boats pursuing them found it prudent to stop. Tomales Beach in Marin County, California, for example, was used to unload ships, but it had only a fifty-foot-wide entrance. Adventurous smugglers in small boats found that they could enter the cut in comparative safety at high tide, but pursuing Coast Guard ships usually decided that they did not want to take a chance on running aground and gave up the pursuit.

As well as unloading directly on land or at a seaside dock, a more subtle method of landing liquor was to move it from the transfer boat to shore underwater on a steel cable that ran from the launch or dory to the shore. If a Coast Guard boat arrived unexpectedly, the workers merely had to drop the cable. It and the attached bottles of booze then sank to the bottom. The smugglers could then come back later at their leisure, drag for the cable, and retrieve the bottles.

Another solution that was used to avoid being caught red-handed with the evidence by the Coast Guard was to simply drop cases of liquor over the side and let them be swallowed up by the sea. One enterprising hijacker found this created an opportunity for him. He learned the techniques of deep-sea diving in order to retrieve liquor loads that were dropped overboard during a pursuit. If the water were shallow enough, a snorkel and fins were often all that was needed to find and retrieve sunken liquor.

Bottles that had been retrieved from the sea actually had some vicarious prestige for drinkers, as they knew that what they were drinking had been involved in a sea-going chase. Some moonshiners who bottled their own "whiskey" used labels that had been soaked in seawater before being attached in order to give some added prestige to their products.

The threat of violence on the high seas was very real as sea-going hijackers in fast boats robbed anyone and everyone they could catch. These pirates preyed primarily on small boats, if possible overwhelming the crew when they went out to sea because smugglers often carried large amounts of cash to make liquor purchases. Sometimes if crews resisted, they were killed and thrown overboard. For protection against pirates, most of the rum-runners' ships were armed with machine guns, rifles, and revolvers that were handed out to the crew if danger threatened.

Violence was not limited to the ocean, and shoot-outs between rum-runners and prohibition agents, or rum-runners and hijackers, also occurred on land with shotguns and machine gun bullets spraying hot lead across sandy beaches.

Some rum-runners installed armor plating around the cockpits of their boats, thinking it a good idea for protection from stray gunfire. Some inventive rum-runners even tried to outfit their crews with suits of armor for protection against bullets, but the added weight and bulk proved to be too cumbersome for working conditions aboard a boat, and also added additional unnecessary overall weight to the boat. The idea of armor was soon abandoned as steel or iron plates added considerable weight that could be more profitably utilized by carrying additional cases of liquor. In truth, rum-running boats needed speed in order to outrun the Coast Guard, rather than physical protection from bullets. The Coast Guard was mostly able to catch the smaller boats that did not have the necessary power to outrun them.

Over the years, nautical tall tales about smuggling started to emerge and many exciting legends grew up around the Caribbean rum-runners. In reality, the trip from the West Indies to the coast of the United States was generally a smooth sea voyage. But, to add some stature to their self-perceived image, some rum-runners turned their voyages into colorful epic adventures, complete with tales of savage gales, fierce hurricanes, skirmishes with hijackers, wild chases by the Coast Guard, and any other narrow escapes and hazards they could think of. Wide-eyed journalists eagerly latched onto and repeated these wild adventure tales, in the process amplifying the rumors and the stories. Eventually even many of the captains started to believe their own nonsense and figured themselves to be swashbuckling pirates.

## 7

# The West Coast States

## (Washington, Oregon, California)

SMUGGLERS HAD SEVERAL choices for bringing illegal alcohol into the United States on the West Coast, smuggling it either by land, water, or air. Almost immediately after Prohibition came into force, smuggling moonshine and legitimate whiskey across the Mexican and Canadian borders became a growth business. Interestingly, some of the most persistent small-time smugglers were members of Congress and other government officials who had diplomatic privileges of entry at border crossings.[1]

## Leaky Borders

Records from Canadian customs showed that the amount of liquor legally exported to the United States from Canada in 1921 was 8,335 gallons. By 1928 this figure had risen to 1,169,002 gallons. Smuggling added substantially more as the potential number of inland border crossings from Canada into the United States included about 400 good or fair roads, 150 passable ones, and maybe 100 backwoods trails.[2]

Canadian liquor was shipped across the border in quantities from a gallon to a truckload. The main supply was often hidden in remote wooded areas just over the border and distributed by automobile, truck, or boat. In winter whiskey was sometimes transported on sleds from Canada across the border, or was sometimes even carried by individuals using snowshoes or cross-country skis.[3]

Some smuggling was quite straightforward. An agent of a bootlegging organization might buy a certain quantity of liquor in Victoria in British Columbia to fill an outstanding order he had. The liquor was then simply put on a power launch and transported by sea down the Strait of Georgia and Puget Sound to Seattle. The agent might pay $2 a quart to purchase the liquor in Victoria and sell it to his customer in Seattle for $5 a quart. The difference was $3 profit per quart for the agent and the boat crew.

The U.S.-Canadian border was 5,525 miles in length and the U.S.-Mexican border was 1,954 miles long. Legitimate liquor flowed across both north and south borders by railroad, truck, automobile, and boat. Some came in under false paperwork and some with the cooperation of corrupt customs officials. More unusual was the man who came across the Canadian border with two dozen eggs. He had drilled a small hole in the end of each egg, blown out the contents, then refilled the shells with whiskey and carefully sealed up the holes.[4]

Most of the liquor smuggled across the border came from Canada, which had its own distilleries and breweries. In addition, several large American whiskey plants were disassembled before Prohibition, moved up to Canada, and resumed operation there.

On the Pacific Coast and in the Southwest, legal whiskey, cut whiskey, and moonshine were in good supply and easily available. Liquor was legal in both Mexico and Canada and didn't become contraband until it crossed the United States border. Thus cargoes of bottles were moved across the border into the United States by car, truck, boat, airplane, or sometimes by more primitive means, such as by raft and mule.

## Mexico

Illegal alcohol imported from Mexico was not a large part of the overall West Coast bootleg business. A few distilling operations had been moved south across the border before Prohibition, but they mostly produced inferior whiskey due to poor regulation and supervision of the process. Whiskey made in Mexico often had an uncertain basis and might be made from rancid potatoes, rotten cactus, and other highly undesirable materials, before being artificially colored and flavored.

Most of the liquor that was smuggled up from Mexico was liquor that was originally exported from Canada, Europe, and the West Indies. Shiploads of this legally-imported liquor were brought to Mexico, then it was moved up from Baja California to California and Arizona where it became illegal.

One method of smuggling was to simply transport the liquor across the border by car or truck. Bottles could be hidden in barrels of flour or sugar, in coffins and hearses, or hidden in a truck bed under a load of grain, fruit, sawdust, lumber, or any other transported goods. Bootleggers coming across the border also hid alcohol in their automobiles under false floorboards or in fake gas tanks. Another method used was to fill the spare tire with alcohol. Decoys were sometimes used, such as having women and children in the car to lull the attention of suspicious customs agents. Some bootleggers even hid their product in school buses to further the appearance of innocence.

Trucks modified for the bootlegging business could carry as much as 600 gallons of alcohol. One particular bootlegger's truck that was used to smuggle alcohol from Mexico was modified to carry 300 gallons in a copper tank hidden under a false truck bed. The tank was only three inches deep and was located just below the bed of the truck, with six-inch sideboards to hide it. The bottom of the truck was boarded up so that Prohibition agents couldn't see the tank from underneath.[5] Another bootlegger successfully shipped smuggled liquor to San Francisco in a black hearse. His theory was that God-fearing Prohibition agents wouldn't imagine that a hearse would be involved in the transport of liquor.

Smugglers also transported illegal booze to the Pacific Coast states by air in planes specially-equipped for smuggling liquor, landing at small local airports in California or Nevada. In the early days of aviation, small planes did not require much of a runway, and some of the smaller transport aircraft could even be landed in agricultural fields or on dry lake beds out in the desert.

The California border with Mexico was about 140 miles long, most of it uninhabited desert, which made it more appealing to smugglers than more populated areas. The smuggled liquor that came across the border by land was investigated by the Border Patrol as part of its mandate to control all types of smuggling. The Border Patrol at the time had a total of 717 agents.

Depending on the payoffs that had been made to corrupt border officers, moonshine trucks might be able to drive through checkpoints without being stopped. To do this, smugglers made arrangements with certain officers that when they were on duty at certain gates on the border, their border crossing would not be hindered. However, bootleggers had to remember to choose the correct gate. The occasional one or two who didn't pay attention to what they were doing were caught and then charged with smuggling.

During the first few years of Prohibition, there was a total of only thirty-five agents to watch the entire Mexican border. Their mission was to catch bootleggers in California, Arizona, New Mexico, and Texas. Similarly, there were only about a hundred agents to patrol and watch the entire Canadian border.[6]

When illegal booze traveled around the end of the land border by boat, it was transferred to a truck on shore and transported to Los Angeles, San Francisco, or Sacramento for processing and distribution. These trucks were typically driven very fast in order to avoid hijackers, county sheriffs, small town policemen, and Prohibition agents.

As well as bringing liquor in themselves, hijacking someone else's smuggled shipments of alcohol was big business for some smugglers. Some hijackers even disguised themselves as policemen to throw off their victims' suspicions. Gangs armed with pistols, rifles, shotguns, and submachine guns hijacked ships at sea, or those docked and unloading their cargo, or trucks that were transporting liquor from the landing areas to bootleggers' warehouses. An unscrupulous gang might simply stop a boat, kill the rum-runners, put the cargo on their own boat, and sink the rum-runners' ship.

Another target for hijackers was the sugar used to make the mash. Hijacking it was a way to make some extra money without any investment. In some instances sugar was hijacked and boldly sold back to the moonshiners it was originally stolen from.

High speed chases and blazing shootouts during these operations often resulted in fatalities. Occasionally deaths were also the result of indiscriminate shooting by Prohibition officers in hot pursuit of the hijackers. This scenario could and did happen anywhere in the country, but it occurred in particular along the Canadian and Mexican borders. Some areas were the locations of so much indiscriminate shooting by hoodlums and law officers that respectable citizens were afraid to drive around in their own cars after dark.

Smugglers bringing alcohol into the United States from Mexico occasionally tried to navigate boats up or across the Rio Grande where it formed the border with Texas. This was a very uncertain method, as in most places the river was too shallow to successfully sail or to row boats that were loaded heavily with cases of illicit liquor. Rafts were sometimes used to try to ferry loads of liquor from one bank of the river to the other, but the water was so low for most of the year that even most of these shallow-draft vessels became grounded on sand bars or mud banks.

Another method used to ferry liquor across the Rio Grande was to tie the end of a rope to a dog and send it swimming across the river, pulling the rest of the rope behind it. After removing the rope from the dog on the other side of the river, confederates could pull barrels of liquor tied together across the surface of the water on the rope. Other smugglers simply waded across shallow parts of the Rio Grande pushing floating barrels filled with bottles of liquor ahead of them.

The easiest way to smuggle liquor from Mexico was to simply drive a load of bottles across the border. Trucks and cars laden with liquor frequently roared across the border between the two countries. Vehicles that were smuggling were met on the American side of the border by gunmen who were essential to protect the liquid cargo from hijackers, customs agents, the Border Patrol, or eager Prohibition agents. To increase the carrying capacity of the vehicles, most of the seats were removed and the additional space was used for storage of cases of liquor. Bottles might also be hidden under the hood, tied under the chassis, or hidden in spare tires. Smugglers' cars and trucks had extra-heavy-duty springs in order to carry the heavy liquid loads without sagging and dragging on the road surface.

Horses, mules, and burros could be used on the smaller, but more obscure, trails. On a larger scale, liquor was smuggled in railroad cars, nominally shipped as hay, cleaning fluid, machinery, or other innocent goods.

A variety of simple methods of transporting small amounts of illegal whiskey were in use in California. One was by wearing a vest-like garment under a jacket or overcoat that contained multiple pockets that could hold booze bottles. One particular problem for Prohibition agents was how to deal with women smugglers who carried bottles under their blouses, because most officers were reluctant to search there.

Another hiding place for small amounts of liquor was in women's high-heeled shoes that were specially constructed with a small container in the heel. This small receptacle could only hold about a full shot of whiskey, but sometimes that was enough to get by. Another small-scale method for carrying alcohol to serve an individual's needs was in a hollow walking cane with a detachable handle. These two devices were used to hold a small amount of alcohol for individual drinks that could be mixed into a glass full of a soft drink at an ice-cream or soft drink parlor.

Though Mexican production of American-type liquors was small, there was a large border trade in mescal and tequila. Women crossed at the official Mexican border-crossings with goat bladders or hot water bottles filled with tequila or mescal tied around their waists under their skirts. Men smuggled small amounts of liquor in special suits that were equipped with multiple pockets that held pint bottles, or they had extra-large pockets to hold bigger bottles, or both. Some coats or jackets were designed to carry as many as forty bottles. Other carrying containers were dummy books with a bottle hidden inside a cut out section, boots with expanding rubber reservoirs around the ankles, ladies muffs with a bottle hidden inside, and baby carriages with false bottoms underneath the baby.

Men also crossed the border wearing carpenters' aprons with deep, wide pockets under their clothes. Some hit on the ingenious scheme of wrapping rubber car inner tubes or garden hoses full of alcohol around their waists under their clothes. Some hung hot water bottles full of bootleg booze on cords around their necks. One interesting method was to wear oversized shoes or boots that had a small space in front of the toes that had small bottles of liquor stuffed up into the front part of the shoes.

Those in search of liquor in Southern California or the lower part of

Arizona or New Mexico could also take a day trip over the Mexican border and easily find a drink in a bar close to the crossing point. One of the more famous watering holes in Juárez, Mexico, was the Kentucky Club, or as it more-formally styled itself "The World Famous Kentucky Club and Grill," south of the Rio Grande, two blocks from the Mexican border at the Paso del Norte Bridge. It was about a thirty-minute walk from El Paso, Texas. The bar opened in 1920, after American Prohibition started, when a Kentucky distillery that made liquor opened up their own club in a place as close to home as they legally could. Rumor has it that bootlegger Al Capone once drank there.

Inside the building, the long, polished mahogany bar was located on a tiled wall that sported a rather unusual feature, a thin, raised trough running the length of it, just above the floor, right below a man's feet if he were sitting. However, the bar was built at a time when men didn't sit on barstools, but stood and drank leaning on the bar. The trough was a convenience for customers who didn't want to leave the bar and lose their place, but needed to relieve themselves. Unfortunately on some days the building was said to have a rather unpleasant strong gamy smell.[7] The Kentucky Club is still open at the same location today, though thankfully the makeshift urinal is not in use.

The Kentucky Club claimed to be the birthplace of the margarita, after a bartender named Lorenzo Hernandez created the drink off the top of his head in the 1930s for a patron named "Margarita." However, it also has to be noted that four other bars in Juárez alone claim the same apocryphal distinction.

## Alaska and the Yukon

As early as the Klondike Gold Rush of 1897–98 Alaska had rigid laws about the importation, manufacture, and sale of liquor. In practice, though, this was a law on paper that was typically ignored and saloons sprang up on every street corner in the booming gold towns. Long before Prohibition, the same techniques that were used by later bootleggers were already in practice. Mattie Silks, a madam from Denver who traveled to Dawson in the Yukon Territory in 1898 to cash in on the Klondike gold rush, sold whiskey made from grain alcohol. Her cost was $60 a gallon. When the alcohol was cut, colored, and flavored, it sold for $130 a gallon.[8] Silks returned to Denver with a hefty profit for only one season's work.

Statistics for 1897 showed that there were 5 breweries and 142 bars in the area of the port at Skagway that did a roaring business. Liquor shipped to Dawson and the Yukon Territory via Skagway was billed through to

Canada in bond, but often by the time it arrived at the border 15 miles or so to the north of Skagway, the whiskey had somehow been mysteriously replaced by water.[9]

As part of their efforts, the WCTU pushed through a bone-dry law in Alaska in 1916. As a result, a variety of ingenious schemes were used by wholesalers to smuggle illicit whiskey past eagle-eyed Canadian customs officers. One method was the use of a specially-built kerosene can. The spigot indeed produced coal oil if it was opened by a curious inspector, but the interior of the can also held a container of whiskey. Another clever smuggling method employed egg crates with false bottoms that hid whiskey bottles underneath. Small barrels of whiskey might also be concealed in bales of hay. To detect them, suspicious customs officials would force long rods into the hay. Some of the kegs shipped in labeled as white lead did not contain white lead at all but were used for the transportation of whiskey.[10]

Radio station KGBU, the first radio station in Ketchikan, in the panhandle of Alaska, went into operation in a house in the red-light district in the early 1900s to inform listeners when the rum-runners were due in town.[11]

## Washington

Early attempts to control liquor in Washington were intended to prevent American Indians from obtaining and possessing liquor when the British government directed the Hudson's Bay Company to reduce the amount of alcohol the company was using as payment to the Indians in trade for pelts. The eventual goal was to eliminate all use of alcohol for trade. A major concern was that overindulgence in liquor might incite the Indians to rebel against British occupation of the area and thus affect the fur trade. All sale of rum to the Indians was forbidden 1831.

Attempts to prohibit drink in Washington had a varied history. In November 1848, the school rules for Port Angeles, Washington, included Rule Number 12, which said that the punishment for drinking "spirituous liquors" at school was eight lashes. Even this, however, was apparently not considered to be as bad as playing cards in school, which rated ten lashes. Obviously these were not pleasant times for students who liked to drink and play cards.

The Territorial Legislature put a referendum on the 1855 ballot to outlaw the sale and manufacture of liquor. Women were not able to vote; nevertheless the vote was close and the measure was defeated by the all-male electorate at 650 to 564.

In 1879 the sale of liquor was prohibited within a mile of the Northern Pacific Railroad during its construction. This was probably an attempt to avoid the saloons, prostitutes, and gamblers of the hell-on-wheels towns that accompanied construction of the Union Pacific railroad some years earlier.

A local option law was passed by the Legislature in 1886 to allow residents of a town to license liquor sales as they saw fit. The Territorial Supreme Court overturned this in 1888, but later allowed a modified version of the law. This allowed cities to charge license fees on saloons and thus generate additional revenue for city treasuries. This remained in effect through 1909, but led to variations in the availability of liquor from town to town.

The State of Washington voted for prohibition in 1914 and outlawed the manufacture and sale of liquor, though not the consumption of it, throughout the state beginning January 1, 1916. Consistent with the typical trend across the country, the majority of urban voters in Seattle and the other major cities voted against it, but the rural population were in favor of Prohibition. A permit system was used to allow limited importation of legal alcohol that had been manufactured out of state by individuals and businesses who had applied for and received permits from their county.

A lack of liquor in the state meant that rumrunners and bootleggers quickly jumped in to supply an ever-increasing demand for alcohol, making use of Seattle's boundary waters and the city's proximity to Canada. In the central part of the coast, the shoreline of Grays Harbor around Aberdeen was a popular spot to unload mother ships carrying illegal liquor. An entire network of manufacturers, distributors, and buyers that ran north into Canada grew up along the coast.

Smuggling, however, didn't always go well. Early in the morning on January 17, 1922, William Morris of Seattle accidentally lost his bearings and ran aground off the coast near Tacoma. He and his forty-foot launch were taken into custody by the Coast Guard, along with sixty-five cases of whiskey and four fifteen-gallon kegs. This alcoholic cargo was valued at $15,000.[12]

Most of the illegal liquor that was brought to shore on the West Coast was immediately taken by car or truck to bootleggers in large cities, such as Los Angeles and San Francisco, though a certain amount stayed in the coastal area and retail facilities were established to provide entertainment and liquor to local inhabitants. Many of these establishments were low-class dancehalls that catered primarily to thirsty loggers and fishermen. The pace of the action and dancing, along with the flow of money extracted from the customer, willing or not, was fast and furious.

As in every other large city, numerous fraudulent schemes from the subtle to the outright obvious took place in Seattle. One of the simpler ones involved a con man who hung around the railroad station when a train came in. He would look over the passengers and select a likely-looking one. He would then go up to the man and say that he could supply a drink for the weary traveler with only a small fee added for his trouble of going to get the liquor. He would take money from the traveler saying he was leaving the station to get the booze and would come right back. Once outside the building, he would, of course, simply keep going, and the expectant customer would wait patiently until he finally realized he had been had and the man was not coming back.

A more subtle scam involved a customer purchasing a cask or barrel of whiskey that had been offered to the buyer at a very good price. As a sign of good faith, the seller would extract the bung, stick in a straw, and invite the customer to taste it for himself. The customer would sip a little of the whiskey and find that this was indeed excellent liquor. It wasn't until after he had made the purchase and tried to drink more of the whiskey that he found out that he had been fooled. A small bottle of good whiskey had been attached inside the barrel under the bunghole and that was what the straw had been placed in. The rest of the barrel was filled with water to give it the appearance of having the appropriate weight.[13]

## Oregon

Like Washington, most of the early laws in Oregon that related to liquor control were intended to prevent American Indians from obtaining and possessing liquor. In June of 1844, Oregon's provisional government enacted a prohibition law designed to "prevent the introduction, sale and distillation of ardent spirits in Oregon." The law was repealed in 1845. In November of 1887 Oregon voters defeated a proposed amendment to the state constitution that would have instituted state-wide prohibition.

On June 6, 1904, Oregon voters approved a local option law that allowed individual cities to go dry if they wanted. This law said that a successful county-wide vote for prohibition would make each precinct in that county subject to a ban on alcohol. In 1905 the city of Hood River was the first to enact prohibition by local option, a measure that was upheld by the Oregon Supreme Court. During the following years, various other counties and cities also enacted prohibition via use of the local option.

Fighting this trend, most bar owners, brewers, and distillers did everything they could to stop women from getting the vote, because the Temperance Movement and women's suffrage had been associated with each other for a long time. The wet supporters knew that when women exerted their influence in the elections, they would use it to eliminate drinking, which many women saw as the great social evil of the day.

Voting rights for women appeared on the Oregon ballot in 1912. When the votes were counted, a majority of 52 percent had voted for women's suffrage. As soon as women achieved voting rights, they started preparations for a prohibition initiative for the 1914 election. This passed, and five years before National Prohibition the voters of Oregon passed an amendment to the state constitution prohibiting the manufacture, sale, or advertising of intoxicating liquor. Individuals could still bring liquor in from outside the state and consume it in the privacy of their own homes, but they couldn't purchase liquor in Oregon and couldn't sell it.

In 1915 the Oregon Legislature enacted a law called the Anderson Act that implemented statewide prohibition, becoming effective on January 1, 1916. On that date, Oregon became a dry state and the era of bootleggers and moonshiners, blind pigs, and speakeasies began.

By the time the Volstead Act went into effect, Oregon bootleggers were already experienced. Portland had always had a special relationship with British Columbia. For most of the 1890s, Vancouver and Victoria had been part of the route to bring opium into the country to supply Chinese communities in various West Coast cities. Smuggling routes were therefore well-established and smugglers were experienced. Only the cargo being smuggled changed.

One interesting piece of excitement took place on February 7, 1932, when a boat named *Sea Island*, crewed by three Canadians, ran aground in Whale Cove on the Oregon Coast. The cove was known locally as Bootlegger Bay, because it was ideal for landing small boats that were sneaking to shore to drop off bottles of illegal liquor in the dead of night. The Canadians unloaded 400 cases of whiskey in the bay and buried them in the sand. Then they set their boat on fire to destroy and hide it, and rode to Portland with the unloading crew. On the way their car turned over near Hebo on Highway 101 and the men were forced to continue on by bus.

Quick-acting police checked the wrecked and abandoned car and were waiting for the bootleggers when they got off the bus. The boat still burning in Bootlegger Bay was suspicious enough that the police began to poke around in the sand and dug up most of the booze, which was moved to the Toledo jail in Lincoln County for storage, along with the three Canadians.

The plot thickened as four men armed with machine guns and welding torches appeared at the jail. They used the welding equipment to burn their way into the jail cells, loaded the Canadians and most of the bottles of liquor into two vans and headed out. The police caught up with them on Highway 18, and arrested most of them. The men with machine guns disappeared into the night in their car.

Trials were held, everyone pled guilty, and sentences of a few months to a few years were handed down. The Canadians went home to Vancouver. The seized bottles were sent to the U.S. Customs House in Portland.

The finale to this debacle occurred later in July 1932, when Prohibition agents gathered in the basement of the building and took turns throwing bottles against the back wall of the elevator shaft. The whiskey ran down the shaft, where it was pumped into the sewer, emptied into the Willamette River, and carried out to sea.

## California

Californians liked their drinks. In the spring of 1917, the California electorate voted down a bill that would have prohibited saloons and the sale of wines and liquor. On November 5, 1918, the voters defeated Propositions 1 and 2 that would have stopped the selling of liquor in saloons and restaurants. Proposition 1 was defeated 341,897 to 256,778 and Proposition 2 lost by about 40,000 votes. Though Californians voted against Prohibition, their elected officials voted for it.[14]

When National Prohibition was enacted, the town of Redding staged an impromptu funeral with a hearse that carried a figure representing John Barleycorn inside. It was led by a local band playing the death march. Vallejo did essentially the same. Santa Monica repeated what was now becoming a common demonstration and, for a grand finale, marched the hearse right off the end of the Santa Monica pier.

Some businesses threw in the towel right away. The El Dorado Brewery, for example, seeing Prohibition coming, started to make non-alcoholic beer, claiming the distinction of being the first brewer in California to make near-beer. The company, covering all their business bases in case near-beer was not popular (which it was not), also made root beer and other soft drinks.[15]

On the other hand, as Prohibition started, the coastal states showed that an unpopular law could not be enforced. Hundreds of thousands of ordinary citizens drank, creating a large demand for illegal alcohol. Citizens reacted to the law by violating it, and an entire industry quickly sprang up to make, transport, and sell booze. Moonshiners and bootleggers were ready to satisfy the market, with bootlegging often tied in to prostitution and gambling throughout the state.

In spite of the high quality of Canadian alcohol, such as Canadian Club, Peter Dawson, or Glen More, only about 10 percent of the alcohol drunk during Prohibition in California originated in Europe or Canada. The other 90 percent, which comprised millions of gallons, was made right in California. The motive of course was profit. A five-gallon can of 180

This primitive still was hidden away in a heavily wooded area in San Francisco. Carefully camouflaged stills like these were hard to find and authorities had to reply on tips from informants or watch for tell-tale smoke from the wood fires used to heat the stills (Library of Congress).

proof alcohol cost approximately $25 to make. This could be converted into ten gallons of 90-proof gin by diluting it with water and adding some juniper berries or juniper oil to produce the gin flavoring, and sold for a handsome profit.

Those Westerners who wanted alcohol soon got it, and bootlegging ran rampant in the big West Coast cities, such as Los Angeles and San Francisco. Bootlegging also flourished on a smaller scale in smaller towns, in the mountains, and in the desert. The majority of bootleggers in California were small timers, often family members making a little extra to pay off the mortgage on the family farm or to buy the wife a new dress. Typical was the bootlegger in California who made whiskey at home from apple brandy colored with pan-fried brown sugar. There were, however, others who were involved with big-time syndicates that were backed by large investors.

## Southern California

Even before World War I, populism and progressivism had created liberal leanings in the West. Southern California tended to be conservative and dry, while San Francisco and the northern part of the state was liberal and wet. The primary reason was that during the late 1910s Southern California was the destination of a large influx of people migrating from the Midwest and South. This generally made the southern part of the state a more conservative place to live. The residents of southern California, for example, tended to follow conservative radio evangelists, such as Aimee Semple McPherson. This trend made southern California identify themselves with the drys, as opposed to the more liberal San Francisco in the northern part of the state, which had a higher proportion of wets. In a similar way a large anti-liquor voting contingent in Oklahoma kept a prohibition law in the state constitution for fifty-two years, until 1959. Liquor by the drink could not be purchased there until 1984.

Los Angeles was one of the large centers of illegal alcohol on the West Coast during Prohibition. The population of Los Angeles in 1927 was 1,300,326 and liquor arrests totaled 8,480. In neighboring Riverside County, a total of 1,867 people were jailed in 1929, with 199 (10.6%) of them for liquor violations.[16]

One of the suburbs of Los Angeles was Hollywood, founded in 1887 by Harvey Wilcox and his wife Daeida, both of whom were strong supporters of Prohibition. The new town was very conservative and passed laws such as one on March 10, 1904, that prohibited drunkenness and disorderly conduct. Another specified that the maximum speed limit on city streets was to be limited to twelve miles-per-hour. The sales of liquor in Hollywood were prohibited, except for that sold by pharmacists on prescription.

After Harvey passed away, Daeida re-married and tried to perpetuate Hollywood as an ultra-conservative Christian community. The concept, however, was doomed, due to the growth of the Hollywood motion picture industry and the influx of people who wanted to live in the pleasant climate of Southern California. Hollywood had been legally dry since 1904, but Hollywood stars and other workers in the film industry encouraged bootlegging after the end of World War I and the introduction of the Volstead Act. One popular punch in the movie colony was called the Hollywood Special. Basically all the guests at a party brought a bottle of something and mixed it all together. Hard drugs were readily available at the time and, in fact, morphine and cocaine were used as popular remedies for the hangovers induced by overindulgence in bad liquor.

Liquor wholesalers in Los Angeles encouraged ranchers to make moonshine and then purchased this "whiskey" from them. Local law enforcement often just looked the other way, as many enforcement authorities were reluctant to stop Prohibition violators who were their friends and neighbors. They figured that most of these moonshiners and bootleggers were decent men who were often just struggling to make a living in hard economic times. Police might go after moonshiners making bad booze in order to put them out of business before they poisoned someone, but they usually didn't bother those who made a quality product.

The desert country of southern California was ideal for hiding moonshine stills, and liquor flowed freely from the Mojave Desert to Los Angeles. According to former State Senator Edwin Grant, in 1925 Victorville in the Mojave Desert was a wide-open town where eager shoppers could find booze, slot machines, bordellos, and willing women.[17] Most desert towns had prostitutes who increased their incomes by selling liquor to their customers.

Three vital ingredients for making moonshine were water, labor, and a hidden location. The Mojave Desert was a vast isolated empty space dotted with abandoned mine tunnels in which a secret still could be set up, and water was available in the form of desert springs and ranch wells. Every canyon in the desert with running water from a desert spring was a potential moonshine site. Still sites using water from the Mojave River might be hidden in tunnels along the river bank.

Stills were often hidden in thickets of willow, mesquite, and cottonwood trees, or were well-hidden among bushes. A liquor stash might be conveniently hidden under sand dunes. One still site in San Bernardino county had an entrance hidden by brush that was the access point into 200 feet of tunnels and rooms that had been hollowed out under some ancient sand dunes.

Many ingenious schemes were used to hide liquor from the law. One farmer stored his bootleg wine in barrels covered with straw and cow manure to disguise the alcohol smell when Prohibition agents were around. Another moonshiner in Helendale, north of Victorville in the Mojave Desert, operated his still in his cow shed, where it was protected by a fierce bull that would not allow revenue agents into the building. Others hid liquor under haystacks or under chicken roosts. One bootlegger in Oro Grande hid his stash of illegal liquor under a trapdoor in his chicken coop. The combination of dirt, hay, and chicken manure spread over the bottom of the coop disguised the opening and discouraged Prohibition agents from performing a detailed search.

The Los Angeles suburb of Wilmington was the site of one highly elaborate moonshine manufacturing operation. In 1923 federal agents raided a farm and found that a large chamber had been excavated twenty feet under a barn, and that it housed all the machinery and distilling apparatus to perform an extensive moonshining operation. The fumes generated inside the chamber were run up a vent inside a windmill and discharged out of the top. Another still was hidden under a trapdoor with bales of hay stacked on top.

Prohibition in Southern California also had its lighter side. One resident of Crestline, in the San Bernardino Mountains north of Los Angeles, raised and sold "high-priced" chickens. When purchased, each carcass was found to be miraculously stuffed with a bottle of moonshine. The technique of hiding booze inside food like this was nothing new. During army war games in Nebraska in 1889, one soldier from the Seventh Cavalry described how a local farmer sold watermelons in the camp. Some sold for 10 cents, but others sold for a dollar. The difference was that each melon that went for a dollar had a pint of whiskey concealed inside it.[18]

Bootleggers had other tricks to disguise their trade. One bootlegger in Needles always wore a heavy gray coat, no matter how warm the weather was. The inside of his coat was lined with dozens of pockets, with each pocket containing a pint or half-pint of liquor for sale. One bootlegger placed a mannequin in his car as a decoy when he was transporting liquor so that it would ostensibly look like he and his wife or girlfriend were a couple driving to Los Angeles.

Two views of a pair of "cowshoes," attachments for regular shoes that left tracks like the hooves of a cow. Bootleggers wore them to disguise their footprints so that Prohibition agents or rivals would not be inclined to follow them to and from still sites (Library of Congress).

On a grander scale, one Los Angeles bootlegger had a lumber truck that had a false panel at the rear, inside the back door, that was constructed to resemble the ends of a stack of two-by-four lumber. If a Prohibition agent opened the back of the truck, he saw what appeared to be the ends of a stack of wood, and didn't bother to inspect further. Behind the false panel, however, was enough space in the interior of the truck to carry seventy cases of Scotch.

Penny Morrow, a constable in Oro Grande, north of Victorville, remembered one jury that was trying a local rancher for bootlegging had three bootleggers empaneled on it. Not surprisingly he was acquitted. In another case the lawyer dismissed everyone who did not drink.[19]

In one of the more unusual legal defenses, when moonshiner

Jack Roche was taken to court, he used the excuse that the quality of the water was so bad in Holtville, near the U.S.-Mexico border, that it had to be distilled to make it fit to drink. Ironically, by law the town was chartered as a dry town. No liquor could be sold in Holtville according to the deeds to individual pieces of property. It did not, however, take much effort to find booze in a local pool hall or movie theater. And a bottle could be found at most hotels simply by asking the bellboy.

As a final note, when San Diego planned to host the Eleventh Annual American Legion Convention in August 1929, among the planned activities were parades, outings, a trip to the beach, and other activities. As part of the activities, the local planning group formed an "Irrigation Committee" and wanted to provide safe liquor (and plenty of it) for the thirsty conventioneers. Around 4,000 gallons of liquor were ordered. Unfortunately the assembled stash of $27,000 worth of liquor was raided and hauled away just before the convention started. Even though the mayor intervened and tried to get the confiscated liquor back, the convention ended up being completely dry.[20]

## Northern California

San Francisco in the northern part of the state was openly wet. The town of Sausalito on the northern side of the Golden Gate, across the bay from San Francisco, was so flooded with liquor that it was said that the only place a man couldn't get liquor was at the local church.

The rest of northern California was also awash in liquor. In Stockton twenty-five blind pigs opened within three weeks of the start of Prohibition. Crescent City, an isolated California town far north on the Pacific coast close to the border with Oregon, had a population of less than 1,000 in 1920, but had ten or eleven operating speakeasies and a large number of bootleggers to supply them. In many cases, local government not only overlooked the problem, but was part of it. For example, fifty barrels of whiskey were donated to the Democratic Party by San Francisco's Board of Supervisors so that they could entertain the delegates to the 1920 Democratic National Convention.[21]

By the summer of 1919, many of the bars and saloon owners in San Francisco had already applied to the city and county to turn their establishments into soft drink parlors in anticipation of Prohibition, but bars and nightclubs still operated openly. Two of the most famous speakeasies in San Francisco were Izzy Gomez', which was housed in a loft on Pacific Street in the North Beach area, and Tait's at the Beach, on the Great Highway near Sloat Boulevard. Smaller and lesser-known drinking places existed literally by the hundreds. In addition, bootleg booze could be freely purchased at most hotels via the house detective, front desk clerk, or the bellboys. The better hotels sold non-alcoholic drink set-ups in the form of ginger ale, orange juice, or fruit punch, and then the customer added his own alcohol out of his own bottle. Set-up and corkage fees, however, might be charged.

Assistant United States Attorney Mabel Willebrandt commented that San Francisco was 85 percent wet. Estimates were that between $5,000 and $20,000 worth of illegal liquor was smuggled into San Francisco every night, distributed to what the police estimated to be 1,492 locations. Even the 1922 San Francisco grand jury declared that the Volstead Act was a farce. Cab drivers and newspaper boys knew all the places to get a drink. Many poolhalls, soda parlors, ice cream parlors, and soft-drink parlors sold liquor under-the-counter.

The largest stills could produce as much as 1,000 gallons of alcohol a day, fed by redwood fermenting tanks that might be as large as 1,000 gallons. A large still could produce 5 gallons in eight minutes, or about 37 gallons per hour. A large commercial still could produce 50 to 100 gallons a day at a cost of 50 cents per gallon. The sales price was $3 to $12, depending on the market at the time, which resulted in a good profit for the bootlegger.

Successful raids by Prohibition agents produced more cases in Northern California than could be handled by the courts. In 1924 courts were adding fifty Prohibition violation cases to the docket each day, while they were behind in dealing with a backlog of 5,000 cases.

Juries were not always sympathetic to federal agents and often found violators not guilty on principle. Not-guilty votes could also stem from other causes. For example, juries might be biased against Prohibition or the government. On a humorous note, in one San Francisco trial the entire jury was arrested for drinking up the evidence during their deliberations.[22]

Many cases had to be dismissed when witnesses would not testify or the evidence disappeared. In one trial in Eureka, for example, the charge was dismissed when a friend of the defendant drilled a hole through the courthouse floor and into the wooden keg that was being held for the trial, and drained away all the evidence.[23] The *Sausalito News* for December 10, 1926, reported that 6,300 gallons of industrial alcohol had been shipped from Sausalito in a sealed and guarded railroad car; however, only 5,100 gallons were received by the consignee in Pittsburgh. The missing 1,200 gallons were never located.

One Prohibition case in San Jose involved surveillance of a warehouse that was full of whiskey. Federal officials put a round-the-clock watch on it to see who would come and retrieve the liquor. After waiting and watching for a month with no results, they gave up the surveillance and went to retrieve the whiskey and confiscate it. They found that there was nothing in the place. The whiskey had mysteriously vanished while the building was firmly under guard.[24]

Some of the mysterious disappearances of evidence may have been due to the fact that in the mid–1920s, the prohibition district of Northern California and Nevada had only thirty-two agents to police a population of 1.5 million. And in 1925 this included checking the 12,000 permit holders who could use alcohol legally, such as druggists, physicians, breweries, and vinegar manufacturers.[25]

Another type of theft occurred when the owners of the American Distillery, near Sausalito, actually stole their own liquor. One of the owners installed some additional plumbing that went unnoticed by federal inspectors. Thus when he wanted a few gallons of alcohol for his own use, he had his own private spigot to drain off whatever he required.

Thieves also stole from each other, from government storage warehouses, and from impound areas of city and county jails. Legal alcohol was sometimes stolen from legitimate distilleries with help from the inside by bribery or simple theft. Baradat's warehouse in San Francisco lost $4,000 to $5,000 worth of liquor to thieves.

Other targets for robbery were the wine cellars and liquor stockpiles of the summer vacation homes and rich estates of San Mateo and Marin County. Thieves often disguised themselves as laundry men or gas meter readers to gain entrance to houses or businesses with valuable liquor available. W.M. Fitzhugh, a wealthy San Franciscan with a house in Portola Valley, lost $30,000 worth of liquor when thieves disappeared with 141 cases of imported whiskey, 68 cases of wines and brandy, and 34 cases of assorted whiskey, brandy, and champagne.[26]

Prohibition agents developed some clever techniques for catching bootleggers and moonshiners. One was the use of unplanned fingerprints. Moonshiners would often use flour dough to seal any cracks or leaks in their stills. When the dough dried due to the heat from the still, the moonshiner's fingerprints would be clearly visible in the baked dough. Surprised bootleggers found that in this way agents could definitely link them to their particular still.

One favorite technique for putting a moonshiner out of business was for a Prohibition agent to padlock the premises. Most of the operations that were padlocked were speakeasies or restaurants, but some were stills in private houses. Often the moonshiner simply cut off the padlock and went back into business.

One of the stranger padlock operations involved an illegal 50-gallon still in the redwood forests of Northern California. The moonshine operation was located inside the cavity of a hollow redwood tree that was twenty-four feet in diameter. The entrance to the cavity was disguised by a piece of canvas painted to look like tree bark. The Prohibition Bureau, however, discovered the still and destroyed it. Afterwards they "padlocked" the tree, and tacked a notice to the canvas that the tree was in violation of the Volstead Act.[27]

## California Wine

During Prohibition, legitimate commercial wine (as opposed to that made at home) generally came from Mexico, California, or France, because wine grapes required specific growing conditions to provide a quality product.

Prior to Prohibition, California was a principle source of wine and the wine industry was of major economic importance to Northern California and the central valleys. Whiskey could be distilled anywhere, but the grapes to produce high-quality wine had to be grown where the soil and climate conditions were suitable. Just prior to Prohibition, the price of grapes skyrocketed. In 1911 grapes sold for as little as $9.50 a ton. By 1921, with an impending shortage, this had increased to $105 a ton.

Prohibition hit the California wine industry hard and several hundred California wineries closed. With the start of Prohibition 150,000 jobs in the wine industry were threatened, grape and wine exports were devastated, and economic chaos loomed over the wine industry.

In 1919 more than 700 wineries were in operation, but by the end of 1933 only 380 wineries remained. The number plummeted from 694 in 1922 to less than 200 in 1925. The industry went from producing 51 million gallons of wine in 1918 to only 3 million in 1925. To symbolize Prohibition and what they saw as the end of the wine business, government agents dumped 35,000 gallons of wine from the North Cucamonga Winery literally down the drain.[28]

One of the looming questions with the arrival of Prohibition was what to do with the land that had been used to grow wine grapes. Raisins made from wine grapes were not suitable for table use, but only for wine making. One proposal was to turn previous vineyards into edible raisin-grape fields or into fruit orchards. The problem with that was that the country did not need more acreage devoted to raisins, as that would cause the price to fall and hurt the raisin suppliers economically. Similarly, fruit growers in California were already starting to remove fruit trees as unprofitable, so more fruit trees were certainly not needed.

Another idea was to raise chickens on land formerly occupied by vineyards. The idea, however, was rapidly dismissed because the poultry industry was already falling on hard economic times and did not need additional sources of supply. Other prohibitionists wanted the government to purchase previous vineyards and give the land to soldiers returning from the war. Critics immediately complained that this would essentially just be a transfer of land through a confiscation program.

As it turned out with hindsight, the acreage devoted to vineyards actually increased to seven times its previous size during the first years of Prohibition. The basic sales price of vineyards increased drastically. Grape-growing land rose from $100 an acre in 1919 to as much as $500 a few years later. Growers who had re-planted their vineyards with fruit trees in anticipation of financial disaster rushed to plant grapes again. California winegrowers increased the acreage devoted to growing grapes from 97,000 acres in 1919 to 680,796 in 1926.

What saved the wine industry was an exception in the Prohibition laws. Under the Volstead Act, the head of each household was allowed to make 200 gallons a year of fermented fruit juice or wine for family use. Thus, a family could make, but not sell or transport, about 1,000 bottles of wine a year. The provision was included in the Act to pacify legislators from New England and California who needed to placate the cultural traditions of their constituents of making hard apple cider and wine for family use. Wineries were allowed to continue making wine vinegar and wine for medicinal and sacramental use on a limited basis.

Not only did breweries and wineries find ways to keep making products during Prohibition and stay in business, but many individuals indirectly supported the industry by turning fruit juice into illegal wine. The immediate reaction of the wineries had been to go out of business, but profits soared as the sales of grapes rebounded. When wine was still legal in 1917, Americans consumed 70 million gallons. By 1925, in line with increased whiskey drinking, this figure had increased to 150 million gallons.[29]

One course of action for wineries that didn't shut down was to make sacramental wine and wine tonic. As sacramental wine was acceptable under the Volstead Act, author Herbert Asbury wryly commented that a lot of people became Jewish rabbis or dressed in the appropriate black garments and wore a beard in order to withdraw wine for religious use.[30] One winery in the sacramental wine business stored 900,000 gallons in a building that covered more than an acre, and had its own rail spur for shipping the finished product. That would seem to be a lot of Communion wine.[31]

Garret and Company, who made wine under their Virginia Dare label, had to relocate from Brooklyn, New York, to Cucamonga, California, due to the business pressures they encountered during Prohibition. They grew grapes in California, but continued to use their Brooklyn address on their labels. They survived Prohibition by making sacramental wine. They also made Virginia Dare Constitutional Tonic, a medicinal product that contained ingredients that were invigorating and stimulating. The label on their bottles particularly recommended the tonic for "... anemia, neurasthenia, convalescence, and building up run-down systems." Neurasthenia was a vague and poorly-defined Victorian-era mental "disease" that supposedly struck men of intellect and exhibited nebulous symptoms of multiple diseases without any organic cause. The disease was later determined to be so nebulous that it did not exist. One time someone at the winery left out the medicinal components of the tonic and substituted simple spices instead. After the word spread, sales could not keep up with the demand.[32]

The amount of wine allowed under the Volstead Act was so small that it was not a profitable part of business for a bootlegger. Bootleggers sold what they promoted as fine wine, but good wines were hard to get even for them. The bottles they sold looked authentic, but the labels used were often bogus imitations of the quality wine manufacturers. What they sold as

**Garrett & Company survived the difficult business pressures of Prohibition by making sacramental wine. They also made Virginia Dare Constitutional Tonic, a medicinal product that contained ingredients supposed to be invigorating and stimulating. When someone at the winery left out the medicinal components of the tonic and substituted spices instead, sales reportedly could not keep up with the demand (author's collection).**

champagne was often only cider with a little grain alcohol added and the mixture pressurized with carbon dioxide. Prohibition agents seized 8,000 cases of illegal champagne in New York in 1926 and when they analyzed it they found that none of it was genuine.[33]

Like the beer and whiskey business, wine for making vinegar was sometimes diverted to illegal use. The government solved that issue by adding acetic acid (vinegar) to the wine before it was shipped. Legitimate manufacturers of vinegar did not mind the addition, but those seeking to sell illegal wine found it to be a problem.

Wineries made the most of what they had. Grapes could take several pressings and a considerable amount of dilution and still be productive. The first pressing was used to produce the highest quality of wine. The second pressing was used to produce "second wine" that was made from the leftovers. The dregs of the dregs were distilled into cheap moonshine.

Another way for wineries to stay in business was to market grape concentrate products during Prohibition, ostensibly for making non-intoxicating grape juice. As a result, a large market emerged for dried grapes that could surreptitiously be made into a reasonable quality of wine. Grapes were pressed into wine bricks and sold with directions on how to make this wine. The processed blocks or bricks were grape juice concentrated down into solid masses about the size of a pound of butter. These grape blocks were available in different varieties, such as port, sherry, burgundy, Rhine Wine, or any other wine variety or flavor the consumer might desire. Accompanying instructions described how to make non-alcoholic, unfermented grape juice by reconstituting the blocks into juice. The manufacturer warned customers not to allow their product to ferment or they would risk making intoxicating wine in the process.

Instructions included a disclaimer that if an individual accurately followed the directions he would end up with wine. That, of course, would be illegal. So the bricks came with explicit instructions for preventing fermentation. With hypocritical glee, suppliers specifically warned consumers that grape concentrate should not be mixed with water, sealed in a jug, and stored for three weeks while being periodically shaken or it would turn into a fermented beverage, namely wine, with an alcohol content of about 13 percent. In essence then, these were "do not" instructions.

Vino Sano grape bricks, made from crushed and dehydrated grapes, were sold starting in the early 1920s with the "warning" that "After dissolving the brick in a gallon of water, do not place the liquid in a jug away in the cupboard for twenty days, because then it would turn to wine." Vine-Glo was another legal product that would turn into wine if stored in a cellar for sixty days.[34] The maker also specified that fermented grape juice was legal in the customer's home, but that it must not be transported.

Grape juice was openly sold in grocery stores, and the associated necessary equipment for home manufacture of wine was available in many stores and other places. Wine could easily be made within the law as it was easy and legal to purchase equipment for crushing the grapes, along with kegs, barrels, bungs, bottles, corks, and all the other supplies needed to produce wine. The accompanying instructions solemnly emphasized ways to stop fermentation, such as to keep the liquid in the refrigerator, to avoid natural yeast that was in the air, to sterilize the liquid by boiling it, and to avoid using yeast. In other words, all the things that someone making wine at home should avoid doing.

Between 1925 and 1929 more than 678,000,000 gallons of home wine were produced, not including wine made from other plants grown at home, such as dandelions, apples, cherries, and other fruit products.

For the convenience of California customers, the railyard in San Francisco had portable grape presses and tanks mounted on trucks that would crush grapes to juice while the customer waited. It was perfectly legal to crush grapes and the crushers figured it was none of their business where the grape juice went after they pressed it.

As a side note of interest, Welch's grape juice evolved from an attempt to use drinks other than fermented wine for communion services after one Methodist church tried using a substitute made from raisins and water. Dr. Thomas B. Welch, a Methodist minister as well as a dentist, improved on that by developing a sterilized bottled grape juice that could be stored without natural fermentation occurring. He named it Dr. Welch's Unfermented Wine. After further development, he marketed Welch's Grape Juice in 1893 as an enjoyable soft drink.

On the other hand, real wine also flourished. In 1933, in Modesto, two brothers named Ernest and Julio Gallo learned how to make wine at the Modesto Public Library by reading about commercial wine-making methods. They rented an old building with a grape press and tanks, and started making wine. With one brother in charge of sales and the other in charge of production, their winery became a business success that continues today.

One of the offshoots of the California wine industry was distilled wine. Swiss immigrant families made their regular allotment of wine, then added more water to the leftovers, fermented the result, and distilled it until the resulting alcohol was 190 proof. The called the result schnapps or brandy.

A popular drink with Italian families was grappa, which was a strong clear alcohol that was distilled by recycling the leftover grapes after filtering wine. Grappa was a type of Italian brandy that was about 110 proof. Some also called it "apple jack." In Mendocino County around Healdsburg it was called "jackass." If it was run three times through a still, a gallon of good wine would produce a fifth of alcohol that was 180 to 195 proof. It was usually cut with water to produce a 90-proof drink. Various flavoring extracts and a little coloring might be added to give the flavor of rum, brandy, or whiskey. Ranches around Stockton sold it for $6 a gallon.

In the end, voters in the 1932 California election voted 1,308,428 to 730,522 to abolish the Wright Act, which was California's enforcement act for the Prohibition Amendment. With that, Prohibition was essentially over in California.

# 8

## The Mountain States

### (Wyoming, Idaho, Montana, Colorado)

In the wide-open spaces of the West, most bootleggers were not the violent criminals and gangsters of the type found in Chicago or New York. Many people in the West did not consider drinking whiskey to be a bad habit and, to some, the Western moonshiner was accepted as a good neighbor and a type of folk hero. However, conversely, moonshiners had to stay on the good side of their neighbors or risk being exposed to federal agents. Another possibility was that a fellow moonshiner might turn in a competitor to try to steal his business.

In the rural West, many bootleggers ran small-time operations that manufactured a few pints or gallons of illegal alcohol. This was mostly a small business of small stills run by small-time bootleggers. If they were discovered, Prohibition agents would either confiscate the still and any moonshine, or smash the equipment and barrels with axes. Occasionally illegal stills became the source of running battles, sometimes literally, between moonshiners and law enforcement officials who sought to shut down stills and destroy them.

In the West, in the early part of the twentieth century, saloons were a profitable business. In mining towns and other male-dominated early towns, the saloon provided a type of social center for unmarried men or miners and loggers living apart from their families, particularly on the long cold nights of winter in the high mountains. Even in establishments where there were no women for entertainment, men could find social interaction in the saloons among their fellow bachelors. They could play cards or billiards or relax and have a social drink or two and some quiet conversation in a convivial atmosphere.

Local chapters of national organizations, however, were soon founded in the mining camps of Colorado, Montana, Idaho, and Arizona to promote national temperance. One of the prominent organizations was the Independent Order of Good Templars, founded in 1850 in Oneida, New

York. The first temperance organization in Arizona was the Arizona Order of Good Templars, founded in 1878 in Phoenix. Local lodges flourished in mining camps after the Civil War when gold and silver mining was a major industry in the West. These lodges attracted many of the professional classes, such as lawyers, mining engineers, ministers, and middle-class merchants. By 1868 the organization had a national membership of more than 400,000. Members of these lodges sponsored lectures, dances, and other celebrations, but always without liquor.

Though these local organizations were well-meaning, efforts were not always as successful as the promoters had hoped they would be. For example, during one year the Good Templars lodge in the booming mining town of Black Hawk, Colorado, expelled half of its members for breaking their temperance vow.[1]

Social reformers who encouraged Temperance organizations felt that providing reading rooms and sponsoring lectures and similar types of entertainment would provide adequate entertainment for lonely bachelors and, after experiencing the joys to be found in them, men would abandon the saloons. Reformers reasoned that as a consequence saloons and liquor would disappear.

The temperance workers' perception was that the saloon was merely a place for most men to find supplies of whiskey and that its patrons were only there to become roaring drunk in as short a time as possible. Temperance supporters chose not to acknowledge that there were men who were only social drinkers and they assumed that anyone who drank anything was a drunkard. They did not, or chose not, to understand that social drinking, particularly drinking beer, was part of the culture from Europe that had accompanied many of the immigrants who worked in the mines. They also ignored, and did not like, the fact that a couple of drinks might be used merely to produce a sense of relaxation and more companionable interaction among many of the working men.

Reformers also ignored other practical aspects of the saloon issue. For example, an ordinance passed in 1906 closed all the saloons in the mining town of Creede, Colorado, on Sundays. The closures didn't, however, last long. City fathers quickly realized that many of the single miners had nowhere warm to go during the freezing winter evenings of the mountains, except to the saloons. As a result, the ordinance was quickly repealed.[2]

As well for the saloons, the sale of liquor was an important part of the profits for bordellos. In fact, the consumption of large amounts of wine and champagne was encouraged as a central part of the business of a parlor house. In many cases this revenue could exceed the income from prostitution. Because of large potential profits, parlor houses might be backed by liquor merchants. A merchant would put up the introductory cost of operating the house and arrange for the initial investment for rent and furniture, with the understanding that the madam would supply only his particular brand or brands of wine and liquor.

Liquor was sold in brothels at a marked-up price that was up to five or six times the proprietor's cost and was thus an extremely profitable part of the house business. A bottle of wine might cost the customer fifteen dollars and a quart bottle of champagne could cost up to thirty dollars at a time when a common miner made three dollars a day and a cowboy made thirty dollars a month.

After South Dakota prohibited the sale of alcohol, the madam of one brothel in Rapid City closed her house permanently. When asked why, she replied that she couldn't run a sporting house and make a profit on creek water.[3]

## Moonshining

In the early settlement of the West, alcoholic drinks appeared mostly in the form of distilled spirits, such as whiskey and rum, as the distances to economically transport other forms of alcohol, such as beer, were too great. Likewise, distilled spirits were popular among bootleggers because they consisted of concentrated alcohol and a smaller volume of liquid that could be easily transported by car or truck. Beer in barrels and kegs, on the other hand, was bulky, heavy, and expensive to ship over long distances except by railroad, thus beer tended to be brewed at local breweries.

Ranching country in the empty reaches of the West provided an abundance of secluded places to make moonshine. Within a week after Prohibition went into effect, small portable stills were on sale throughout the country. If a still was located around ranch buildings, the equipment could be easily concealed in a secret storage cellar with a trapdoor under a barn or other outbuilding.

Other tricks were used to conceal illegal stills. One rancher protected his still by having it concealed in the same pasture as his bad-tempered bull to discourage investigation by revenue agents or other law officers. Another hit on the trick of locating his still behind the cattle pens where his cows were corralled at night. Prohibition agents coming up the road in the dark saw only a dead-end road that ended at the cattle pens. The constant movement of cattle inside the pens also quickly wiped out any car or truck tracks going through the pens to the still. Moonshiners near Denver placed decaying animal carcasses near their stills, so that the telltale scent of the mash was disguised by the more potent and disgusting smell of rotting flesh.

Sometimes illegal stills in the West were buried underground under a thick cover of trees in mountain forests. This one had a roof made from discarded railroad ties covered by sheets of tin. Prohibition agents could sometimes find these hidden stills by sitting on high ridges and watching for columns of smoke rising, often indicating a moonshine still being heated by a wood fire. Moonshiners then defeated this tactic by using kerosene or propane stoves that did not give out visible smoke (author's collection).

Illegal stills for making moonshine liquor in the mountains were sometimes buried underground in forested areas to avoid being found by revenue agents who worked for the government. A typical size for one of these dugouts was eight feet by twelve feet. The rafters were held up by large logs or discarded railroad ties, with a tin roof that was covered with dirt, branches, small bushes, and other local materials for disguise. A trapdoor in the side or top of the structure allowed access to the interior.

Still sites were often located underground below thick stands of pine trees deep in the forests of the West to avoid detection. To counter this tactic, law enforcement officials sat on high ridges and watched for telltale columns of smoke curling up from the forests below, which often indicated that a moonshine still was being heated by a wood fire.

One trick used to thwart Prohibition agents was the use of dummy trucks. A truck carrying sugar or other bootlegging supplies that was being pursued by Prohibition agents drove at night with its lights on to where an empty truck or one loaded with some innocuous farm supplies waited in hiding. The sugar truck would drive to a place of concealment behind a hill, a barn, or a grove of trees and quickly turn off its lights. Taking its place, the dummy truck turned on its lights and sped off, pursued by the Prohibition agents. If the agents caught up with the dummy truck and stopped and searched it, they obviously would not find what they were looking for. This same trick could also be used by cars or trucks carrying finished moonshine liquor.

When revenue agents found a still they either destroyed it or padlocked it. Hidden supplies of bootleg liquor were either confiscated, retained for evidence at a subsequent trial, or destroyed by punching axe holes in the cans and barrels. Much of the illegal liquor was simply poured down the nearest drain or storm sewer or, in the case of a backwoods still, out onto the ground.

## Wyoming

Colorado outlawed the possession, manufacture, and sale of alcohol in 1914. Idaho followed in 1915. Nebraska, South Dakota, and Montana did the same in 1916, and Utah followed in 1917. Wyoming became the only wet state left in the Rocky Mountains. As a result, towns along Wyoming's borders did a thriving business with customers who drove in from its neighboring states to purchase their liquor supplies.

Wyoming was a state full of wide open spaces and Wild West sentiments, but it succumbed to Prohibition in 1919, when the legislature passed a state law banning alcohol. As in many other states, enforcement of prohibition in Wyoming was difficult because a large proportion of the population didn't obey the law. Bootlegging was quick to follow and as early as August 1919 enforcement agents in Laramie arrested five men and a woman, and confiscated 400 gallons of illegal liquor.

Enforcement of the Prohibition law in Wyoming was haphazard, and sometimes violent. One example occurred when the body of a local rancher named Frank Jennings was found dead in his car near Laramie with five bullet wounds in his body. After a detailed investigation, three state Prohibition agents were arrested and charged with the killing. One of them finally confessed and said they had thought they were following a car driven by a couple of well-known local bootleggers. As they chased the car, one of the agents started shooting at it with a rifle. All three agents were eventually convicted of manslaughter and sentenced to the state prison.

Another violent incident occurred in October of 1922 in Cody when the town marshal tried to arrest a federal Prohibition officer for drunkenness after the man had been partying with two women and a bottle of Canadian whiskey that had been stolen from the county sheriff's evidence locker. In the ensuing fight, the marshal broke the agent's jaw and the agent shot the marshal in the leg. The town judge fined the Prohibition agent $100 for public intoxication.

Casper, Wyoming, grew to be one of the biggest centers for vice in the Rocky Mountains in the 1920s, with illegal gambling and liquor readily available in most bars and restaurants. Wyoming's large oil drilling and refining industry, along with mining, ranching, and the railroad attracted a lot of single men to Casper's alcohol and prostitution. Some illegal liquor was made from dried apricots and sugar. A popular local drink with a powerful kick was "Casper moon."

As happened in many other towns across the West, in 1933 Casper's mayor, the police chief, and the Natrona county sheriff were accused of corruption and conspiring with local bootleggers to violate federal Prohibition laws. All three were charged in federal court with taking regular payments from bootleggers and bar owners.[4]

## Colorado

One of the first saloons in the West was set up in the open air in the 1820s in the far northwest corner of Colorado near where the states of Colorado, Utah, and Wyoming come together. The location was Brown's Hole, which was first used as a rendezvous point for fur trappers in the mountain valleys of the West, and was later used as a part-time hideout by outlaw Butch Cassidy and his wild bunch.

The people of Colorado were on the early forefront in their efforts to introduce prohibition to their state. On November 3, 1914, voters decided 129,589 to 118,017 in favor of a constitutional amendment to turn the state dry. Though legal wrangling over the constitutionality of the provision dragged on through 1915, the legislation was eventually held to be legal and Colorado enacted statewide prohibition on January 1, 1916, four years before National Prohibition started. As a result, the production and importation of all intoxicating alcoholic beverages was outlawed except for religious and medicinal purposes. Denver, which had actually voted against the legislation 38,139 to 29,553, had to go along with the rest of the state's wishes.[5]

During World War I prohibitionists argued that grain should be used for food for the troops and not squandered on producing alcohol. This patriotic sentiment was apparently popular with the general public of Colorado and the state voted accordingly to become completely dry. Though this satisfied the temperance supporters, the rest of the population was not necessarily happy with the idea, because this meant total abstinence from alcohol. This was not temperance, but a total ban, which of course was not appealing to moderate and social drinkers.

The campaign to ban liquor had been conducted with rallies, brass bands, and fiery speeches, but when January 1, 1916, arrived, there was little open unrest and the potential demonstrations that the police expected never occurred. The state's 1,500 saloons, 12 beer breweries, and 500 hotels, restaurants, and drugstores that sold liquor shut down quietly.

In order to survive, breweries had to turn to other business ventures. Coors Brewery, which was located in Golden, just west of Denver, relied on producing other products, such as ceramics and nonalcoholic beverages, until Prohibition was repealed. In the process, the company became the world's largest supplier of malted milk to soda fountains and candy companies.

## Denver

Immigrant Germans who were accustomed to drinking brought their brewing and drinking habits with them. A traditional German holiday, Bock Beer Day, came to Denver in 1874. Three thousand glasses of beer were drunk at the celebration when the population in 1870 was less than 5,000 people.

As also happened on the national level, when prohibition came to Denver in 1916 many Germans lost their jobs in the brewing industry. As a result of the new law, dozens of manufacturers, wholesalers, and distributors were forced to close. Denver and the rest of Colorado headed into a long dry spell from 1916 until 1934.

In 1900 Denver had boasted 334 saloons, and by 1910 there were 410. But by 1920 the official number of saloon in Denver had dropped to zero.[6] The oddest side-effect of shutting down the saloons in Denver was that hundreds of cats suddenly became homeless. They had been kept as barroom pets, surviving on scraps from free saloon lunches while they were tasked with controlling the rat population.

Gambling, drinking, and prostitution were closely intertwined, and those who wanted to indulge themselves in Denver had easily been able to find women, drink, and games of chance before the saloons closed. At the same time that Prohibition took effect, however, the county sheriff seized the opportunity to close the red-light district in Denver and eliminate all the gambling, women, and opium dens. Thus, when Colorado went dry, the red-light district on Market Street quickly faded away and by 1916 all the bordellos were officially gone.[7] Most of these vanished underground, but almost any taxi driver, hotel clerk, or friendly policeman could direct a customer in search of a safe establishment to find a drink.

Although the effect of Prohibition in Colorado was to restrict drinking, it did not totally eliminate it. Police reports state that in 1916 out of a total of arrests of 10,045 there were 566 arrests for Prohibition violations (5% of the total). In addition, there were 1,605 arrests for drunkenness (16% of the total). In 1918 the number of arrests for drunkenness were not much different at 1,423.[8]

The law allowed dispensing alcohol for medicinal purposes through a permit system. The amount was two quarts of hard liquor and six quarts of wine per household per month, which would seem to be quite a generous amount. Denver city auditor Fred Stackhouse noted in 1917 that the city issued 59,339 liquor permits to individuals. Prohibition supporters, however, found this to be unacceptable and campaigned hard over the next couple of years for the complete restriction of alcohol, except under extenuating circumstances.

Another loophole in the law allowed beer and spirits to be imported for personal use from wet states. Thus, starting in 1916, an estimated $3,000 to $5,000 of whiskey a month poured into Denver and the rest of the state from the wet state of Wyoming to the north.[9] One bootlegger in Denver was arrested for "importing" 2,000 pints of whiskey into the city in wooden boxes labeled as olive oil and salad dressing, underneath a layer of containers of real salad dressing packed in sawdust.[10]

Like the Pacific Coast states, legitimate (but illegal) liquor also flowed into Denver from Mexico and Canada. To support the illegal production of wine, railroad cars full of grapes were regularly shipped to Denver from California. These grapes were supposedly being used for consumption as food, but judging from the amount of grapes sold there must have been a lot of residents who really enjoyed their fruit.

To accommodate law-abiding citizens who wished to meet for social gatherings, Denver issued licenses for soft drink shops, ice cream parlors, and billiard halls. The fee for a business license was $25. There is evidence that at least some of these ice cream and billiards parlors were fronts for illegal drinking. For example, the license of M. Engbar on West Colfax Avenue was suspended for "violating the prohibition law." There were other similar citations as well.[11]

Vacant buildings that had previously been saloons soon re-opened as pool halls, soda shops, restaurants, candy stores, cigar stores, and soft-drink parlors. Some didn't try to be part of the charade and simply became speakeasies. Others just kept going as before. Gahan's at the corner of 15th Street and Larimer in Denver, directly opposite the old city courthouse and police station, converted its premises from a saloon into a restaurant. All through Prohibition, however, it kept its back room open with a well-stocked bar and brand-name liquor.[12]

Many drugstores, of course, supplied whiskey for medicinal purposes, with the pharmacist left to be the judge of the patient's need. If someone came into the drug store and said they were ill and needed a drink, the druggist was obligated to provide for the customer's medicinal needs.

Even though the temperance movement was strong in Colorado, alternative ways to obtain a drink soon appeared in the major cities of Denver, Colorado Springs, Pueblo, and Cripple Creek. Drinking continued in back rooms or in the numerous "soft drink parlors" that soon opened. Sometimes not even that subterfuge was necessary. When the front doors of Jim Ryan's Monte Carlo saloon in Denver were closed by prohibitionists, customers continued to frequent the establishment, but entered by an alternate door that was around the side of the building.

Prohibition was probably more of a nuisance than a problem in Colorado. To the dismay of the Prohibitionists, dry laws had little impact on human nature. For example, the Italian population of Denver regarded wine and spirits as a healthy part of their culture and diet. Thus when Prohibition became the law they made and drank their own wine in the basement, or frequented the back rooms of taverns that had been converted to soft-drink parlors. Bootleggers soon started supplying wine to other thirsty Denver residents, and the Italian speakeasies in North Denver continued to provide plenty of red wine with their spaghetti dinners.

Like any other part of the country, Colorado had liquor hijackers. But the strategy of stealing someone else's booze instead of making it wasn't always successful, and the joke sometimes turned on the miscreants. Reporter Forbes Parkhill related a story of how police raided a Denver bootlegger during Prohibition and confiscated a hundred five-gallon kegs of red wine. Somehow, on the way to the evidence locker at the police station, five of the kegs disappeared. Word spread among the newspaper community that the kegs would be opened that night. The first keg was drunk in five minutes. But when the thirsty reporters moved on to the second keg, they found out that it was vinegar. So were the remaining three kegs. It turned out that to fool policemen or Prohibition agents looking for illegal booze, the bootlegger had hidden his kegs of real wine behind a false front of kegs containing vinegar. Unfortunately for the reporters, the misappropriated booze consisted of four of the kegs of vinegar and only one of real wine.[13]

The trail of illegal liquor showed up everywhere. The Arabian Bar had a wine press in the cellar that was used during Prohibition.[14] When the furnishings of the bordello on Market Street in Denver that belonged to

Madam Mattie Silks were auctioned off in 1919, a coffin was found in the basement of the building in the wine room. Those in the know suspected that the coffin had been used to transport illegal liquor. Coffins were occasionally used for shipping bootleg whiskey as most people would not suspect that a coffin and hearse were being used to transport liquor.[15]

## The Rest of Colorado

One of the towns in Colorado that was founded on temperance principles was Colorado Springs, which was established as the resort town of Fountain Colony by General William Palmer in 1871. Palmer's wife, Queen, was a Quaker by religion and talked him into outlawing liquor in all the houses within the city limits. Thus all the town deeds contained a clause that if "intoxicating liquors" as a beverage were manufactured or sold on the premises, the property would revert back to the original town company.

The town founders and residents were actually not opposed to drinking on moral grounds, and even General Palmer was not opposed to having a drink or two. The main reason for the liquor ban was the intention of the founders to keep out saloons and liquor that they felt would foster drunks and lower property values.[16]

In spite of temperance efforts, the liquor ban in the new town never worked successfully. Sales of the early Fountain Colony lots were poor, which was blamed on the disapproval by potential purchasers of the liquor ban in all the Colorado Springs Company deeds. This led to endless and futile controversy and discussion. The situation was finally resolved to everyone's satisfaction by locating saloons and bawdy houses in nearby Colorado City, which was about two miles west of downtown Colorado Springs. An estimated twenty-seven saloons were soon in operation there, providing drinking and dancing, along with gambling houses and prostitution.

Occasional efforts were made to circumvent the liquor ban. For example, the civic leaders of Colorado Springs organized a private club, called the El Paso Club, that allowed members to keep private stocks of liquor in the club's lockers. When the club moved its location in 1890, the mayor and civic government decided that their liquor was not the same as the liquor covered by the liquor ban, and opened a member's bar in the new building.[17]

Another hypocritical method of obtaining a drink in Colorado Springs was a repeat of a system for providing a drink that had been used as far back as Maine in the 1840s. At the southeast corner of Pikes Peak Avenue and Tejon Street in downtown Colorado Springs was a room with nothing in it but a hole in the wall covered by a vertical partition that rotated on a wheel, with an attached tray at the bottom. This was called the "Wheel of Fortune." A man wanting a drink placed a coin on the tray and rotated the wheel. As the other side of the partition came around, the coin had magically been replaced by a glass of whiskey. Nobody was seen or heard to speak. This contraption was also nicknamed the "Spiritual Wheel" because of the miraculous appearance of the glass of whiskey where the coin had previously been.

The Colorado Springs Company found out about this magical wheel and brought a legal suit against the owners. The controversy went to the highest court in the land and, in 1879, the U.S. Supreme Court decided that the forfeiture clause in all the town deeds was valid. The owner of the Spiritual Wheel sold his property in disgust and left town.[18]

The time between ratification of the Eighteenth Amendment and the date when the Volstead Act went into effect was one year. A provision of the Volstead Act allowed the continued possession of alcoholic beverages that had been purchased before July 1, 1919. In other words, drinking liquor was still legal, but making and selling it was not. As a result, many individuals and businesses with foresight purchased and stored plenty of alcoholic beverages before Prohibition went into effect.

Some wealthy individuals stocked their personal cellars with as much booze as they could. One of these far-sighted men was Spencer Penrose, the owner of the lavish Broadmoor Hotel in Colorado Springs. In 1919, anticipating National Prohibition, Penrose purchased 2,400 cases of some of the finest and rarest liquor from Europe and America, and put it in storage in New York. He purchased a further 1,000 cases for his private wine cellar in Colorado. When Prohibition was repealed, he shipped the liquor from New York to Colorado in two box cars and stored it in his cellar. Needless to say, he employed burglar alarms and a full-time security guard to protect it.[19]

In practice there were very few speakeasies in Colorado Springs, though the town did have many small-time bootleggers. A bottle or two of some kind of liquor was usually available at the local college fraternity and homecoming dances, where hip flasks were fashionable among both alumni and students. Also the nearby town of Colorado City freely provided drinking, and was only fifteen minutes from downtown Colorado

*Opposite:* The cover of *Frank Leslie's Illustrated Newspaper* from July 7, 1877, showed an ingenious device used in Colorado Springs to obtain a drink. The contraption was a rotating wheel in the wall known as "The Wheel of Fortune" or "The Spiritual Wheel," due to the sudden way in which a coin placed on the wheel and the wheel rotated was magically changed into a glass of beer or whiskey that emerged from behind the wall (Library of Congress).

COLORADO.—EVADING THE LIQUOR LAW IN COLORADO SPRINGS, AS WITNESSED BY THE MEMBERS OF THE FRANK LESLIE TRANSCONTINENTAL EXCURSION PARTY.
FROM A SKETCH BY HARRY OGDEN.—SEE PAGE 304.

Springs by streetcar. Other means of obtaining a drink in Colorado Springs were as simple as going to the public bar that was in the back of the billiard hall in the La Font House on Huerfano Street (now re-named Colorado Avenue).

Colorado City, just west of Colorado Springs, was the home of numerous saloons and bawdy houses that sold liquor as part of their operations. The town was established in 1859 as a supply town for travelers and miners headed via nearby Ute Pass for the gold camps of South Park in central Colorado. By 1888 there were twenty-three saloons in the town to serve a population of only 1,500.[20]

The residents of Colorado City were primarily working-class. Most were associated with the local railroad shops located in town, and the mills that processed gold ore from nearby Cripple Creek in the mountains. It was a rough Western town long before Colorado Springs was founded with its anti-liquor laws and elite citizenship. Though most of the residents of Colorado City were good, hard-working citizens, their town was largely overshadowed by saloons, dance halls, and brothels.

In spite of the red-light district's popularity with the male segment of the population, there had always been attempts to limit liquor in Colorado City. In 1894 the Woman's Christian Temperance Union (WCTU) submitted a petition to limit the hours of operation of all saloons, bowling alleys, and "other resorts." Only 152 people signed the petition, but that was taken by city authorities as a mandate to proceed. However, in 1902 there were still twenty-seven saloons and more than thirty combined saloons and gambling halls in operation.[21]

In 1906 a city ordinance was passed that mandated that saloons had to be closed from midnight to 6 a.m., and all day on Sundays. The new law didn't seem to have much effect as twenty-two saloons remained in business. As a parallel effort, the mayor told all the "working girls" in the saloons to leave town within ten days. Both the saloon-keepers and their girls refused to move.

This was still the Old West and sometimes lawlessness was used to fight lawlessness through violence. In January of 1907 a suspicious fire broke out in the saloon district of Colorado City and wiped out many of the beer halls on Saloon Row. Three more unexplained fires broke out in January of 1909 and burned most of the red-light district, including many of the remaining saloons and brothels. Most were rebuilt, but by this time city officials, who realized that they needed the revenue from taxes on liquor and monthly fines from the women, turned a blind eye to the re-appearance of drinking and prostitution.[22]

The WCTU carried out a vigorous campaign to vote Colorado City a dry town as a method of stopping prostitution. In retaliation, several saloon-keepers banded together and purchased a section of land a few blocks directly north of the main saloon district which was located on Colorado Avenue. Here they founded a new town named Ramona and some of the bars and women moved there. The town of Ramona was named after local author Helen Hunt Jackson's character and popular novel of the time of the same name. Soon there were four saloons in operation in the new town, and a population of 300 that followed them. The saloons even cooperated to operate a bus service for the convenience of its patrons, using an old truck to ferry them to the saloons.

The town of Ramona hired a chief of police, a city marshal, a city detective, and a jailer, even though in practice all the functions were carried out by the same man. The jail was a small tent that never seemed to house any occupants. The *Colorado Springs Gazette* called it "a degraded, besotted little sinkhole," and the town received the alternative nicknames of "Whiskeytown" and "Whiskeyville." The town of Ramona was eventually annexed by nearby Colorado Springs in 1917 and the saloons all disappeared.

Pueblo, Colorado, to the south, turned out to be a hotbed of moonshining after the start of Prohibition. To fill the demand for alcoholic beverages, bootleggers Pete and Sam Carlino started to supply illegal whiskey and eventually controlled bootlegging in almost the entire state.[23] Sam Carlino became the biggest bootlegger in Colorado during Prohibition.

Pete (Pietro) and Sam (Salvatore) Carlino lived in Vineland in southern Colorado, where the Carlino family grew sugar beets on their ranch in the early 1900s, after their arrival from Sicily. By 1917 Sam and Pete were distilling "Sugar Moon," a popular homemade local moonshine made from sugar beets.

One recipe for Sugar Moon was to mix 120 pounds of beet sugar, 50 gallons of spring water, and a pound-and-a-half of yeast and let the mixture stand for ten days at 80°F while it fermented. The resulting liquid was distilled to produce alcohol. Colorado produced a large crop of sugar beets each year, making the inexpensive beets ideal for manufacturing powerful low-cost liquor.

The Carlino family was not successful and in 1917 lost their farm to foreclosure. They moved to Sugar City and continued to farm sugar beets and make bootleg whiskey. The Carlinos' bootlegging business did well and after 1926 they were the undisputed suppliers of illegal liquor in the southern half of Colorado. Some of the liquor was distributed through Pellegrino Scaglia's grocery store in Pueblo; some was distributed through John Cha's soft drink parlor in downtown Trinidad.[24]

The Carlinos had moonshine stills hidden around the countryside and even secreted in caves. The quantity of moonshine that was being manufactured and shipped was large. On March 6, 1929, federal agents intercepted a truck south of Denver that was loaded with fifty-five kegs of moonshine, making it the biggest federal bust for several months and a big loss for the Carlinos.

In the wake of their success, the Carlino's decided to expand their bootlegging business north from Pueblo into Colorado Springs and Denver. By 1930 Pete Carlino was doing business in Denver and was trying to control the entire state. He intimidated many of the competing local bootleggers by hijacking their supplies and threatening to bomb their stills.

By now supply was outpacing demand and the price for moonshine fell. In 1926 local moonshine went for $3 a pint, but by 1931 the price was down to $1 a pint and $7 a gallon. In an attempt to end the price competition, Pete Carlino tried to organize the bootleggers. His idea was to form a bootlegger's trust and fix the price at $10 a gallon and $2 a pint. In addition he wanted 25 cents from every gallon to go into a defense fund to help arrested bootleggers pay their legal fees. He organized a bootlegger's meeting for representatives from the different factions on January 24, 1931, at La Palmatre Restaurant on West 38th Avenue in Denver. The police found out about it and twenty-three police officers armed with machine guns surrounded the place and arrested twenty-nine of the bootleggers for vagrancy. Though a trial date was set, most of the defendants were released for lack of cause, and others received only suspended sentences.

Not everyone appreciated the fact that the Carlinos were trying to muscle in on Denver's bootlegging territory. Rivalry between various moonshine factions included gang-style warfare, shoot-outs involving professional assassins, the mysterious disappearance of participants, and the bombings of bootleggers' houses and stills. Shotgun drive-by shootings occurred that were worthy of the violence in Chicago.

In the end, Sam Carlino was gunned down in his home on West 33rd Avenue in Denver on May 8, 1931, shot in the back by employee Bruno Mauro, one of the Carlino employees who operated a whiskey still.[25]

Pete Carlino did not end up any better. He was finally captured by a dozen police officers armed with sawed-off shotguns on June 18, 1931, and taken to the Denver jail. He was released while he was awaiting trial. During a trip to the Colorado State Penitentiary in Cañon City on September 10, 1931, to visit two of his associates who were in prison, he was forced off the highway, driven to a secluded back road outside Pueblo, and shot dead in gangland-style. An anonymous phone call to the Pueblo police told them where to find the body. His body was not found for three days, by which time it was in a state of advanced decomposition.[26]

Denver continued to be a center of gangland violence throughout 1932. Further violence occurred when Joe Roma, a Denver bootlegger, was cut down at his home in a hail of bullets on February 18, 1933.[27] This type of gang rivalry and violent warfare mostly faded away after the end of Prohibition in 1933.

For years nearly every city in Colorado had passed ordinances against brothels, gambling dens, and saloons, in the hopes of limiting drinking and other vices, but the large amount of money that flowed into city treasuries from licenses, fines, and arrests was difficult to ignore. Caught on the horns of a dilemma, some city fathers decided that it was more effective to isolate this type of business to one part of a town and control it, instead of shutting the saloons down completely. Pueblo, for example, passed a city ordinance in 1895 that created the Pueblo Saloon District, which concentrated and controlled the saloons in one area of town.

Other towns approached the problem differently. Fort Collins, for example, repealed its ordinances against saloons in 1875, which led to a natural increase in those establishments. By 1883 the number of saloons had grown to thirteen. In an effort to try to eliminate some of these dens of iniquity, the city raised the fees for liquor licenses from $300 to $1,000. This was apparently an effective tool as the number of saloons soon dropped to six.

Prostitution often went along with drinking, and vice versa. In 1913 an ordinance passed in the gold-mining town of Victor prohibiting women from entering or working in saloons and other places where intoxicating liquors were sold. Other ordinances adopted Prohibition in the city. In Silverton, in far southwest Colorado, prostitution continued during Prohibition with women offering bootleg liquor as part of their services. In response, city authorities required them to pay a weekly fine, just like the bootleggers.

In 1909 voters in the mining town of Cripple Creek in central Colorado decided that the town should remain wet, voting down an ordinance to close the saloons. City officials accordingly changed their strategy and tacitly licensed women to operate through a series of monthly fines and health exams. In the Cripple Creek area, where moonshining was popular, some of the liquor was traded for food and other supplies during the hard economic times of the Great Depression. Much of this illegal booze went to the saloons of Cripple Creek where it was rebottled and given a fancy label in the basement of a saloon to enhance the profits of some of the saloon-owners.

When Colorado went dry in 1916, sixteen saloons in Cripple Creek, eleven in nearby Victor, and two in the tiny town of Goldfield closed their doors. This put over 150 men out of work in the mining district and cost the city of Cripple Creek $11,700 in annual liquor licenses.

Large quantities of the sugar beets that were grown along the Arkansas and South Platte rivers were shipped to Leadville where distilleries hidden in the nearby hills and mountains transformed the product into illicit "Leadville Moon." The resulting whiskey was distributed in 5-gallon cans that sold for $10, and was available on many street corners. The whiskey was transported to customers all over the state by bootleggers driving Ford and Chevrolet sedans equipped with special springs to handle the heavy liquid loads. Two of the apocryphal ingredients rumored to be in Leadville Moon were black powder and old miners' overalls.

Al Capone appeared briefly in Colorado around Trinidad and Aguilar at the south end of the state. Known for his association with major mafia crime families in New York and Chicago, Capone fit in perfectly with many of the Italians in the area during the 1920s and 1930s. Using tunnels dug under the streets of Trinidad, liquor sales and other illegal operations became a way for these Italian families to gain power in the area.

The town of Cañon City, southwest of Colorado Springs, had no saloons, possibly because the town was the home of the Colorado State Penitentiary. Serious drinkers, however, didn't have to go far to find liquor. For their convenience, a suburb just outside the town to the south called Prospect Heights contained bars that were open day and night. To indicate the leanings of the suburb, the town's only mercantile store included a combination bar, hotel, and brothel.

## Temperance Colorado

Not all towns in Colorado were in favor of liquor at all, and some were founded on definite temperance principles. When the dry town of Greeley was founded as the Union Colony in 1870 by Nathaniel C. Meeker, agricultural editor of Horace Greeley's *New York Tribune*, he intended it to be a farming community like a New England village. Meeker decreed that there would be "no fences and no rum." For two years communal cattle roamed freely until residents complained that the cattle were ruining the fields and their 250,000 strawberry plants. Greeley then relented and allowed fencing. The colony was fenced from the outside and had gates across all the roads leading into the town.

No saloons were allowed within the city limits of Greeley and all alcoholic beverages were banned. Property deeds banned the sales of liquor forever. For the convenience of drinkers, however, an enterprising businessman set up a saloon in a sod hut just outside the town limits. In retaliation, a group of angry temperance residents marched out to the place and "accidentally" set it on fire.

The town of Greeley prospered with sugar beets and potatoes, but stayed a dry town. In fact, the restriction of the consumption, production, and distribution of liquor in the town was in all the property deeds until

**While the police commissioner and several policemen keep watch, Prohibition agents pour a barrel full of bootleg liquor into a sewer following a raid (Library of Congress).**

1969 when the ban was finally lifted. There were no liquor stores in Greeley until that time and residents had to travel to nearby towns or taverns beyond the restricted area.

The nearby town of Longmont, founded as the Chicago-Colorado Colony in 1870, did not initially allow the sale of alcohol on Colony land. In this town, however, attempts at banning liquor were apparently not as successful or popular as in Greeley as the ban on liquor was removed within two years.

Prohibitionists had promised that Prohibition would end drunkenness, but also vice, crime, and other social ills. Instead, they claimed that public libraries with easy chairs, couches, newspapers, reading rooms, games halls, public restrooms, and water fountains would be enough to substitute for the saloon for male drinkers. However, it gradually became apparent that Prohibition in Colorado was not working and, in 1926, a referendum was placed in front of the voters to end Prohibition.

Though the ballot issue failed 154,672 to 107,749 it was obvious to the anti-liquor faction that not everybody was happy with Prohibition. Many people who simply wanted to have a drink or two in the privacy of their own homes without interference from the government felt that Prohibition was an infringement on their personal rights. Many Colorado residents came to believe that Prohibition made criminals of ordinary citizens, along with threatening their health, lowering morality, and endangering young people who should not be drinking. Liquor manufacturers, distributors, and retailers correctly claimed that their businesses had supported the economy, provided thousands of jobs, and financially supported the government through liquor licenses and taxes.

Several groups, including the Colorado Medical Society, petitioned the state for changes in the law. By 1932 support for the repeal of prohibition in Colorado was strong and Colorado voters decided that prohibition should end on the last day of June 1933. In December 1933, National Prohibition was repealed.

## Idaho

As in the rest of the West, saloons sprang up by the hundreds in the mining camps of Idaho. The number of men far outweighed the number of women, making this a man's world, where saloons were a major source of entertainment. The general view of saloons did not change until women began to arrive in the West. Women saw saloons as hotbeds of vice and degradation. Along with the drinking was the related gambling, prostitution, dancing with lewd women, and the use of strong tobacco. In the 1880s, women took up the cause of closing the saloons.

Shepherds in Idaho brewed a home-made liquor called "sheepherder's delight." It consisted of raw alcohol, a plug of tobacco, some prune juice for color and taste, and a dash of strychnine to give it a jolt.

## Montana

Montana's Prohibition law went into effect on January 1, 1919. This legislative effort was somewhat academic, as National Prohibition was ratified only fifteen days later.

Butte's 210 saloons had to close, along with the town's three breweries, the Butte, the Centennial, and the Tivoli. A number of saloons in Butte, however, ignored the law and kept their doors open throughout Prohibition. A network of underground tunnels dug beneath the city was ideal for bootleggers and their product to move around undetected.

By June of 1921 federal officials estimated that Butte led the nation in per capita consumption of illegal alcohol.[28] To try to stop, or at least slow, this flood of liquor and lawlessness, the federal government sent a number of agents to Butte to enforce the Prohibition laws. Some were bribed to leave bootleggers alone. Others mysteriously disappeared and were never seen again.

A large amount of illegal liquor came into Montana across the border from Canada. The road between Coutts on the Canadian border in Canada, and Great Falls, Montana, became known locally as the Bootlegger Trail. Rumrunners sped across the open range in fast touring cars to stay ahead of the police officers' slower Ford Model Ts. A full carload of alcohol of about fourteen barrels of beer and five cases of whiskey was worth about $2,500 in 1928. This was a time when the average family income for a year was about $2,600.

On the other hand, "Red Lodge Moon," which was made in Montana, was a liquor that was so good that companies in Canada were said to bottle it for export to the United States as bonded whiskey.

Though some women had always been drinkers, most very rarely drank in public before Prohibition. The problem was that in small towns there were no places for women to drink without being seen and recognized. Throughout the West, including Butte, saloons were male-only establishments where men led a hard-drinking social life that took place behind closed doors. The only women found in saloons were prostitutes, and to emphasize that, laws were passed to make criminals of women who frequented places where drinking occurred. This was nothing new, however. Legislation was passed in 1887 in Helena, Montana, backed by the WCTU, that prohibited the sale of liquor and the employment of women in variety houses.

Enforcement of Prohibition in Montana was difficult. The state's remoteness and abundant supply of wheat were ideal conditions for bootlegging to thrive. Although the general perception was that bootlegging was a masculine activity dominated by gun-toting gangsters, many Montana women were in fact quick to cash in on the illegal liquor trade. Women around the state manufactured moonshine and operated home speakeasies and roadhouses to supplement their family income. Because making moonshine could be done at home in the kitchen, making illegal alcohol was an attractive business for single or working-class women who needed to add to their family income or for widows who could not easily work outside the home. One Montana resident recalled that her mother was involved in the sales of liquor that accompanied her laundry business of washing clothes for miners who lived in boardinghouses. When the clean clothes were returned, liquor bottles that cost fifty cents a pint or two dollars a gallon were hidden among them.

Two men showing off their small home-made still, one holding a bottle of some liquid that was probably liquor from the still. The piping on the still is galvanized iron and the body of the still also looks like it is galvanized. Galvanized stills, though easy and cheap to make, could leach lead into the alcohol made in it and poison the drinker (Library of Congress).

One of the interesting stories of women bootleggers was that of Josephine Doody, a former dance-hall girl who brewed moonshine at her remote cabin on the southern edge of Glacier National Park. After her husband, Dan, a park ranger, died in 1919, she remained at their homestead and became famous for her moonshine. She was known as "The Bootleg Lady of Glacier Park." Some of her best patrons were men working on the Great Northern Railway. The train would stop at Doody Siding, and each toot of the whistle would mean an order for one gallon of moonshine that Josephine delivered across the Flathead River in a small boat. She died of pneumonia in 1936.

Montana did not repeal some of the liquor laws enacted for Prohibition until 2005. This step allowed distilleries to begin producing small batches of alcohol for limited distribution. The first legal distillery in Montana was RoughStock Distillery near Bozeman, which opened in 2009. As a point of interest, the Montana Department of Commerce reported that approximately 20 percent of the barley grown in Montana in 2014 was used for alcohol production.

# The Southwest

## (Arizona, New Mexico, Utah, Nevada)

A POPULAR DRINK IN THE Southwest, particularly in Texas and in Oklahoma, was chock (or choc) beer, also known as Old Hen. This peculiar name was derived from the Choctaw Indians who brewed the stuff. It was made from molasses mixed with water, yeast, and hops, then spiced up with shelled corn and raisins. The mixture sat and fermented for three weeks, then was strained, bottled, and corked. It reportedly tasted terrible, but was very powerful and drinking only a couple of bottles was reputed to be enough to make inexperienced drinkers pass out. But, if this was not strong enough for confirmed Southwestern lushes, drinkers were known to add snuff to the bottles and bury them in hot sand in order to produce further fermentation.[1]

## *Arizona*

Arizona had definite wet tendencies for a dry state. The first commercial building in a new town was usually a brewery, more typically built in the form of a combination of brewery and saloon. The saloon was in the front of the building and the brewery was located in the back. Having a brewery in town solved the problem of transportation, because beer did not travel well over long distances.

Prior to the start of Prohibition, Arizona first regulated liquor in 1864 with the Howell Code, which assessed a tax on vendors of wines and distilled spirits. At the time Arizona gained statehood on February 14, 1912, states, counties, and cities in the United States had the option to vote themselves dry if they wished. In 1914 Arizona was the thirteenth state to do this, with statewide prohibition starting on January 1, 1915. Unfortunately the amendment to the Arizona constitution that achieved this was not well thought through and did not address issues such as wine used for religious purposes or alcohol used for scientific purposes, such as to preserve biological specimens.

Other issues in the amendment were also not covered adequately. For example, under the law, alcohol could not be imported into Arizona. One example of the problems created by this was the question of what would happen if a friend who came to visit from New Mexico brought a bottle of wine across the border for dinner with his host. Would the New Mexican be criminally liable for bringing in the liquor, or the Arizonan for accepting it? Or both of them?

A more serious issue was that the new law had an immediate impact on the brewing industry, which was currently very successful, by throwing all the employees out of work. Another ballot initiative appeared in 1916 to try to correct these issues. This amendment was written better and gained substantial support.

Many Arizonans, however, refused to give up their enjoyment of drinking, and the prohibition law was widely violated. The enthusiastic sheriff of one Arizona county reportedly seized 152 stills within one three-month period in 1925. He also arrested 183 people for federal alcohol violations and 80 for state violations.

As in other states, serious problems were caused by moonshine that was not properly prepared or distilled. Some moonshine contained toxic lead compounds from poorly built stills or from careless distillation. People who drank it suffered from paralysis, blindness, and death from these undesired toxic additives.

One type of liquor specific to the Southwest was tequila, though this tended to be a local beverage because drinking it was an acquired taste. Tequila was reputed to have originated in Tequila, Mexico, and was distilled from the blue agave cactus plant (*Agave tequilana*). The first mescal distillery was licensed to José Antonio Cuervo in Jalisco, Mexico, in 1821.[2]

Some saloons offered a powerful drink called "cactus wine," which was made from tequila and peyote tea. The combination must have been literally mind-blowing as peyote was a drug used by American Indians to produce hallucinogenic effects. Peyote was collected from a small, spineless pincushion cactus named *Lophophora williamsii*, that looked somewhat like a small gray-green carrot top sticking out of the ground. When the peyote button was peeled, dried, and chewed it caused brilliantly-colored hallucinations that were interpreted in some native cultures to be spiritual and religious visions. The plant grew freely in the Chihuahuan Desert of Mexico and was commonly found in a wild state in the desert country of the lower Rio Grande valley.

The other fiery Mexican alcohol that crossed the southern border of Arizona was mescal, which was distilled from the fermented juice of several different species of agave cactus, the final product depending on the particular species of agave used. Mescal was usually run through the still only once, which left it in the form of a rather rough fiery drink. Tequila was distilled twice, which gave it a much smoother taste. Both types of liquor were humorously nicknamed "cactus juice" by Arizona oldtimers.

Another version of liquor drunk in the Southwest was *mula*, a strong, clear, distilled alcohol that was made in New Mexico, Arizona, and the southern California desert country. Raisins, prunes, potatoes, and sugar were boiled in a large vat, then yeast was added and the mixture allowed to ferment. The distilled product received its name because it supposedly had a kick like a mule.

Because Arizona shared a direct border with Mexico, individuals wanting to find a drink easily slipped across the border to the state of Sonora, Mexico, directly to the south. The ability to find a drink there, however, varied with the particular governor that was in office at the time. One governor might be in favor of open drinking, but the next governor to be elected might be in favor of prohibition and would not allow drinking.

One of the gateway border towns was Nogales, which actually straddled the international border. The section of border between the part of the town of Nogales in Sonora and the part of Nogales in Arizona was a geographic curiosity; there were thus two towns of Nogales (Ambos Nogales) which existed as twin cities on either side of the border. International Avenue ran east-west on the border, with one half of the street in Mexico and the other half in the United States. After Arizona introduced prohibition, which outlawed the production and sale of alcohol, some saloon owners took advantage of the unusual geography of Nogales and built their saloon buildings such that they also straddled the border. Patrons who were tired of sipping a soft drink in the north part of the saloon and wanted to enjoy a real drink of mescal simply moved to the south end of the bar where the drink was legal.

On August 27, 1918, International Avenue was the setting for the Battle of Ambos Nogales, which led to a permanent fence being built down the middle of the street, thus separating Ambos Nogales into two distinct cities, one on either side of the border.

As well as traveling to Mexico to find a drink, there were ingenious ways to transport liquor across the border. One bootlegger and his partner near Yuma took a mule across the border to Mexico, loaded it up with bottles of liquor, and encouraged it to wander back over to the California side of the border where they captured it again. The smugglers figured that if the Customs men caught the mule, they would lose only the liquor. And the unfortunate mule.

Like some of the other Western states, Arizona was in favor of National Prohibition and was among the earlier states to ratify the

This postcard from 1899 shows Nogales divided into two towns. The international border runs through the middle of the photograph, with the dry United States side in Arizona on the right and the wet side in Mexico on the left. Some saloons were built straddling the border and patrons could enjoy either soft drinks or hard liquor, depending on which end of the building they were in (author's collection).

Eighteenth Amendment, which it did on May 24, 1918. Like the residents of other states, Arizonans expected that the banning of alcohol would promote morality and reduce crime, along with improving health, protecting young people, and reducing domestic violence. What happened, of course, was quite the opposite. Health was threatened by drinking questionable rotgut liquor, ethics and morals underwent a radical new shift in perspective, crime rose with the wars among bootleggers, and violence increased. Young people were actually endangered by drink and the new direction in loosened morals. Like many other states, Arizona finally realized that Prohibition was not working for them and over three-quarters of the voters agreed to repeal Prohibition.

## New Mexico

In the November election of 1917, the citizens of New Mexico voted themselves dry by a wide margin. When the law went into effect on October 1 of the following year, most of the saloons closed. Some became soft drink parlors or other similar businesses, some became other businesses completely, and some continued operating as speakeasies. Local breweries often became soft drink manufacturers.

One speakeasy in Santa Fe that was housed in a building that had three levels used a rather unusual approach to its clientele. The first floor was for low-class drinkers who were looking for cheap rot-gut booze at the lowest price. The second floor was higher class and appealed to those who desired a little more decorum and wanted something that at least resembled halfway decent liquor. The third and top floor, on the other hand, appealed to those who wanted the best in their liquor and who had plenty of money to pay for it.[3]

The illegal distilling of whiskey in New Mexico started on a small scale. The limited size of these operations can be judged by the fact that one of the first liquor cases that was prosecuted involved only two quarts of homemade whiskey that was sold by a clerk in a grocery store in Albuquerque.

Some of the first bootleg alcohol in New Mexico was produced in small stills using raisins as a base. This resulted in a subsequent rapid increase in the price of raisins that was blamed on bootleggers buying up all the available supply. The larger stills that followed that had eighty to a hundred gallon capacities tended to use the more traditional grains to make the mash. One of the largest stills in New Mexico had a capacity of 310 gallons, but stills with a capacity of a hundred gallons or less were preferred by bootleggers because this smaller equipment could be fairly easily dismantled, moved, and re-assembled in a new location in case of an impending raid by Prohibition agents.

Though some speakeasies manufactured their own liquor, most had arrangements with local bootleggers to supply them with product. Bootlegging started in New Mexico on a small scale with the sale of stocks of liquor that had been purchased and stored away before Prohibition. When these stocks ran out, liquor was either manufactured in a local still or was imported from across the border from Mexico. Some of the alcohol came from Agua Prieta on the Mexico-Arizona border via Douglas, Arizona. Depending on the current inclinations of the governor of the state of Sonora, if liquor was not freely available there for export, illegal liquor flowed instead across the border from Juarez in Chihuahua, Mexico, to El Paso, Texas.

Efforts to suppress the liquor traffic resulted in gun fights and shootouts on the streets of El Paso, but they mostly had no other effect. In one incident along the Rio Grande, when smugglers surrounded by an early morning fog were surprised by troops from the Border Patrol, they became so confused that they started shooting at each other. The result was that the troops simply waited and watched while the smugglers shot each other down.[4]

In a goodwill effort to help the United States cope with the flow of illegal alcohol during Prohibition, the Mexican government formed a ten-mile zone along the border in which Americans were not allowed to purchase liquor. This ban, however, was mostly ignored and was not particularly effective. At the same time, liquor prohibitions were suspended again in Sonora, so in effect more Mexican liquor in the form of tequila and mescal was able to flow freely across the border.

Another method for bootleggers to obtain alcohol was for them to simply steal it. Before Prohibition started, some wealthy individuals had laid in stocks of liquor while it was still legal. These people became easy targets for theft. As early as March 1919 thieves broke into the house of Frank Jordan in Grant County and made off with thirty-one cases of whiskey. One of the largest thefts occurred in 1921 at a ranch owned by Henry Garzina near Roy, where thieves stole liquor valued at ten thousand dollars.[5]

The wine industry entered an economic crisis when Prohibition was first enacted, but quickly bounced back. Wineries were still allowed to make wine vinegar or wine for religious purposes. Though most of the wine in the United States was produced in California, wine-making could be carried out wherever the climate was suitable for grapes. This small vineyard and tiny adobe winery were in an arid portion of central New Mexico (author's collection).

Another ploy was to steal from other bootleggers. Thieves figured out where a moonshiner had located his still and then stole from it when they could. Thieves also figured out where bootleggers kept their stocks of finished liquor that was ready for sale and stole it. Sometimes a buyer of illegal alcohol and the seller did not meet, but the seller stashed a few bottles or kegs of whiskey in a secret agreed-on place. The buyer would then pick the liquor up at another time. Rival bootleggers could simply trail the shipment and steal it when it was left in place.

Though Prohibition violations were intended by law to be a cooperative effort between federal, state, and local law enforcement, in practice most of the enforcement efforts in the West were left to federal Prohibition agents. One reason was that local law enforcement officers often did not wish to investigate and arrest people that they knew and considered to be neighbors and friends. The second reason was purely economic. The enforcement program was vastly under-funded from the beginning and local officials figured that the fines that came in from arresting bootleggers would hardly pay for the efforts of enforcing Prohibition laws.

## Utah

The Latter-Day Saints entered the Salt Lake Valley on July 24, 1847, following their leader Brigham Young. Utah was unusual among the states as the Mormons did not drink alcohol. However, Young declared that drinking beer was acceptable when water that was heavily polluted was the only available drinking supply. Partly because of this, Mormon settlers started brewing beer almost as soon as they arrived in the Salt Lake Valley. The first documented brewery in Utah was at the Hot Springs Hotel and Brewery, built on land that was later taken over by the Utah State Prison. The Mormons also distilled alcohol for medicinal use.

Brigham Young never drank whiskey and totally despised those who made it. Though Mormons were not allowed to partake of alcohol, Brigham Young was also pragmatic enough that he thought that "fleecing the gentiles" traveling through the state by selling them whiskey was just good business.

Extensive drinking started in Mormon towns following the California gold rush of 1849 and the transcontinental railroad started bringing would-be prospectors from the East to the desert state. After United States troops arrived in Salt Lake City in 1857 during what was called the Utah Expedition or the Utah War, outside pressures on the state increased and drinking became more prevalent. Main Street in Salt Lake between the 200 and 400 blocks south was called Whiskey Street by Brigham Young himself.

In 1861 when Mark Twain visited Utah, which was then still part of the Nevada Territory, he mentioned a type of powerful pioneer whiskey named "Valley Tan" or "Mormon Whiskey," which was made only in Utah by Mormons. The drink was said to be so raw that it was also appropriately nicknamed "leopard sweat." This powerful brew was the basis for a popular rhyme of the time: *"Valley Tan, Valley Tan, Maketh glad the heart of man."*[6]

When the Anti-Saloon League started preaching to church leaders about the evils of alcohol and saloons, 600 saloons were operating in Utah. The Hotel Utah, one of the best hotels between Denver and San Francisco, opened in 1908. It was mostly owned and built by the Mormon Church, with a lavish bar that was one of the best in the West. Profits from the bar were used to pay off the costs of construction of the building.

On February 8, 1917, Governor Simon Bamberger signed a law-making Utah the twenty-third state to adopt statewide Prohibition. As the deadline date of August 1 for the law to take effect drew near, liquor was sold at bargain prices and finally almost given away at any price. The *Salt Lake Tribune* estimated that hundreds of thousands of dollars worth of liquor were acquired and stored in the cellars of Salt Lake residents. The new law, however, recognized that there was a legitimate need for some products that contained alcohol, such as patent medicines, flavoring extracts, pure grain alcohol for scientific and industrial purposes, and wine for sacramental purposes.

In 1921 church president Heber J. Grant specified church policy to include absolute abstinence, a policy that was in line with the national temperance movement. In spite of this, during the latter years of Prohibition bootleggers and moonshiners were active in Utah. Between 1923 and 1932, Prohibition agents seized over 448 distilleries, 702 stills, 332,000 gallons of mash, 25,000 gallons of spirits, 8,000 gallons of malt liquors, and 13,000 gallons of wine. As in other communities and states this was probably only a small percentage of what was actually being produced, because almost every community and every neighborhood in the larger cities housed an illegal still.

One of the easiest types of bootleg alcohol to produce was known as sugar whiskey. It required only a 100-pound bag of sugar, a sack of cornmeal, and a sack of yeast, which were mixed together and boiled in fifty-gallon drums.

Though Utah did not have the gang warfare and mayhem that plagued the Eastern cities, occasional incidences of violence occurred during shootouts in which undercover agents were attacked and bootleggers were shot.

## Nevada

Most of the liquor drunk in Nevada during Prohibition reached the state by way of San Francisco, either arriving by ship over the Pacific or made in the state.

Las Vegas was established in 1905 as a station, repair yard, and housing facility for employees of the Union Pacific Railroad. To discourage the use and spread of liquor, the railroad confined the sales of alcohol to one square block, "Block 16," that was located a few blocks northeast of the railroad depot. Though the railroad management was opposed to alcohol for its employees, it was practical enough to realize that selling alcohol generated some profitable business among the passengers of their trains.

As Las Vegas was still developing as a city, many of Block 16's saloons rented out their back rooms to prostitutes. Popular saloons included the Gem, the Red Onion, the Star, the Arcade, and the Red Front. These dens of iniquity were humorously called "resorts," after the brothels that most of them contained. Block 16 became the center of the town's gambling, drinking, and prostitution, and it was not unusual to see highly intoxicated men stumbling about in the saloon district.

The question of statewide prohibition appeared on the Nevada ballot in November 1918. The issue passed with nearly 60 percent of the people voting for it. Thus prohibition in Nevada started on December 17, 1918, a little over a year before National Prohibition went into effect.

Even though prohibition became law under the statewide referendum of 1918, almost all disregarded it in Las Vegas, and most of the saloons, including the "Queen of Block 16," the Arizona Club, defied the ban.

Violations of the prohibition law started in Las Vegas in early 1919, only several weeks after Nevada's state law went onto the books. In February, A.P. Chamberlain was the first person convicted for having several bottles of liquor in his downtown hotel room. A local judge fined him $125, gave him a suspended sentence and, in the best tradition of the Old West, ordered him to leave town and not return.

Las Vegas in 1920 was an isolated desert town of only 2,300 residents, which helped the town to avoid strong enforcement of Prohibition laws. Due to the small size and its remote location, the town had no federal building, federal court, or office space for Prohibition agents. The closest federal agents were based in Los Angeles. Though Las Vegas had a city ordinance that banned alcohol, saloons operated openly. Fines for violating the city law were considered to be part of the cost of doing business.

The problems of enforcing Prohibition in Nevada became even murkier when in 1923 the Nevada legislature decided to repeal the state prohibition law. As a result, police officers in Nevada did not enforce the state

**Ingenious drinkers came up with many innovative ways of carrying enough liquor to have a drink or two when visiting a speakeasy or an ice cream parlor. A woman seated at a table in a soda shop in 1922 is pouring alcohol into a cup from a hollow cane (Library of Congress).**

law any longer, but in addition they were not technically bound to enforce the National Prohibition law. After 1923 local police essentially left Prohibition enforcement to federal agents. Federal agents did conduct raids and investigated illegal bootlegging, but they had to do so with their own resources. For example, on February 6, 1928, federal Prohibition agents raided a group of saloons in Block 16 and arrested twelve men and women. Among them were Mayor Fred Hesse, who was arrested for operating a still to supply local bootlegger James Ferguson, who was also arrested.

Many of the liquor violators did not carry out large-scale operations and many of the small bootleggers in Nevada made only a couple of gallons of booze at a time. But, in spite of the small size of Las Vegas, bootlegger R.C. McKay had a 100-gallon and a 350-gallon still operating on his ranch outside of town and 500 gallons of alcohol stored in his home.

Another prominent bootlegger was Lon Groesbeck, who smuggled liquor into town in the false bottom of his car. His place of business was the Northern Hotel in downtown where he sold bottles of liquor from his room. He was arrested in January 1920, for having transported twenty-three pints of illegal whiskey into the state. On January 7, Groesbeck pled guilty and a justice of the peace fined him. The judge also gave him ninety days in the county jail, but suspended the sentence on the condition that he leave town. The district attorney refused to accept the sentence and took the case to the District Court, where a judge reinstated the jail sentence. The judge's order was handed to the original judge, then to a sheriff's deputy about an hour later. However, when the deputy arrived to pick up Groesbeck, the defendant and his car were long gone.

Though Las Vegas did not have the level of mayhem that plagued Chicago, violence did occur from time to time. Two examples will serve to illustrate the type of violence that took place in Las Vegas over illegal whiskey. The first was when Joe Santini was ambushed as a result of a dispute over the local liquor trade. On the night of April 22, 1932, Santini left the pool hall he owned and walked back to his house. Just as he finished closing the gate behind him, a flashlight shone in his face and someone asked if he was the proprietor of the place. When Santini replied in the affirmative, a gunman fired a single shot that struck the pool hall owner in the abdomen. Santini stumbled back to his business and collapsed soon after re-entering the building. He was rushed to a hospital, but died from his wound within a few days.

As a result of the shooting, one of Santini's close friends, Vittorio Decimo, traveled to town in order to investigate his friend's killing. He made the mistake of staying at the same small house where his friend had been gunned down. On the night of May 29, 1932, Decimo was killed by a single shot to his head while lying in bed inside the Santini home. Despite a vigorous search for suspects, both killings remained unsolved.

The second act of violence involved a falling out between two partners who were in the business of illegal liquor. John Hall from North Carolina and John O'Brien were both new arrivals in Las Vegas. Hall wanted to become a bootlegger and O'Brien approached him with a business proposal. If Hall would put up the money for the wholesale purchase of moonshine for $2 per gallon, O'Brien would repay Hall with fifty cents on the dollar. Hall was interested and the two men agreed to the deal.

One night in early June 1931, Hall and O'Brien drove to meet O'Brien's moonshine contact, taking with them $680 (equivalent to about $13,000 in 2021) in a coffee can. The meeting with O'Brien's contact did not work out and when Hall awoke the next morning, he was missing the $680. O'Brien swore that he had not taken the money. Hall did not believe him, but remained silent at the time.

After visiting a place where O'Brien sold bootleg liquor, O'Brien started to leave in his car. Hall, who had been drinking heavily, pulled out a revolver and emptied it into the driver's side of the vehicle. O'Brien was hit in the back by three .38 slugs. He was taken to a local hospital where he died of his wounds. Hall escaped, but was caught, went to trial, and was eventually executed in the gas chamber.

Violence often occurred as a result of drunkenness. On the afternoon of November 22, 1921, a young man by the name of Nick Dugan had fourteen drinks of moonshine over a period of several hours. Around five or six in the afternoon, he stumbled over to Fremont Street in downtown Las Vegas and burst through the door of Lambert's Cafe, where he started yelling obscenities at a waitress. Another customer, Marcus Wherle of Las Vegas, rose from his table and told Dugan to shut up and get out. Dugan pulled a revolver and turned on Wherle. "You going to make me?" Wherle hesitated then grabbed Dugan's wrist to wrestle the gun from his hand, but not before Dugan pushed the barrel of the gun against Wherle's side and pulled the trigger.

Dugan testified at his own trial, saying that he did not remember anything after about five o'clock on November 22. After five hours of deliberation, the men of the jury returned a verdict of voluntary manslaughter due to Dugan's state of extreme intoxication and his lack of memory of the homicide.

Las Vegas was not the only town in the state with Prohibition problems. A little further to the south of Las Vegas in Boulder City, where workers for Hoover Dam lived, bars, liquor stores, and gambling were prohibited in order to prevent workers at the dam from drinking and gambling.

By the early 1930s federal agents had increased their attention to enforcement of Prohibition, even though Prohibition was not popular in Nevada and had little support. One poll of residents showed one of the highest rates of opposition to the law in the country.

# 10

# Unintended Consequences

In the early 1900s Mayor Martin Behrman of New Orleans said, "You can make it illegal, but you can't make it unpopular."[1] He was speaking about prostitution rather than the banning of alcohol, but the same was true of drinking during Prohibition.

In the final analysis, Prohibition was a failure. Prohibition was forced upon the country by well-meaning but misguided zealots in an effort to try to maintain what they saw as traditional family values against the forces of increasing urbanization and industrialization, and the onset of modern changes in contemporary society. As a result, temperance reform was generally more popular in rural areas than in the urban environment. It was also partly a Victorian backlash against the immigration of non–Protestants from Europe who brought with them customs and values that were not welcomed by most evangelical Protestant churchgoers.[2]

Promoters from the dry faction, including members of the WCTU and ASL, were surprised that their efforts were not enthusiastically supported by the entire population. Consumption of alcohol did indeed rapidly drop to an estimated two-thirds of the level before Prohibition; however, this figure soon reversed and started back upwards again. Prohibition led to a pattern of less frequent, but much heavier, drinking. Instead of having a quiet drink of wine with dinner, consumers became binge drinkers, swigging what they could when they could, and the consumption of home-made wine soared. The demand for alcoholic beverages in general became so great that the supply never surpassed the demand.

Prohibition turned many previously law-abiding citizens into law-breakers. Thousands of Americans rebelled against Prohibition, not only breaking the law, but having fun while they were doing it. Drinking alcohol became a new fad that was considered wild, crazy, and daring.

Part of the attraction was that when drink became forbidden, it suddenly became desirable. The Eighteenth Amendment created a nation of lawbreakers as previously law-abiding citizens flouted Prohibition and continued to drink. Carrying a concealed flask of spirits, knocking at the door of a speakeasy and whispering a password, and drinking in the back seat of a car became the symbols of a changing society.

The supporters of Prohibition also did not anticipate the high financial costs to society that was the direct result of their efforts. When the Eighteenth Amendment went into effect, local saloons, along with the breweries and distilleries that supported them, were forced to close, thus throwing all their employees out of work. When the amendment was ratified, the United States had almost 180,000 licensed saloons, 1,217 breweries, and 507 distilleries.[3] The new law essentially wiped out an industry that employed hundreds of thousands of individuals. The result was that unemployment skyrocketed. The associated loss caused government tax revenues to plummet, while the farm industry was crippled by the loss of their huge market for corn and grain.

Breweries had to turn to manufacturing alternative products if they wished to survive. Anheuser Bush in St. Louis, the makers of Budweiser beer, survived by making a variety of different products, including soft drinks, corn syrup, and egg products. One of their new product lines was making truck bodies.

One example of a relatively minor, but unexpected, outcome of Prohibition, was that farmers who relied on bees to pollinate their crops suffered because of the illegal activities of moonshiners. Beehives were lost when moonshiners stole or destroyed them to gain access to the honey for producing illegal alcohol. Interestingly, the sugar in pure honey was so concentrated that fungi and bacteria could not live in it, hence producing a long storage life without any degradation. However, if the honey was diluted with water, it provided an excellent medium for yeast and fermentation, because it consisted of simple sugars.

## Clogging the Courts

Unforeseen and unintended consequences of Prohibition quickly became apparent. The dry faction and members of Congress who voted for the amendment believed that everybody would be so happy to have Prohibition that there would only be a few prosecutions for violations of the law. As a result, no new jails or additional courts were planned, and no additional government prosecutors were appointed to deal with any potential Prohibition violation cases.

The result turned out to be quite the opposite of what was expected. During Prohibition, cases involving liquor violations made up 40 percent of all the cases before American courts.[4] The federal courts were rapidly overwhelmed by the number of liquor violations awaiting trial. The

Volstead Act made every violation a jury trial so the court system was inundated with a flood of petty cases over inconsequential violations. And federal penitentiaries quickly ran out of space to house those who were convicted. By 1924 the population of federal prisons was almost double what it was at the start of Prohibition.

During the first six months of 1920, prosecutors were faced with dealing with 7,291 federal cases of violations of the Volstead Act. By June of 1920, the district attorney of Chicago reported a backlog of 568 cases. By 1921, the number of federal cases had ballooned to 29,114.[5] In 1925, the number of people arrested for violating the Volstead Act was estimated to be more than 76,000.[6] During the first six years of Prohibition, federal agents arrested 313,940 alleged violators. In 1928 alone federal agents arrested 37,181 suspected violators.[7] Probably an equal number of people were arrested and tried at the local level.

In 1925, during the height of Prohibition, federal agents seized 29,087 illegal stills.[8] Between 1921 and 1925 the Prohibition Bureau seized almost 697,000 stills nationwide.

As one example of what happened in a big city in the West, Appendix 4 shows specific details of the annual frequency of alcohol violations from Denver, Colorado, from 1920 to 1929. Arrests for the violation of Prohibition understandably dropped substantially in 1921 immediately after Prohibition took effect, but soon rose back up again. Arrests for violation of the Volstead Act were up to around 5 percent when bootlegging started in earnest, and continued to rise as the 1920s progressed. The number of arrests for drunkenness rose from 1921 to 1922, and then remained fairly constant at around 16 percent of the total arrests.

By 1923 United States attorneys were spending about half of their time on cases that involved liquor violations. Depending on the particular region of the country, the amount of time might be much higher. In the Southern District of Alabama, for example, prosecutors devoted as much as 90 percent of their time to liquor-law violators. Luckily for prosecutors about two-thirds of the cases were settled quickly by pleas of guilty, because there were far too many violators to be able to take them all to trial by jury.[9]

As associated problems, there weren't enough qualified jurors for all the cases waiting to be tried, and government chemists were so overwhelmed that they were unable to analyze all the liquor that the police had seized as evidence for court cases.

Another problem for the Prohibition Bureau was that the law was often enforced haphazardly or not at all, and liquor crimes were difficult to prosecute successfully. Guilty individuals who did make it to trial were often not convicted because of technicalities and loopholes in the law, evidence that disappeared, claims of improper search and seizure, witnesses who disappeared or refused to testify, bribery, plea-bargains, or law officials who looked the other way.

A jury trial required at least a day to be heard, but cities such as Denver might be filing five to ten new cases every day. Because state and federal courts were overcrowded, dismissing cases and accepting plea bargains for guilty cases were essential to keeping the system moving.

Juries tended to be lenient towards liquor violation cases, making enforcement and punishment of obviously guilty offenders very difficult. Often men on a jury were reluctant to indict others for breaking the same law that they themselves were breaking at home. Some police officers also tended to be lenient. If someone was making liquor for their own use at home, or was making wine for religious purposes, the police often tended to look the other way.

So many cases clogged the federal courts in the Southern District of California that 800 to 1,000 minor cases a year had to be transferred to the state courts. This strategy helped to relieve the congestion in the federal courts, but all the local courts were still overloaded with too many cases. It was ironic that attempts to prevent crime caused by alcohol created more crimes than were originally caused by the liquor violations. By 1928 approximately half of the cases that went to the courts in Denver were for prohibition violations.

## The Rise of Organized Crime

Along with the rise in the number of individuals who flaunted the law by manufacturing, purchasing, and consuming illegal alcohol, another of the changes in American society was the mass takeover of bootleg liquor production and distribution by organized crime. Prior to Prohibition, criminal organizations and gangs primarily concentrated their activities on prostitution, gambling, and theft. After 1920 they added bootlegging as a result of Prohibition and the desire to cater to a profitable, though often violent, black market for alcohol.

As law enforcement capabilities broke down under a wave of crime, the underworld took over the importation, manufacture, distribution, and sales of illegal liquor. Criminal gangs were already well-organized in areas such as gambling and prostitution, and were able to easily add dealing in bootleg liquor to their inventory of skills.

Prohibition was the start of widespread organized crime in America. Hoodlums who had been involved in small-time prostitution, extortion, and gambling became big-time mobsters, and smuggling illegal booze moved from a cottage industry to a large one that was bold and well-organized. Criminal organizations dealt in huge shipments of illegal alcohol that were worth thousands of dollars. The larger syndicates operated their own distilleries and cutting plants.

Professionals criminals, drawn by the huge profits to be made, quickly worked their way into the business side of supplying alcohol. Before Prohibition, alcohol had been cheap. In 1914 the price of a cocktail at a first-class bar might cost 15 cents. By 1920, after Prohibition was in force, the price had risen to 40 cents to 60 cents in cheap saloons that served dubious rotgut, and to $1 to $2 for better liquor in a fine restaurant. A fancy speakeasy might charge as much as $3 for a glass of quality whiskey. As a result, it was very profitable to violate the liquor laws and large fortunes were made by moonshiners and bootleggers. One Chicago gangster who went into business with a legitimate brewer made $50 million within the first four years of Prohibition.

After only the first year-and-a-half of Prohibition, bootlegging was a $1 billion-a-year industry. By the middle of the 1920s bootlegging had grown to be a $2 billion-a-year industry.[10] By 1926 the sales of bootleg liquor had reached $3.6 billion annually, which was approximately the same as the federal budget for that year.[11]

Organized crime in the Roaring Twenties was structured as any other business, with centralization and commercialization of the product. Bootlegging empires created their own sales organizations, along with importation and distribution systems, backed by their own purchasing, security, and transportation departments. The organizational structure of crime included "bosses," "enforcers," and "soldiers," who corresponded in more conventional business organizations to executives, mid-level managers, and production workers.[12]

The vast business machinery of the underworld mostly ran smoothly. Gang leaders held formal business conferences, usually attended by representatives of the police, and agreed among themselves on the division of territories, with each gang having its own protected sphere of activity. The fierce competition for maximum profits naturally led to violence and rival gangs came head-to-head in competition for business and exclusive distribution territories. Violence usually started only when one gang encroached upon another's territory or tried to take it over. Some criminal elements hijacked booze shipments or waylaid buyers who often carried thousands of dollars on them, as this was a cash business. Hijackers even hijacked other hijackers.

The newspapers idealized many criminals into cult heroes and made gangsters out to be heroic figures, just as dime novelists had done earlier with notable Western criminals such as Jesse James and Butch Cassidy.

With the backing of the media, many criminal leaders developed gallant public personas, somewhat like had been done with Robin Hood and Billy the Kid.

Probably the most well-known crime boss was Alphonse "Al" Capone. Capone arrived in Chicago from Brooklyn in 1921, at the age of 22, and went to work for Johnny Torrio, one of the leading figures in the city's underworld.[13]

Chicago was already the center of flourishing criminal activity long before Al Capone and Prohibition arrived, and was considered by some to be the crime capital of the world. Racketeering, gambling, and political corruption were common, along with other forms of vice, including brothels and prostitution. From 1900 to 1911, for example, the luxurious Everleigh Club, run by sisters Ada and Minna Everleigh, was the fanciest and most expensive bordello in the country. The Club boasted an orchestra with a gold piano, a wine cellar, an art gallery, and brass beds with inlaid marble. Chicago in the 1920s was also the center of a vast railroad network that was ideal for the distribution of illegal liquor.

Capone rose quickly in the underworld. By 1924 he controlled the flow of illegal alcohol in an estimated 10,000 speakeasies in Chicago and nearby Cicero, and made an annual profit estimated at $3 million.[14] Capone said he was trying to provide people with what they wanted. He once said, "Public service is my motto. I've tried to serve them decent liquor and square games.... I'm sick of the job. It's a thankless one and full of grief."[15]

In early 1925, Torrio was shot and wounded by a rival gang, and moved to New York, leaving Al Capone to take over the crime organization in Chicago. Competition among various criminal organizations led to open threats, killings, and gang warfare. Capone lived in a heavily-fortified home and traveled in a custom-built armor-plated Cadillac that had bullet-proof windows and weighed seven tons. He was surrounded by bodyguards carrying machine guns.

A major change in fighting liquor crime came in May of 1927 when the U.S. Supreme Court ruled that Manly Sullivan, a bootlegger, could not claim that his income from illegal activity was not taxable, nor that filing a federal tax return on income earned from criminal acts would violate his Fifth Amendment rights against self-incrimination. Using this ruling as a basis, Capone was tried, convicted, and sentenced in October of 1931 to a year for carrying a gun, followed by ten years in federal prison for not paying taxes on the profits of his illegal enterprises. In 1930 the Internal Revenue Service estimated that he made $10 million from prostitution, $10 million from narcotics, $25 million from gambling, and $50 million from bootlegging.[16]

Capone spent the next eleven years in prison, first in Atlanta and then in 1934 at the maximum security prison on Alcatraz Island in San Francisco Bay, at the time the most secure prison for dangerous criminals in the country. Capone was eventually released in 1940 and died at his home in Florida in 1947 after suffering a stroke.

Another of the leading bootleggers was George Remus. Remus was a pharmacist and lawyer who had come to America from Germany as a child. He worked for a while as a criminal lawyer defending bootleggers before he decided that it would be more profitable to be one. As one of the leading bootleggers who operated the largest illegal alcohol operations in America, Remus became rich, famous, and powerful.

Remus owned several of Kentucky's best distilleries, along with operations in other states. He was known to own at least eight distilleries, and may have owned others that were kept secret. He also owned a bonded warehouse and a drug company. Through this network he was able to distill, store, and dispense any amount of alcohol for medical use, provided he had the correct government permits. Alcohol routinely went missing between the warehouse and the drug company, and was diverted to a network of retail bootleggers.

Remus specialized in medicinal whiskey and made millions of dollars by selling medicinal alcohol illegally to liquor dealers and speakeasies. Eventually his scheme was exposed by an undercover agent and he went to prison for three years. Remus was also notorious for the fact that after he got out of prison in 1927, he shot his second wife after she embezzled part of his fortune and took up with the agent who had exposed him. He was acquitted at his trial on the grounds of temporary insanity.[17]

## Graft and Corruption

The United States Government had created the Prohibition Bureau to enforce the Volstead Act. Prohibition agents and cooperating local law enforcement throughout the country were charged with seizing warehouses full of whiskey, busting up stills, smashing countless bottles of liquor, and taking axes to beer barrels while dumping the contents into gutters, sewers, and storm drains. In practice, however, agents found it difficult to enforce a law that thousands of Americans did not believe in or take seriously, and that they did not obey.

For some obscure reason, lawmakers made the Prohibition Bureau an agency of the Department of the Treasury instead of the Department of Justice. Due to intense lobbying by the Anti-Saloon League to try and fill the positions for agents with men with strong anti-liquor sentiments,

After a successful raid by Prohibition agents, the problem was often what to do with the large quantities of confiscated liquor. Much of the time it was impounded in a government warehouse, but it often disappeared from custody and vanished into the black market. Here, however, Prohibition agents are immediately pouring bottles of illegal alcohol down a storm drain to dispose of it (Library of Congress).

Prohibition agents were political appointees and were exempted from the normal Civil Service requirements of government employees. Thus, depending on the administration in power, agents might be Republican or Democrat. During the first year of the Bureau's operation, most of the agents were Democrats, as Woodrow Wilson was president. They were then replaced by Republicans when the Harding administration took over in 1921.

The initial budget was set at $2 million to hire 1,520 agents. From its formation, however, the Prohibition Bureau was underfunded and understaffed. In 1921 the bureau's budget was only $7.1 million, which turned out to be woefully inadequate. For most of 1920s, the budget was between $9 million and $13 million. By 1930 there were 3,000 Prohibition agents to cover the entire country.

Potential prohibition agents were not required to possess any special education or other qualifications and many prohibition agents were hired who never should have been appointed to the position. They were not properly trained and most had no prior police experience. And in 1927 they only earned $1,860 a year for a Junior Prohibition Agent, $2,400 for a Prohibition Agent, and $3,000 for an Investigator.[18] Such a situation was ripe for graft and corruption.

To make the situation worse, several states were reluctant to commit funds to such an unpopular program. Though the law technically called for cooperative enforcement efforts between the states and the federal government, most of the states were happy to evade any responsibility and leave enforcement to the federal government. In many instances state budgets did not allow for enforcement efforts or were insufficient for the task. In 1927 the State of Utah spent only $160 on enforcement. Nevada spent less than $1,000.[19] Colorado lawmakers were allowed to appropriate up to $5,000 annually from the state budget.

Official records showed that the Prohibition Bureau was riddled with corruption throughout the 1920s. As a result, hundreds of agents were fired every year for their involvement with the criminal enterprises they were investigating. Between 1920 and 1930, out of the 17,816 people who worked for the Prohibition Bureau, 1,587 (or about 9%) were fired for various causes, including false statements on employment applications, criminal records, extortion, bribery, embezzlement, theft of liquor, graft, and a variety of other reasons.[20]

Lincoln Andrews, who was in charge of prohibition enforcement, testified before a congressional committee during January and February of 1926 that 875 agents had been dismissed for bribery, extortion, immoral conduct, intoxication, and falsification of records.[21] Prohibition agents were known for such lax enforcement that in most cities it was possible to find a drink in less than half-an-hour.

Some Prohibition agents and other enforcement officials made more money by overlooking illegal liquor than they could ever have hoped to acquire by legal means during their lifetimes. In order to do business, bootleggers bribed politicians, legislators, detectives, police officers, judges, and even Prohibition agents. One way was to supply small bribes in the form of bottles of liquor, so that even the local cop on the beat could make a little extra money on the side by re-selling them. The cost of these bribes was simply added into the price of the liquor bootleggers sold and passed on to the customer.

Bootleggers also bribed lawyers, police officers, sheriff's deputies, tax collectors, court clerks, and anyone else who might be in a position to help them. Other people who were bribed were those involved in distribution of legal alcohol, including truck drivers, guards, salesmen, office personnel, and warehouse workers.

Many enforcement officials in low-paying positions broke the laws they were sworn to uphold. One simple method was to sell a government permit that authorized the purchase of alcohol that had been manufactured for sacramental or medicinal purposes to a bootlegger or other criminal. In this way the bootlegger could legally purchase drinkable alcohol from government-approved manufacturers or from legal government warehouses. The temptation and the potential profits were enormous.

Other irregularities were that prohibition agents escorted liquor trucks, protected smugglers and helped them unload their cargo, accepted bribes to supply information about impending raids, allowed real beer to be shipped as near beer, and sold withdrawal permits for alcohol and whiskey. Some law enforcement officials sold the liquor they had confiscated during raids to bootleggers, speakeasies, and to the public. Even though official government salaries were less than $3,000 a year, some agents were able to purchase country homes, real estate investments, speedboats, and expensive cars, furs, and diamonds to lavish on their women.

Distributing illegal liquor on a large scale also required police cooperation. One investigation in Philadelphia in 1928 showed that many police officers had saving of tens of thousands of dollars, somehow supposedly accumulated from their meager annual salaries.

Corruption spread to every branch of the government that dealt with Prohibition, including congressmen. Several dealers kept supplies of liquor in the basement of the Capitol and in the Senate and House buildings in Washington, in order to provide congressmen with prompt service. It is also curious to note that Prohibition agents were not allowed to issue search warrants for federal buildings.

Instances of bribery also occurred among agents of the Customs Service and the Border Patrol guarding the Mexican and Canadian borders. Even the Coast Guard tracking down smugglers by sea was not immune to corruption. Boats smuggling liquor were occasionally escorted into port by Coast Guard patrol boats and sailors sometimes helped to unload cargoes of liquor. Within the first two years of Prohibition, seven warrant officers and thirty-six enlisted men were convicted of cooperating with bootleggers and smugglers.[22]

In 1927 the Coast Guard seized the rumrunner *Federalship* and towed it to San Francisco, in the process confiscating 12,500 cases of Scotch whiskey. The cargo was stored in a federal warehouse for safekeeping. But when a check was later made on the cargo, the entire amount had mysteriously disappeared.

Certainly not all prohibition agents were dishonest, and most did the best they could with the limited legal tools they had to work with. One favorite technique to put a bootlegger out of business was to padlock his illegal premises, such as stills and speakeasies. This was a method that was easy, inexpensive, and not particularly dangerous. It required only a court order, a padlock, and a length of chain. A more real hazard was that revenue agents were sometimes injured when an illegal still or a batch of volatile illegal alcohol caught on fire or exploded during a raid.

## Increased Violence

Another unforeseen effect of Prohibition was an increase in the violence that became associated with the illegal liquor trade. Throughout the 1920s newspaper headlines trumpeted stories of gangland murders. Bodies might end up in some remote area out in the woods or in a nearby river. Hymie Weiss (birth name Earl Wajciechowsky), a lieutenant in the Dion O'Banion gang in Chicago, developed the less-than-subtle technique of forcing a victim into a car and taking him for a "one way ride" to the location of his own murder.[23] Gangsters and the police were often involved in high-speed chases, gun battles, and mass arrests. The newspaper-reading public was shocked, fascinated, and disgusted at the same time.

Violence was not restricted to intergang warfare. In 1929 the Treasury Department announced that forty-five federal agents had been killed in the line of duty. The job of Prohibition agent was dangerous, but work was often so hard to find that men were willing to face the risks of the job. More disturbing was the fact that 137 civilians were killed by Prohibition agents, some of them in self-defense, and others during raids and other enforcement efforts. This did not include the large number of deaths of moonshiners and law enforcement officers during local raids and confrontations. Some agents, assuming that everyone they dealt with was guilty of something, tended to shoot first and ask questions later.

Dale Frances Kearney, an agent for the Prohibition Bureau, was killed by four shotgun blasts while investigating bootleggers in Aguilar, a small town near Trinidad in Colorado, on July 6, 1930. His killer was never apprehended or even identified. He was the first federal agent to be killed in Colorado and, as a result, federal officers cracked down on local bootleggers and padlocked many of their illegal operations.[24]

Innocent citizens also sometimes got caught in the crossfire. For example, Senator Frank Greene of Vermont was walking in Washington, D.C., when he was accidentally hit in the forehead by a bullet during a shootout between Prohibition agents and bootleggers. He did eventually recover, but that was beside the point.[25]

Chicago gained the dubious notoriety of the capital of gangland slaughter and the murder rate in Chicago rose steadily year by year. There were sixteen murders in 1924, forty-six in 1925, and seventy-six in 1926. In

1928 Chicago reported nearly twice as many murders as New York City. Very few were solved or the culprits brought to trial.[26] Like the larger cities of the East, violent crime also occurred throughout the West, but the statistics were not quite as bad. In 1928 Los Angeles had seventy murders, as compared to 498 in Chicago and 182 in Philadelphia.[27]

One of the lethal tools used by both sides of the law was the Thompson submachine gun, which was nicknamed "the chopper," or "the ack-ack" for the noise it made. The Thompson was popular with Prohibition agents, the police, the FBI, and criminals for being lightweight, portable, easy to use, and its capability for fully automatic firing. Bullets could pierce a quarter-inch of steel. It was also affectionately known as the "Chicago typewriter," the "Chicago organ grinder," and the more descriptive "annihilator" and "street sweeper."

The Thompson submachine gun, better known as the "Tommy gun," was invented by John T. Thompson in 1918 during World War I. This powerful but compact machine gun was supposed to change the dynamics of the war, but it was perfected too late. One nickname was the "trench broom" for its intended use during World War I as a weapon with a high rate of fire. Thompson founded the Auto-Ordnance Company in 1916 for the purpose of developing his "auto rifle"; however, final development was completed too late and the war ended before the prototypes could be tested in Europe. The gun's subsequent use by both law enforcement officers and criminals, and its later portrayal in gangster movies of the Roaring Twenties, made it the best-known weapon of its type.

Chambered for the Colt .45 automatic pistol cartridge, the gun could be fired either as a fully automatic or a semi-automatic weapon. Automatic weapons fall into two categories, semi-automatic and full automatic. Semi-automatic weapons reload the chamber and cock the gun each time that the gun is fired. To fire a semi-automatic gun the trigger has to be pulled for each shot. By contrast, a fully automatic weapon continuously reloads the chamber and fires until all the ammunition in the clip is expended. Handguns commonly referred to as "automatics" are in reality semi-automatic in operation. Fully automatic weapons are subject to strict control by the federal government and are, practically speaking, unobtainable for the average citizen.

The rate of fire of the Thompson was between 600 and 800 rounds a minute, and even up to 1,200 rounds per minute for some models. Ammunition was supplied in 20-shot magazines, and more typically in 50- and 100-round drums that locked in place in front of the trigger guard. The drums could be changed in about four seconds.

With a short barrel and a removable butt stock, the gun weighed about ten pounds. Held with both hands, it could be fired from the hip or from the shoulder, though it was somewhat inaccurate at ranges over fifty yards as the bullets tended to spray in all directions. The first Thompson submachine guns were manufactured by Colt's Patent Firearms Manufacturing Company for the Auto-Ordnance Company.[28]

The Tommy gun finally went into full production in 1921, but as World War I had ended many surplus guns piled up. One could be purchased by civilians for $200. Tens of thousands were sold and shipped via the U.S. mail. Advertising for the gun promoted the concept that ordinary people would feel much safer if they had the protection afforded by this type of weapon. In 1929 a Thompson submachine gun could be legally purchased by mail order for about $175. With the serial number filed off it could also be purchased on the black market, and the guns ended up with murderers, bank robbers, and ordinary crackpots.

Other firearms used by both bootleggers and law enforcement agents were ordinary deer rifles and automatic shotguns loaded with buckshot. The winner in a shootout was usually the side with the most guns.

## Cars and NASCAR

To evade prohibition agents, bootleggers typically drove cars and trucks loaded with liquor at high speeds at night with their lights off along back roads that might be dirt or unpaved, and often had only a single lane. To accomplish this, drivers had to have exceptional driving skills.

Bootleggers preferred big powerful touring cars, such as Studebakers, Hudsons, Chryslers, and other large sedans for transporting liquor. Other favorite models used for transport were specially-modified Packards, Cadillacs, or trucks. Probably the most popular was the Packard roadster. The cars looked normal on the outside, but contained modified supercharged engines for greater power and speed. These cars were sometimes called "whiskey sixes," because they were outfitted with powerful souped-up six-cylinder engines.

The insides of the transport cars were modified to hold as many bottles of moonshine as possible. As well as filling the trunks and secret compartments, most had the passenger and rear seats removed, and even some of the floorboards, to make room for the maximum amount of liquor. A big sedan could typically carry about thirty cases of bottles. The powerful Marmon automobile could be retrofitted to hold up to seventy-five cases of liquor. Most cars could hold two layers of five-gallon cans with up to 120 cans carefully stacked in the back without any of them showing above the bottom of the window.

To counteract all this weight, heavy-duty suspensions and springs were added to make the cars ride in a normal way without the rear ends

Remains of a borrowed Stutz touring car after running into a tree at a speed of seventy miles an hour, in which the bootlegger driver was killed.

Bootleggers and moonshiners had to be able to drive fast on back roads without their lights on at night to be able to outrun Prohibition agents. Some drivers weren't as good as they thought they were and the result was frequently a crash. This is the remains of a Stutz touring car after it crashed into a tree at 70 miles an hour on July 29, 1924. The driver was killed in the accident and the fifty gallons of corn liquor he was carrying were destroyed (Library of Congress).

sagging or dragging on the ground. Other accessories were powerful spotlights to blind any pursuers, and thirty-foot chains that were dragged behind the cars to raise huge clouds of dust along dirt roads and obscure the visibility for any pursuing police cars. Bootleggers usually carried extra gasoline and oil so that they would have to make fewer stops during a trip.

As part of attempts to catch illegal shipments of alcohol, bootleggers and Prohibition agents often became involved in chases and gunfights. Attacks by rival gangs were common and both sides carried guns at the ready in case of trouble. Shotguns, automatic weapons, and submachine guns were part of their standard equipment, and violent shootouts often resulted in deaths. Attempts to outrun pursuers and the use of evasive maneuvers during a high-speed chase sometimes meant that moonshiners died when their cars rolled, crashed, and caught fire when they failed to hold to the road.

When Prohibition came to an end, driving and racing these fast cars on makeshift tracks continued as a popular recreational pastime on weekends. Fast and dangerous driving required the best drivers and their skills eventually created a culture of car racing which evolved into the popular National Association for Stock Car Auto Racing (NASCAR) in 1947.

## Liberated Youth and Emancipated Women

In spite of efforts by the prohibition forces to try to hold back progress, change inevitably occurred in the youth of the United States. Attempts to create a happier time in the aftermath of World War I and the unpopular Eighteenth Amendment led to a change in the moral attitudes of many young people. Men became dashing "sheiks" who lasciviously kissed the palms of young women they called "shebas." The name "sheik" became popular among America's youth after sultry movie star Rudolph Valentino became established as the sex symbol of the decade in the motion picture *The Sheik* (1921). Another name given to a young woman who smoked, drank, and had a casual attitude towards the interaction between the sexes was a "flapper."

The 1920s produced the Jazz Age and associated dramatic changes in the lifestyle of young people. Personifying the era was the flapper, who dominated college campuses throughout the country with her chin-length bobbed hair and short dresses. An editorial in the Colorado Springs *Gazette* for February 13, 1924, criticized the modern college students who drank in defiance of the Volstead Act, smoked, played cards, and indulged in immorality (a subtle way of saying sex). Prior to Prohibition, drinking among college-age students had not been a serious problem. Now, college boys were expected to have a flask and offer their date a drink or two. Some women students smoked openly between classes and maids in college dormitories often complained about the smell of stale cigarette smoke in the rooms. The new dance craze, the Charleston, that was sweeping the country was considered highly unladylike by the older generation. Necking and petting were common practices among young couples. The writings and theories of Freud and others along the same lines were common topics of discussion.

These changes were part of the new youth movement. For the first time young singles could go on a "date," where a boy and a girl could go out together by themselves without parental supervision or an adult chaperone present. Previously, courtship was strictly chaperoned and was intended to lead to marriage, but the new dating was simply a casual way to go out in private with someone of the opposite sex and have some fun at places like a movie theater or a speakeasy.

Part of this new freedom involved the automobile. High school and college boys now had access to a car and carried a hip-flask. Early models of automobile were open to the air, but the newer models had enclosed tops that created a degree of privacy, particularly in the back seat. Some parents, who were concerned over what their offspring might be doing in them, referred to cars as "devil wagons." They may have had a point as some others called the back seat of a car a "struggle buggy." The increased availability of automobiles also offered women a new freedom to travel as they wished.

One of the changes in American youth that was brought about by Prohibition was drinking, which became popular and respectable among young women. Rather than encouraging people to stop drinking, Prohibition made them want to drink. Reformers did not anticipate that once alcohol became illegal it would take on an aura of glamour. Prior to the start of Prohibition, women typically did not drink in social situations, and then perhaps only took a small glass of wine or sherry. After Prohibition started, people drank with a frantic desire to get drunk and enjoy themselves. Drinking champagne made people feel naughty.

After Prohibition became law, women had the right to vote and they enjoyed their newfound freedom. The Jazz Age resulted in a loosening of morals, exactly the opposite of what Prohibition advocates had intended. For the first time, it was acceptable for women, particularly young women, to drink. Drinking became romantic and glamorous and adventurous, and a young man on a date wouldn't be caught without his pocket flask of gin. Any young man going to a party without a hip-flask was considered to be a poor sport. Guys who drank so much they passed out were considered to be heroes. Tipsy youths staggering around led to a corresponding increased disrespect for the law, such as vandalism and truancy.

Prohibition actually did more harm than good in this respect, and the Volstead Act provided a challenge to many college men throughout the country. Students drank partly due to poor examples by their parents who flaunted the law, and partly due to the simple challenge of being told by the law that they were not allowed to drink.

Before the mid–1910s, no respectable woman was allowed in a saloon and few women were drinkers at home. But after 1920 and the onset of Prohibition, drinking illegal liquor was seen as exciting. Glamorous college co-eds carried silver flasks tucked into their garters and rolled stocking-tops. By the end of the 1920s a poll at Yale showed that 71 percent of its students (and presumably their female companions) admitted to drinking.[29] Some people even enjoyed the risk and thrill of having been in a real raid at a speakeasy.

Prohibition also promoted the undesirable new drinking pattern of drinking less often, but very heavily when doing so. People didn't go to a speakeasy to leisurely sip their drinks. They went to guzzle them quickly

One of the popular fads that during the years of Prohibition was carrying a dainty flask of booze in a woman's garter. This, along with the cloche hat this woman is wearing and a raised hemline, was one of the characteristics of a sophisticated flapper in the 1920s (Library of Congress).

while they could. The new practice of drinking simply to become drunk became a popular habit.

In the days of the Old West most men drank beer or straight shots of whiskey. During Prohibition, cocktails became popular because bootleg alcohol had to be mixed with soft drinks and fruit juices to disguise the rough taste of poor-quality liquor. These sweetened drinks were also more palatable to women than raw liquor, and added to their desire to drink. Men and women now drank forbidden cocktails together at bars or in discreet candle-lit alcoves. Parties in private homes with a group of friends with men and women drinking and dancing became a popular pastime for people of all ages. Bellhops ran up and down hotel stairs carrying soda and ice buckets. Drinking took on an aura of sophistication and sexiness, which was the opposite of what the Prohibition supporters wanted.

Another freedom for women that emerged during Prohibition was smoking, and long cigarette holders became popular. Smoking was also a habit that became associated with female emancipation. As late as the early 1900s a woman could be arrested for smoking in public. One such woman was arrested in 1904 in New York for smoking on Fifth Avenue.[30] Seattle had a smoking prohibition for women from 1893 to 1911. Advertisements showing women smoking did not appear in women's magazines until 1927, and it wasn't until as late as 1929 that the restriction against women smoking in railroad dining cars was finally removed.[31]

Another practice that emerged from the permissive atmosphere of the speakeasies was the increased use of recreational drugs. The expanded acceptance of drinking also led to experimentation with drugs, a practice that had not been popular before Prohibition, and the use of hashish, marijuana, cocaine, and other drugs became popular for some. One popular 1920s song was titled, "You Cannot Make Your Shimmy Shake on Tea." "Tea" was a nickname for marijuana.

For those with a sense of humor, Prohibition could be celebrated in 1919 with various songs, such as "Prohibition Blues," performed by popular singer and comic actress Nora Bayes with lyrics written by humorist Ring Lardner and music by Bayes.

The new freedoms enjoyed by women included a radical change in popular dress fashions, which became unrestricted and boyish. The bloomers, corsets, thick black stockings, voluminous petticoats, and heavy floor-length woolen dresses of only a few years earlier were replaced by loose silk underwear and translucent silk stockings rolled beneath the knee and held up by garters. Rolling the stockings below the knee was one way to indicate that a woman was not wearing a corset. Chests were flat, often bound to create the new popular flat look, waists were worn low, and skirts rose above the knees. Arms and legs were now on tantalizing display.

Before World War I women could be arrested for not wearing a corset. In the 1920s young, liberated women refused to wear them. One justification was they claimed that men would not dance with them if they wore a corset. Many dance establishments had "corset check rooms," so a girl on a hot date could leave home wearing a corset, but remove it and check it before a dance.

The weight of a woman's typical daily clothing in the 1920s was reduced from perhaps around thirty to forty pounds to about two pounds, consisting of a light-weight chemise or teddy made from lace, silk, rayon, or crepe de chine (also called artificial silk), with silk stockings, underneath a dress made from thin fabric. A teddy was the name for a one-piece women's undergarment consisting of a combination of chemise top and loose panties. Slight variations resulted in the step-in or camisole knickers.

Hair was shortened, bobbed, and dyed or bleached. This new style of short hair was partially caused by the needs of World War I. Women who nursed men on the battle front did not have time to take care of their long Victorian-style hair and found it more convenient and time-saving to wear it short. Also, women working in wartime industrial manufacturing plants shortened their hair because of the possibility of it becoming dangerously entangled while working around moving heavy machinery. This shortened hair then became part of the image of the flapper of the 1920s.

The 1920s saw the rise of Madison Avenue and mass advertising, which led to an attitude of consumerism and a need to improve a woman's self-image. In Victorian times the use of makeup was essentially restricted to stage actresses and prostitutes, and women who wore makeup were considered to be of loose morals. As part of the new look of the 1920s, fingernails were varnished and lipstick was worn by the daring. Makeup, in the form of face powder and rouge, became acceptable for the first time for the average woman and cosmetics started on the way to becoming a multi-million-dollar industry.

Popular fashion accessories for flappers were bangles and long strings of beads. The most daring accessory of all was a tiny gold spoon or a box that contained cocaine, worn on a thin necklace.[32]

Going to speakeasies stimulated a new kind of informal socializing. Popular dances in the speakeasies were the Charleston (and its spin-off the Shimmy) and the Black Bottom. Both dances involved lively kicks and skipping, along with vigorous movements of the knees. More shocking to the previous generation was an explicit vigorous wiggling of the backside.

Some of the new women were obsessed with creating and maintaining a thin figure. A youthful boyish figure was achieved by strict dieting and exercise, sometimes enhanced by drugs, such as the use of nicotine.

Smoking cigarettes was promoted as a healthy aid to gaining and keeping a fashionably slim figure, which was the ideal of the times.

The patterns of courting changed. The 1920s were a time of increased sexual experimentation, which included the popularity of "petting parties." The increased availability of cars that became part of going on a date in the 1920s, led to automobile parties and provided an unchaperoned young couple with a place for courting and as a surrogate bedroom on wheels, or at least the opportunity for serious necking. The name of one popular cocktail was "between the sheets." For the very daring, there was casual sex before marriage with a lowered fear of pregnancy due to expanded methods of birth control. As women became more emancipated, divorce became more socially acceptable and more common. The new liberated women could now support themselves, thus they had the freedom to escape from unhappy marriages without the pressures of economic disaster. As a result, the number of divorces doubled between 1914 and 1929.

Young people in general welcomed these change in attitudes. As would be expected, however, some drank too much, used too many drugs, became promiscuous, drove dangerously fast, and died young.

## The End of Prohibition

Prohibition did not accomplish what reformers with good intentions had hoped. The Prohibition law was unpopular, widely ignored, and easily broken. Though drinking did initially decrease, it rapidly increased again and, at the same time, organized crime increased and so did disrespect for authority and flaunting of the law. By the end of the 1920s liquor was flowing freely and crime was flourishing. The general feeling around the country was that Prohibition was not something that the public wanted.

Instead of improving the nation's health and quality of life, as was intended, Prohibition resulted in one of the most crime-ridden eras in the history of the United States. Bombings and murders increased. Extortion and bribery were rampant. In the 1920s there were some 500 gangland murders in Chicago. And bootleg liquor, with its associated manufacture and distribution, was part of the cause. Violations of the Volstead Act were flagrant, widespread, and encouraged.

The voices calling for repeal grew louder and more insistent. One factor was a law that created even more severe penalties for violating the Volstead Act. At the beginning of Prohibition, violations of the Act were treated as misdemeanors. The punishment was six months in jail and a $1,000 fine. In 1929, in a further attempt to halt violations of the law, the drys forced through tough new legislation, called the Increased Penalties Act, or the Jones Act, that provided a much more severe punishment for violators.

Named after one of the sponsors of the bill, Wesley L. Jones of Washington, the new law increased the penalty for most Volstead violations from the level of misdemeanors to felonies. First-time offenders, such as purchasers of illegal alcohol, were subject to a maximum of five years' imprisonment and a fine of $10,000. Even witnesses to the sale or transport of liquor were considered to be violators of the law because failure to report a felony was also a felony. This harsh new punishment angered the public, and even the news media started to campaign against misguided and excessive enforcement of the law. The "Jones Five and Dime Law," as it was popularly called, was now so harsh that it made Prohibition even more difficult to enforce. Courts and prisons were flooded with Prohibition cases, many of which involved respectable middle-class citizens. The

Not everyone was in favor of doing away with drink. By the time that Prohibition was repealed, it had fallen out of favor with the majority of the country. This automobile, covered with sayings and banners supporting repeal of the Eighteenth Amendment, is obviously part of a celebration parade (National Archives).

Jones law was so effective in mobilizing resistance to the Volstead Act that some historians have wondered if that might not have been the underlying intention.

One of the last straws, however, as far as the public was concerned, occurred on February 14, 1929, when Chicago's mob warfare culminated in the St. Valentine's Day Massacre. Four gunmen dressed as policemen, but thought to be part of Al Capone's gang, machine-gunned seven men against the back wall of the SMC Cartage Company garage on North Clark Street at ten-thirty in the morning. The seven were lined up and executed in gangland style. Five of the victims were known gangsters, one was a gang accomplice, and the other was a car mechanic.

Despite investigation by the police, none of the witnesses would testify and none of the killers was brought to trial. The crime ended up as just another of Chicago's unsolved gangland murders. To this day the debate continues about the details of what actually happened. The effect of the St. Valentine's Day Massacre, however, was to create a backlash against Prohibition and its violence, and it set off a public outcry across the nation that focused the unwanted attention of the federal government on suppressing bootleggers and crime.

An equally grim event happened just before New Year's Eve of 1929 when a Coast Guard cutter opened fire on a rum-runner in Narragansett Bay, killing three of the four people aboard. Combined with the Jones law and the St. Valentine's Day massacre, this apparently unwarranted violence, along with widespread official corruption and overcrowding of the nation's jails, contributed to public feelings that ran high against these events and contributed to the opposition towards Prohibition.

The final factor was an economic one. Prohibition was expensive to enforce and efforts were costing both the government directly and the country indirectly, at the same time that hundreds of millions of dollars in tax revenues were being lost. Taxes should have been flowing in to the government from bars, nightclubs, breweries, wineries, and distilleries. The ultimate insult to the ordinary taxpayer was that bootleggers and moonshiners were making millions of dollars from illegal liquor and paying no taxes, at the same time that legitimate businessmen were forced to lay off honest workers.

Then the stock market collapsed on October 29, 1929. The stock market crash did not cause the Depression, but was an outcome of the severe economic problems that had been building in the country. A year later the nation's banking system collapsed. Businesses failed, banks closed their doors, and the country was faced with massive unemployment and homelessness. Nineteen thirty was worse than 1929, and 1931 was worse than 1930. Unemployment soared rapidly. In Michigan, for example, rising as high as 34 percent.[33] Federal income tax collections plummeted 60 percent in the three years after 1930. The worst effect was in the cities, but the downturn also affected the rural population.

President Herbert Hoover was vague on his stance on Prohibition. Drys thought he was dry as he supported enforcing the law and obeying the Constitution. The wets felt that Hoover was not against repeal or letting citizens vote for an amendment. Hoover had said that Prohibition was "a great social and economic experiment, noble in motive and far-reaching in purpose."[34] Noble words indeed, but few knew Hoover's real position on the subject.

At the President's request, Congress authorized the National Commission on Law Observance and Enforcement, also known as the Wickersham Commission, to study and investigate crime and enforcement of the Eighteenth Amendment. The committee spent a year and a half investigating whether Prohibition was being enforced or even could be enforced, along with its relationship to crime and corruption. The committee's preliminary report, issued in January of 1930, told everybody what they already knew: prohibition was not working, many of the public were disregarding and resisting the law, enforcement officials were understaffed and some were corrupt, courts were overloaded, major criminals were seldom prosecuted, and only the small-scale offenders went to prison. The commission also noted to nobody's surprise that enforcement of the Volstead Act was cumbersome, inefficient, and ineffective.[35]

The commission danced around the issue of whether Prohibition was really working, but did note in the report, "It is axiomatic that under any system of reasonably free government a law will be observed and may be enforced only where and to the extent that it reflects or is an expression of the general opinion of the normally law-abiding elements of the community."

The surprise to everybody was that the Commission opposed the repeal of Prohibition and in fact recommended maintaining it. The group felt that basically the problem could be solved by stronger enforcement, and merely suggested spending more money for enforcement. At issue, of course, was the money spent on federal agents to enforce Prohibition, the cost of which was far greater than the initial optimistic estimates, due to the huge increase in crime associated with the manufacture and distribution of illegal liquor.

By 1932 a strong backlash had built in the United States and all these factors combined to put pressure on the government for the repeal of Prohibition. Organized labor looked towards the government to revive the economic impact on the country by allowing a revitalized liquor industry to provide badly-needed jobs in the brewing and distilling industries. The liquor industry had always been big business. At the start of Prohibition alcohol had been the fifth largest industry in the nation. At the time that Prohibition went into effect, the United States had approximately 178,000 saloons, 1,200 breweries, and over 500 distilleries.[36] Prohibition put workers in these industries into the unemployment lines and forced the saloons out of business. In Denver alone, two breweries and 400 saloons closed their doors. Some were torn down, some became restaurants or stores, and some turned to serving soft-drinks and ice cream, or became billiard parlors, in order to survive.

On top of this, the federal government was losing large amounts of tax revenue. The supporters of Prohibition had assumed that an increase in the sales of non-alcoholic beverages would replace the tax money that came from alcohol sales, but this did not happen. Allowing alcohol to be made and sold again would produce revenue and jobs for farmers who grew corn, barley, hops, and other crops that were turned into alcohol. The fact that legalizing liquor would create thousands of much-needed jobs helped to convince many of the politicians who believed in dry principles.

The abolition of Prohibition was used as a strong campaign issue by the Democrats in the 1932 election. They won and, nine days after taking office, President Franklin D. Roosevelt urged Congress to amend the Volstead Act to allow the manufacture and sale of beer … "and to provide through such manufacture and sale, by substantial taxes, a proper and much needed revenue for the government."[37] After only a month in office, on March 23, 1933, Roosevelt signed the Cullen-Harrison Act that ended Prohibition by allowing the manufacture and sale of 3.2 beer (3.2% alcohol by weight or 4% by volume) and wine. This became effective on April 7, 1933.

By the time it was obvious that Prohibition was doomed, even the original supporters were openly admitting that it had failed. They had hoped that they would be supported by public opinion that would recognize the evil effects of alcohol. Instead of which drinking increased, the speakeasy replaced the saloon, a vast army of lawbreakers appeared, regular citizens ignored the law, respect for the law lessened, and crime increased to a level never seen before. On December 5, 1933, the Twenty-First Amendment to the Constitution was ratified, and gave each state the right to restrict or ban purchase or sale of alcohol. Mississippi was the last state to repeal Prohibition in 1966. The full text of the Twenty-First Amendment is contained in Appendix 1.

With the end of Prohibition, speakeasies closed or became fashionable legitimate nightclubs, such as 21, El Morocco, and the Cotton Club. Perversely, as the drys had initially hoped, Prohibition did mark the end of the saloon as a drinking place. However, after repeal, saloons were

The old-time saloons may be gone but their legacy lives on in the West in such as this beautifully-made bar and back bar surrounded by ornately-carved pillars that is still in use in Wyoming. The mounted animal heads are still a popular male-oriented bar decoration (author's collection).

replaced by bars, cocktail lounges, nightclubs, and restaurants that served liquor.

To try to avoid a return to the old days and the bad connotations of the saloon, several states declared that the names "bar" and "saloon" were unacceptable for common usage. For example, after Prohibition ended, the Colorado legislature outlawed the use of the word "saloon" for public drinking places. The alternative names of "cocktail lounge" or "tavern," however, were acceptable. Essentially only the name had changed, though admittedly the new bars and cocktail lounges were not the same as the old-time saloon, which was devoted only to drinking, and was often dark, smelly, and reeked of stale beer, old cigar smoke, and worse.

A few people continued to make and smuggle bootleg alcohol, but their reason was now strictly financial. The country was still deep in the grip of the Depression and out-of-work people needed money to survive. This illegal liquor was often traded locally for food or sold to local bars or to wholesale distributors, who did not pay taxes on it, thus resulting in more profit for them.

When Prohibition ended, tax revenue from alcohol started to flow again into the coffers of the federal government. In 1934 this provided nearly $750,000 a day.[38] During the first year after repeal, the government collected $258,911,332 in alcohol taxes, a figure that was almost 9 percent of the total federal revenue.[39]

Unfortunately, the end of Prohibition didn't mean the end of crime. Gangsters simply reverted back to their old standbys of prostitution, gambling, and extortion. Also on the downside of repeal was the fact that drunk driving and the associated fatalities increased. In January of 1934 fatalities increased over 11 percent, as compared to January of 1933. During 1933 fatalities involving alcohol increased by 40 percent.

# Postscript

Pᴿᴏʜɪʙɪᴛɪᴏɴ ʜᴀs ʙᴇᴇɴ described as "the legislated imposition of teetotalism on the unwilling."[1] It was in essence a widespread social experiment that was an attempt by a vocal minority to regulate what they considered to be a vice in others. The unintended result was that Prohibition promoted criminal behavior, along with bribery, blackmail, and official corruption. It deprived the government of tax revenue and forced limitations on individual rights.

Other countries that experimented with Prohibition had similar results. Finland tried prohibition in 1919 and repealed it in 1932 because rum-running and similar smuggling enterprises made it apparent that regulation was not working. In 1964 the state of Majarashtra (including Bombay) in India abandoned Prohibition after fourteen years.[2]

Prohibition in the United States lasted for almost fourteen years and concluded officially on December 5, 1933. When Prohibition ended, the general feeling was that the cure for what the Prohibition supporters believed to be the social problems of the time was worse than the disease. Promoters of Prohibition had expected that outlawing alcohol would lead to lower crime rates and higher morality, and promote happiness, better health, increased prosperity, and salvation for their fellow-man. Instead they ended up with bootleggers, rumrunners, moonshiners, hijackers, gangsters, racketeers, criminals with machine guns, corrupt police and judges, crooked politicians, and speakeasies.

One frequently unperceived aspect of Prohibition was that supporters often associated alcohol with anyone who looked, spoke, or acted differently than them. Part of the background that led to Prohibition involved Protestant concerns over the waves of largely Catholic immigrants who brought their traditional drinking customs with them from Europe. Exploitation of the prejudices of the rural population through propaganda campaigns, coupled with an unfounded fear of foreigners and their cultural ways, had persuaded many voters to support National Prohibition.

It must be admitted, however, that the old-time saloon was not a very

When Prohibition was repealed on December 5, 1933, happy drinkers crowded the bars to celebrate. Contrast this photograph with the earlier one in Chapter 5 taken at the start of prohibition where the patrons all seem deep in gloom. From the perspective of these drinkers above, "Happy days were here again" (author's collection).

desirable place. Though much has been said about the saloon being a refuge for male companionship and a type of working man's club that was the scene of wise and witty conversation among companions and hosted by a friendly bartender, the reality was that by the late 1910s most low-class urban saloons were grimy, noisy, and disreputable, and were populated by idle riffraff who were mostly drunk. The saloon was often the breeding ground of crime and violence, and was used as the meeting place of criminals. The premises were often dingy and dirty, contained battered tables and chairs and unwashed glassware, and was permeated with offensive smells and appalling sanitary facilities. Often the home of pimps and prostitution, the old-time saloon encouraged drunkenness, often with vile liquor that had been bottled in the basement or purchased from a questionable source. The inner-city American saloon probably sank to its worst incarnation between the late 1880s and 1917, when almost all of them closed with Prohibition.

One important point that the temperance cause overlooked was that the saloon, in spite of its obvious shortcomings, did provide immigrants with a familiar setting to find congenial companionship with fellow immigrants. Surrounded by the new and unknown, including often even the language, immigrants found something familiar in the saloons to help them to adapt to their new country. Group drinking was part of the customs and culture of the home countries of many of these men, making the saloon a familiar place to find male bonding and companionship.

The fond expectations of Prohibition supporters were that banning the manufacture and sale of alcohol would result in social harmony, reduced crime, and enhanced productivity. Instead, drinking continued anyway, fueled by liquor smuggling and the manufacture of bootleg alcohol, both which resulted in a predictable increase in serious crime. By 1927 deaths from alcoholism in the United States had increased by 150 percent.[3]

Before Prohibition, most heavy drinking was done in saloons and restaurants, and drinking in most American homes was not perceived to be a problem. After Prohibition, home brewing and distilling became common. *Time* magazine even published a recipe for making gin in its November 22, 1926, issue.

Prohibition was essentially unenforceable, because the small handful of agents that were tasked with enforcement were unable to police the drinking habits of millions, including those who chose not to obey the law. Thus a generation of lawlessness arose almost immediately. One of the few groups that did embrace Prohibition was the military, because the army realized that they needed clean-living soldiers with clear thinking in order to be and remain effective.

The amendments that started and ended Prohibition were in themselves unusual. The Eighteenth Amendment was the only time that the Constitution had been amended to restrict a citizen's freedom. The Twenty-First Amendment was the only one in United States history to repeal another amendment. In 140 years, the Eighteenth Amendment was the only one to ever be repealed.

Federal law still does not permit production of distilled liquor without a permit, because the distillation of alcohol requires skill and knowledge, and mistakes in the process could harm the consumer if it is not performed properly, as many victims of rotgut booze in the 1920s found out at their peril. Nonetheless, moonshining and bootlegging didn't end with Prohibition, but continued on.

Some moonshiners in the United States continue to produce illegal liquor even today because the tax on alcohol is high. Currently moonshining still persists, primarily among the rural populations of Alabama, Georgia, South Carolina, and Mississippi, but also in Virginia and Pennsylvania. The quantities produced are generally small because large commercial distilleries can buy the required supplies in bulk and produce liquor at a low cost. In reality, even with taxes added, the cost of legal alcohol is not much higher than the cost of moonshine produced in small quantities.

As an added inducement and as with any banned activity, some consumers revel in the illegality of it all and like to drink moonshine just for the fun of it. At an office Christmas party that the author attended some years ago, the hero of the event was the company sales manager, who brought an unmarked Mason jar with a clear alcoholic liquid in it. The rumor was that it was illegal moonshine and the office drinkers reveled in the wickedness of trying the fiery liquid. The manager later confided to the author that he had merely gone to a local liquor store and purchased some beverage grain alcohol and then decanted it into the Mason jar.

On December 5, 1933, in the wake of the repeal of Prohibition, jazz bands played and legal drinkers stepped up to the bar in licensed establishments.

To paraphrase the popular old song, "Happy days were here again."

# Glossary

## Some Slang Terms from Prohibition
## and the Roaring Twenties

*Age*—to mature raw whiskey or other alcohol into the finished product over time

*Bead*—bubbles that formed on the top of liquor when shaken, used as an indicator of the strength (proof) of the alcohol

*Bee's Knees*—anything wonderful

*Bimbo*—originally a promiscuous woman, then applied to a flapper who was perceived to be dumb

*Blind Pig*—another name for a speakeasy, mostly an Eastern U.S. term

*Bootlegging*—an alcohol smuggler, derived from early smugglers carrying illegal liquor in bottles hidden in the tops of their boots

*Booze*—illegal alcohol, usually of a dubious quality

*Brandy*—distilled fermented fruit juice

*Charred barrels*—oak barrels burned on the inside, used to store whiskey during aging to add flavor and the typical golden color

*Chicago Typewriter*—slang name for a Thompson submachine gun

*Denatured Alcohol*—denaturing was the process of adding noxious chemicals to drinking (ethyl) alcohol to make it unfit and unsafe for human consumption; the commonest denaturant was wood alcohol

*Distilling*—the process of selectively heating alcohol to extract and concentrate it from the mash

*Drys*—individuals who wished to prohibit drinking and ban all alcohol

*Ethyl alcohol*—also known as ethanol, made by fermentation of sugar by yeast to produce drinkable alcohol used for beverages

*Flapper*—a free-spirited young woman in the 1920s who smoked, drank, used cosmetics, wore light-weight silk clothing with no corset, and was freer in her relationship with the opposite sex than the previous generation. For what it is worth, in France around the turn of the century, "flapper" was a name for a streetwalker

*Gams*—shapely legs on a woman

*Gat*—slang name for a pistol, derived from the name Gatling Gun, a machine gun designed by Dr. Richard Jordan Gatling from North Carolina in 1862

*Giggle Water*—slang name for an alcoholic drink

*Gold Digger*—a woman interested only in a man's money

*Gorilla*—slang name for a gangster or thug with the strength of a gorilla

*Gun Moll*—the mistress of a gangster, a female gangster groupie

*Hooch (also spelled hootch)*—a slang generic name for moonshine whiskey, often implying bad liquor; the name is supposed to have been derived from poor-quality whiskey made by the Hoochinoo Indians of Alaska

*Jazz Baby*—another name for a flapper

*Jazzbo*—a pet name for a flapper's lover or a ladies' man

*Malt*—grain soaked in water to allow it to sprout

*Mash*—mixture of malt and yeast that ferments to produce alcohol

*Moonshine*—liquor distilled at night and transported by the light of the moon to avoid detection by law enforcement agents

*Ossified*—drunk as a skunk

*Pineapple*—slang for a hand grenade or other small explosive device

*Roadhouse*—a speakeasy or nightclub at the side of a road in the country

*Rod*—firearm

*Rotgut*—raw low-quality or contaminated liquor that was named for what it did to the insides of a drinker

*Sheba*—female version of a sheik

*Sheik*—a romantic image young men tried to attain; from Rudolph Valentino's 1921 movie *The Sheik*, establishing him as a major sex symbol and whom young women saw as the ultimate in romantic fantasy

*Speakeasy*—an illegal drinking place that sold alcoholic drinks; the quality of speakeasies varied from low dives to exotic nightclubs that were frequented by the rich. Also called a "blind pig" or a "blind tiger"

*Tommy Gun*—Thompson submachine gun

*Torpedo*—an armed thug

*Trigger Man*—a shooter for a gang

*Upchuck*—what drinkers did after imbibing too much bad booze: vomit

*Wets*—individuals who enjoyed drinking and wished to continue the use and availability of alcohol

*Whoopee*—having fun

# Appendix 1

## The Eighteenth and Twenty-First Amendments to the Constitution of the United States

*The Eighteenth Amendment*

Proposed December 18, 1917. Ratified January 16, 1919. Effective January 16, 1920.

*The Eighteenth Amendment: Liquor Prohibition*

Section 1. After one year from the ratification of this article the manufacture, sale, or transportation of intoxicating liquors within, the importation thereof into, or the exportation thereof from the United States and all territory subject to the jurisdiction thereof for beverage purposes is hereby prohibited.

Section 2. The Congress and the several States shall have concurrent power to enforce this article by appropriate legislation.

Section 3. This article shall be inoperative unless it shall have been ratified as an amendment to the Constitution by the legislatures of the several States, as provided in the Constitution, within seven years from the date of the submission hereof to the States by the Congress.

*The Twenty-First Amendment*

Proposed February 20, 1933. Ratified December 5, 1933.

*The Twenty-First Amendment: Repeal of Federal Liquor Prohibition*

Section 1. The eighteenth article of amendment to the Constitution of the United States is hereby repealed.

Section 2. The transportation or importation into any State, Territory or possession of the United States for delivery or use therein of intoxicating liquors, in violation of the laws thereof, is hereby prohibited.

Section 3. This article shall be inoperative unless it shall have been ratified as an amendment to the Constitution by conventions in the several States, as provided in the Constitution, within seven years from the date of the submission hereof to the States by the Congress.

# Appendix 2

## The Sources of Various Alcoholic Beverages

| Beverage and (% alcohol) | Base Material |
|---|---|
| Beer—3–6% (up to 10%) | cereal grains, typically barley |
| Bourbon—40–55% | primarily corn |
| Brandy/cognac—40–50% | distilled from wine |
| Gin—38–45% | fermented grain mash, flavored with juniper |
| Grain alcohol—95–99% | various cereal grains |
| Rum—40–57% | sugar cane or molasses |
| Rye whiskey—40–55% | rye grain |
| Schnapps—30–40% | fruit flavor added to grain alcohol |
| Tequila—40–45% | blue agave plant from Mexico |
| Vodka—40–55% | cereal grains or potatoes |
| Whiskey—40–55% | barley, corn, rye, or wheat grain (Scotch whiskey [spelled whisky] is distilled in Scotland two or three times, then aged for a minimum of three years in oak barrels) |
| Wines—12–18% | grapes, berries, and other fruits and plants |

# Appendix 3

## The Percentage of Alcohol
## in Various Patent Medicines

The following are the percentages of alcohol found in some of the popular over-the-counter patent medicines (proof is twice the alcohol content. i.e., 23 percent alcohol is 46 proof).

| | |
|---|---|
| Ayer's Sarsaparilla | 26% |
| Boker's Stomach Bitters | 43% |
| Burdock Blood Bitters | 25% |
| Colden's Liquid Beef Tonic | 26% |
| Drakes' Plantation Bitters | 33% |
| Faith Whitcomb's Nerve Bitters | 20% |
| Flint's Quaker Bitters | 23% |
| Golden Liquid Beef Tonic | 27% |
| Hoofland's German Tonic | 29% |
| Hooker's Wigwam Tonic | 21% |
| Dr. J. Hostetter's Celebrated Stomach Bitters | 44% |
| Jaynes Carminative | 23% |
| Kendall's Balsam | 61% |
| Luther's Temperance Bitters | 17% |
| Lydia Pinkham's Vegetable Compound | 21% |
| Paine's Celery Compound | 21% |
| Peruna | 28% |
| Psychine | 15% |
| Warner's Safe Tonic Bitters | 36% |
| Whiskol | 28% |

# Appendix 4

## Data from Denver, Colorado, Showing
## the Frequency of Alcohol Violations in the 1920s*

| Year | Total Arrests | For Drunkenness | | For Violating Prohibition Law | |
|------|------|------|------|------|------|
| 1920 | 12,947 | 1,847 | (14.3%) | 655 | (5.1%) |
| 1921 | 19,649 | 3,163 | (16.1%) | 271 | (1.4%) |
| 1922 | 18,667 | 4,031 | (21.6%) | 887 | (4.7%) |
| 1923 | 17,288 | 3,111 | (18.0%) | (not given) | |
| 1924 | 19,825 | 3,003 | (15.1%) | 1,303 | (6.6%) |
| 1925 | 20,356 | 2,982 | (14.6%) | 1,360 | (6.7%) |
| 1926 | 18,109 | 2,916 | (16.1%) | (not given) | |
| 1927 | 18,485 | 2,835 | (15.3%) | 1,390 | (7.5%) |
| 1928 | 20,459 | 3,620 | (17.7%) | (not given) | |
| 1929 | 19,450 | 3,343 | (17.2%) | 1,581 | (8.1%) |

*(data derived from Secrest, Hell's Belles, 317–320)

# Chapter Notes

## Preface

1. Asbury, *The Great Illusion*, 144.

## Chapter 1

1. Rose and Cherpitel, *Alcohol*, 22.
2. Brown, *Saloons of the American West*, 71.
3. Martin, *Whiskey and Wild Women*, 182.
4. Noel, *The City and the Saloon*, 24–25.
5. Joseph G. Rosa, *They Called Him Wild Bill: The Life and Adventures of James Butler Hickok* (Norman: University of Oklahoma Press, 1974), 137.
6. West, *The Saloon on the Rocky Mountain Mining Frontier*, xiv.
7. Parker, *Deadwood*, 187.
8. Thomas G. Thompson, *Lake City, Colorado: An Early Day Social & Cultural History* (Oklahoma City: Metro Press, 1974), 41.
9. Dary, *Seeking Pleasure in the Old West*, 127.
10. Asbury, *The Barbary Coast*, 116.
11. MacKell, *Red Light Women of the Rocky Mountains*, 248.
12. Noel, *The City and the Saloon*, 34–35.
13. Mabel B. Lee, *Cripple Creek Days* (Garden City: Doubleday, 1958), 17.
14. Furnas, *The Life and Times of the Late Demon Rum*, 84.
15. Joe B. Franz and Julian E. Choate, Jr., *The American Cowboy: The Myth and the Reality* (Norman: University of Oklahoma Press, 1955), 77.

## Chapter 2

1. Erdoes, *Saloons of the Old West*, 233.
2. Erdoes, *Saloons of the Old West*, 232.
3. Asbury, *The Great Illusion*: 25–26.
4. Kobler, *Ardent Spirits*, 20.
5. Okrent, *Last Call*, 7.
6. Erdoes, *Saloons of the Old West*, 233.
7. Musto, *Drugs in America*, 9.
8. Furnas, *The Life and Times of The Late Demon Rum*, 82.
9. Asbury, *The Great Illusion*, 34–35.
10. Armstrong and Armstrong, *The Great American Medicine Show*, 44.
11. Asbury, *The Great Illusion*, 58.
12. Furnas, *The Life and Times of the Late Demon Rum*, 169.
13. Furnas, *The Life and Times of the Late Demon Rum*, 170.
14. Asbury, *The Great Illusion*, 60.
15. Furnas, *The Life and Times of the Late Demon Rum*, 175.
16. Holland, *The Joy of Drinking*, 75.
17. Asbury, *The Great Illusion*, 61.
18. Edwards, *Alcohol, the World's Favorite Drug*, 79.
19. Burns, *The Spirits of America*, 118.
20. Furnas, *The Life and Times of the Late Demon Rum*, 284.
21. Brown, *Saloons of the American West*, 138.
22. Asbury, *The Great Illusion*, 39.
23. Asbury, *The Great Illusion*, 96–97.
24. Furnas, *The Life and Times of the Late Demon Rum*, 284.
25. Asbury, *The Great Illusion*, 98.
26. Furnas, *The Life and Times of the Late Demon Rum*, 305.
27. Kobler, *Ardent Spirits*, 154; Asbury, *The Great Illusion*, 39.

28. Furnas, *The Life and Times of The Late Demon Rum*, 80–82.

29. Furnas, *The Life and Times of The Late Demon Rum*, 82–83.

30. Altman, *The Decade That Roared*, 14.

31. Dasgupta, *The Science of Drinking*, 4.

32. Asbury, *The Great Illusion*, 62.

33. Asbury, *The Great Illusion*, 85.

34. Okrent, *Last Call*, 54.

35. Okrent, *Last Call*, 56–57.

36. Kreck, *Hell on Wheels*, 152.

37. West, *The Saloon on the Rocky Mountain Mining Frontier*, 106.

38. Armstrong and Armstrong, *The Great American Medicine Show*, 43.

39. *Daily Miner's Register*, December 18, 1863.

40. Furnas, *The Life and Times of The Late Demon Rum*, 80–81.

41. Palmer, *Inebriety*, 29.

42. Palmer, *Inebriety*, 98.

43. Furnas, *The Life and Times of the Late Demon Rum*, 268–269.

44. Asbury, *The Great Illusion*, 90.

45. Asbury, *Carry Nation*, 80–81.

46. Asbury, *The Great Illusion*, 124.

47. Furnas, *The Life and Times of the Late Demon Rum*, 258–259.

48. McCullough, *Bone Dry*, 42.

49. Milner, *Oxford History of the American West*, 508–509.

50. Asbury, The Great Illusion, 121.

51. Walker, *One Eye Closed, The Other Red*, xiii.

52. Okrent, *Last Call*, 99.

53. Asbury, *The Great Illusion*, 133.

54. Walker, *One Eye Closed, The Other Red*, 22.

55. Asbury, *The Great Illusion*, 134.

56. Walker, *One Eye Closed, The Other Red*, 23.

57. Bauer, *Gentlemen Bootleggers*, 39.

58. Kobler, *Ardent Spirits*, 199.

59. Walker, *One Eye Closed, The Other Red*, 30.

60. Moore, *Anything Goes*, 24.

61. Asbury, *The Great Illusion*, 148–149.

62. Gateley, *Drink*, 373.

63. Okrent, *Last Call*, 118.

## Chapter 3

1. Bauer, *Gentlemen Bootleggers*, 69.

2. Hibbs and Settles, *Prohibition in Bardstown*, 71.

3. *Smithsonian*, Sept 2021, 52, 5, 88.

4. Kobler, *Ardent Spirits*, 19.

5. Asbury, *The Great Illusion*, 285.

6. Asbury, *The Great Illusion*, 267.

7. Asbury, *The Great Illusion*, 223.

8. Asbury, *The Great Illusion*, 224.

9. Okrent, *Last Call*, 200.

10. James Petersen, *The Century of Sex* (New York: Grove Press, 1999), 105.

11. Bauer, *Gentlemen Bootleggers*, 58.

12. Okrent, *Last Call*, 194.

13. Altman, *The Decade That Roared*, 18.

14. Moore, *Anything Goes*, 26–27.

15. Okrent, *Last Call*, 195.

16. Marlin Gardner and Benjamin H. Aylworth, *The Domestic Physician and Family Assistant* (Cooperstown: H. and E. Phinney, 1836), 59.

17. Lydia M. Child, *The Family Nurse: or Companion of the American Frugal Housewife* (Boston: Charles J. Hendee, 1837), 4.

18. Furnas, *The Life and Times of the Late Demon Rum*, 181.

19. Brown, *Saloons of the American West*, 139.

20. Gateley, *Drink*, 216.

21. Bauer, *Gentlemen Bootleggers*, 201.

22. Asbury, *The Great Illusion*, 229.

23. McCullough, *Bone Dry*, 36.

24. Walker, *One Eye Closed, The Other Red*, 28.

25. Kobler, *Ardent Spirits*, 225.

26. Asbury, *The Great Illusion*, 265.

27. Kobler, *Ardent Spirits*, 227.

28. Bauer, *Gentlemen Bootleggers*, 88.

29. Walker, *One Eye Closed, The Other Red*, 494.

30. Okrent, *Last Call*, 334.

## Chapter 4

1. Bauer, *Gentlemen Bootleggers*, 207.

2. Walker, *One Eye Closed, The Other Red*, 51.

3. Okrent, *Last Call*, 8.

4. Furnas, *The Life and Times of the Late Demon Rum*, 66.

5. Dabney, *Mountain Spirits*, xv.

6. Furnas, *The Life and Times of the Late Demon Rum*, 75.

7. James Petersen, *The Century of Sex* (New York: Grove Press, 1999), 105.

8. Kobler, *Ardent Spirits*, 295.

9. Bauer, *Gentlemen Bootleggers*, 66.

10. Burns, *The Spirits of America*, 219.

11. Walker, *One Eye Closed, The Other Red*, 41.

12. Asbury, *The Great Illusion*, 273.

13. Moore, *Anything Goes*, 27.

14. Brady, *Materials Handbook*, 55.

15. Walker, *One Eye Closed, The Other Red*, 494–495.

16. Bauer, *Gentlemen Bootleggers*, 67.

17. Asbury, *The Great Illusion*, 280.

18. Rickey, *Forty Miles a Day on Beans and Hay*, 201.

19. Asbury, *The Great Illusion*, 287.

20. Rickey, *Forty Miles a Day on Beans and Hay*, 312.

21. Dasgupta, *The Science of Drinking*, 217.

22. Bauer, *Gentlemen Bootleggers*, 65–66.

23. Walker, *One Eye Closed, The Other Red*, 422.

24. Walker, *One Eye Closed, The Other Red*, 41.

25. Burns, *The Spirits of America*, 221.

26. Armstrong and Armstrong. *The Great American Medicine Show*, 193.

27. For further information on Abrams and his peculiar machines, see Chapter 8 of Jeremy Agnew, *The Electric Corset and Other Victorian Miracles: Medical Devices and Treatments from the Golden Age of Quackery* (Jefferson, NC: McFarland & Company, 2021).

## Chapter 5

1. Okrent, *Last Call*, 207.

2. Brown, *Saloons of the American West*, 140.

3. T.E. Van Evra, "One Man's Experience in Early Leadville." *The Trail*, Dec 1918, 20–23.

4. Asbury, *The Great Illusion*, 113.

5. Furnas, *The Life and Times of the Late Demon Rum*, 259–260.

6. Walker, *One Eye Closed, The Other Red*, 313.

## Chapter 6

1. *Shoreline Length* at coast.noaa.gov

2. Okrent, *Last Call*, 160; Asbury, *The Great Illusion*, 249.

3. Walker, *One Eye Closed, The Other Red*, 37.

4. Okrent, *Last Call*, 171–172.

5. Walker, *One Eye Closed, The Other Red*, 358.

6. Okrent, *Last Call*, 162.

7. Altman, *The Decade That Roared*, 20.

8. Okrent, *Last Call*, 161.

9. Kobler, *Ardent Spirits*, 313.

10. Altman, *The Decade That Roared*, 21.

11. Walker, *One Eye Closed, The Other Red*, 162.

12. Walker, *One Eye Closed, The Other Red*, 307.

13. Walker, *One Eye Closed, The Other Red*, 123.

14. Okrent, *Last Call*, 336.

15. Asbury, *The Great Illusion*, 246.

16. Okrent, *Last Call*, 278.

17. Walker, *One Eye Closed, The Other Red*, 163–165.

## Chapter 7

1. Asbury, *The Great Illusion*, 259.

2. Asbury, *The Great Illusion*, 257.

3. *Fredericton Daily Mail*, Jan 4, 1920.

4. Kobler, *Ardent Spirits*, 240.

5. Walker, *One Eye Closed, The Other Red*, 213.

6. Asbury, *The Great Illusion*, 257.

7. atlasobscura.com/places/kentucky-club

8. Morgan, *Good Time Girls*, 84.

9. Berton, *The Klondike Fever*, 160.

10. Berton, *The Klondike Fever*, 252.

11. Morgan, *Good Time Girls*, 276.

12. Portland *Morning Oregonian*, Jan 18, 1922.

13. McCullough, *Bone Dry*, 34–35.

14. Walker, *One Eye Closed, The Other Red*, 16, 26.

15. Walker, *One Eye Closed, The Other Red*, 22.

16. Walker, *One Eye Closed, The Other Red*, 283, 486.

17. Walker, *One Eye Closed, The Other Red*, 77.

18. Rickey, *Forty Miles a Day on Beans and Hay*, 105.

19. Walker, *One Eye Closed, The Other Red*, 80.

20. Walker, *One Eye Closed, The Other Red*, 288–289.

21. Walker, *One Eye Closed, The Other Red*, 390.

22. Altman, *The Decade That Roared*, 17.

23. Walker, *One Eye Closed, The Other Red*, 266.

24. Walker, *One Eye Closed, The Other Red*, 445–446.

25. Walker, *One Eye Closed, The Other Red*, 64.

26. San Mateo *News-Leader*, March 5, 1920.

27. Altman, *The Decade That Roared*, 173.

28. *Los Angeles Times*, Jan 20, 1920.

29. Okrent, *Last Call*, 180.

30. Asbury, *The Great Illusion*, 239.

31. Okrent, *Last Call*, 183.

32. Walker, *One Eye Closed, The Other Red*, 280.

33. Asbury, *The Great Illusion*, 238.

34. Altman, *The Decade That Roared*, 18.

## Chapter 8

1. West, *The Saloon on the Rocky Mountain Mining Frontier*, 137.

2. MacKell, *Brothels, Bordellos, & Bad Girls*, 200.

3. Martin, *Whiskey and Wild Women*, 182.

4. Tom Rea, *Booze, Cops, and Bootleggers: Enforcing Prohibition in Central Wyoming*. WyoHistory.org, 2016.

5. Noel, *The City and the Saloon*, 109.

6. Noel, *The City and the Saloon*, 116.

7. MacKell, *Brothels, Bordellos, & Bad Girls*, 235.

8. Secrest, *Hell's Belles*, 317.

9. *Denver Post*, February 13, 1916.

10. *Denver Post*, January 15, 1919.

11. Secrest, *Hell's Belles*, 317.

12. Erdoes, *Saloons of the Old West*, 248

13. Parkhill, *The Wildest of the West*, 123.

14. Noel, *The City and the Saloon*, 129.

15. Parkhill, *The Wildest of the West*, 282.

16. Sprague, *Newport in the Rockies*, 317–318.

17. Sprague, *Newport in the Rockies*, 226.

18. Ormes and Ormes, *The Book of Colorado Springs*, 51.

19. Sprague, *Newport in the Rockies*, 347.

20. MacKell, *Brothels, Bordellos, & Bad Girls*, 74.

21. MacKell, *Brothels, Bordellos, & Bad Girls*, 79, 82.

22. MacKell, *Brothels, Bordellos, & Bad Girls*, 202–205.

23. Carlino, *Colorado's Carlino Brothers*, 19.

24. Carlino, *Colorado's Carlino Brothers*, 39, 56.

25. Carlino, *Colorado's Carlino Brothers*, 110, 170, 172.

26. Carlino, *Colorado's Carlino Brothers*, 128, 138–140.

27. *Denver Post*, Feb 19, 1933.

28. Morgan, *Wanton West*, 252.

## Chapter 9

1. Kobler, *Ardent Spirits*, 399.

2. Gateley, *Drink*, 269.

3. McCullough, *Bone Dry*, 25–42.

4. McCullough, *Bone Dry*, 31.

5. McCullough, *Bone Dry*, 34.

6. Erdoes, *Saloons of the Old West*, 87.

## Chapter 10

1. Rose, *Storyville*, 182.

2. West, *The Saloon on the Rocky Mountain Mining Frontier*, 133.

3. Asbury, *The Great Illusion*, 116.

4. Lawlor, *Rum-Running*, 89.

5. Bauer, *Gentlemen Bootleggers*, 73.

6. Dabney, *Mountain Spirits*, xiv.

7. Asbury, *The Great Illusion*, 169.

8. Dabney, *Mountain Spirits*, xiv.

9. Asbury, *The Great Illusion*, 169–170.

10. Bauer, *Gentlemen Bootleggers*, 98.

11. Okrent, *Last Call*, 274.

12. Altman, *The Decade That Roared*, 43.

13. Moore, *Anything Goes*, 29.

14. Brown, *Saloons of the American West*, 139; Moore, *Anything Goes*, 30–31.

15. Moore, *Anything Goes*, 20.

16. Francis J. Clauss, *Alcatraz, Island of Many Mistakes* (Menlo Park, CA: Briarcliff Press, 1981), 38.

17. Kobler, *Ardent Spirits*, 301–306.

18. Walker, *One Eye Closed, The Other Red*, 454.

19. Asbury, *The Great Illusion*, 171.
20. Kobler, *Ardent Spirits*, 259.
21. Asbury, *The Great Illusion*, 177.
22. Asbury, *The Great Illusion*, 183.
23. Altman, *The Decade That Roared*, 48.
24. Carlino, *Colorado's Carlino Brothers*, 84.
25. Kobler, *Ardent Spirits*, 276.
26. Moore, *Anything Goes*, 36.
27. Walker, *One Eye Closed, The Other Red*, 282.
28. Johnson and Haven, *Automatic Arms*, 59–60.
29. Moore, *Anything Goes*, 72.
30. Zeitz, *Flapper*, 6.
31. Moore, *Anything Goes*, 72–74.
32. Moore, *Anything Goes*, 73.

33. Altman, *The Decade That Roared*, 97.
34. Bauer, *Gentlemen Bootleggers*, 232.
35. Walker, *One Eye Closed, The Other Red*, 466–467.
36. Harris, *This Drinking Nation*, 86.
37. Walker, *One Eye Closed, The Other Red*, 504.
38. Bauer, *Gentlemen Bootleggers*, 225.
39. Okrent, *Last Call*, 361.

## *Postscript*

1. Okrent, *Last Call*, 11.
2. Furnas, *The Life and Times of the Late Demon Rum*, 341.
3. Brown, *Saloons of the American West*, 140.

# Bibliography

Agnew, Jeremy. *Alcohol and Opium in the Old West: Use, Abuse and Influence.* Jefferson, NC: McFarland, 2014.

Agnew, Jeremy. *Medicine in the Old West: A History 1850–1900.* Jefferson, NC: McFarland, 2010.

Altman, Linda J. *The Decade That Roared: America During Prohibition.* Brookfield, CT: Twenty-First Century Books, 1997.

Armstrong, David, and Elizabeth M. Armstrong. *The Great American Medicine Show.* New York: Prentice-Hall, 1991.

Asbury, Herbert. *The Barbary Coast.* New York: Pocket Books, 1947.

Asbury, Herbert. *Carry Nation.* New York: Alfred A. Knopf, 1929.

Asbury, Herbert. *The Great Illusion: An Informal History of Prohibition.* Mineola, NY: Dover, 2018.

Barrows, Susanna, and Robin Room (editors). *Drinking: Behavior and Belief in Modern History.* Berkeley: University of California Press, 1991.

Batchelor, Bob. *The Bourbon King: The Life and Times of George Remus.* New York: Diversion Books, 2019.

Bauer, Bryce T. *Gentlemen Bootleggers: The True Story of Templeton Rye, Prohibition, and a Small Town in Cahoots.* Chicago: Chicago Review Press, 2014.

Berton, Pierre. *The Klondike Fever: The Life and Death of the Last Great Gold Rush.* New York: Alfred A. Knopf, 1958.

Bordin, Ruth. *Frances Willard: A Biography.* Chapel Hill: University of North Carolina Press, 1986.

Bordin, Ruth. *Woman and Temperance: The Quest for Power and Liberty, 1873–1900.* New Brunswick: Rutgers University Press, 1990.

Brady, George S. *Materials Handbook.* New York: McGraw-Hill, 1963.

Brown, Robert L. *Saloons of the American West.* Silverton, CO: Sundance Publications, 1978.

Burns, Eric. *The Spirits of America: A Social History.* Philadelphia: Temple University Press, 2004.

Carlino, Sam. *Colorado's Carlino Brothers: A Bootlegging Empire.* Charleston, SC: History Press, 2019.

Carter, Annie. *These Granite Hills.* Divide, CO: unpublished manuscript, 1989.

Crowley, John W. *Drunkard's Progress: Narratives of Addiction, Despair, and Recovery.* Baltimore: Johns Hopkins University Press, 1999.

Dabney, Joseph E. *Mountain Spirits: A Chronicle of Corn Whiskey.* New York: Charles Scribner's Sons, 1974.

Dary, David. *Seeking Pleasure in the Old West.* Lawrence: University Press of Kansas, 1995.

Dasgupta, Amitava. *The Science of Drinking.* Lanham, MD: Rowman & Littlefield, 2011.

Edwards, Griffith. *Alcohol, the World's Favorite Drug.* New York: Thomas Dunne Books, 2000.

Erdoes, Richard. *Saloons of the Old West*. New York: Alfred Knopf, 1979.

Furnas, Joseph C. *The Life and Times of the Late Demon Rum*. New York: Capricorn Books, 1973.

Gateley, Iain. *Drink: A Cultural History of Alcohol*. New York: Gotham Books, 2008.

Hansen, James E. "Moonshine and Murder: Prohibition in Denver." *Colorado Magazine*, 50, 1, Winter 1973, 1–23.

Harris, Jonathan. *This Drinking Nation*. New York: Four Winds Press, 1994.

Hibbs, Dixie, and Doris Settles. *Prohibition in Bardstown: Bourbon, Bootlegging and Saloons*. Charlestown: American Palate, 2016.

Holland, Barbara. *The Joy of Drinking*. New York: Bloomsbury USA, 2007.

James, M. Lynn, James O. Schreck, and James N. BeMiller. *General, Organic, and Biological Chemistry: Chemistry for the Living System*. Lexington, MA: D.C. Heath, 1980.

Johnson, Melvin M., Jr., and Charles T. Haven. *Automatic Arms: Their History, Development and Use*. New York: William Morrow, 1941.

Kobler, John. *Ardent Spirits: The Rise and Fall of Prohibition*. New York: G.P. Putnam's Sons, 1973.

Kreck, Dick. *Hell on Wheels: Wicked Towns Along the Union Pacific Railroad*. Golden, CO: Fulcrum Press, 2013.

Lawlor, Allison. *Rum-Running*. Halifax, Nova Scotia: Nimbus Publishing, 2009.

MacAndrew, Craig, and Robert B. Edgerton. *Drunken Comportment: A Social Explanation*. Chicago: Aldine Publishing, 1968.

MacKell, Jan. *Brothels, Bordellos, & Bad Girls*. Albuquerque: University of New Mexico Press, 2004.

MacKell, Jan. *Red Light Women of the Rocky Mountains*. Albuquerque: University of New Mexico Press, 2009.

Martin, Cy. *Whiskey and Wild Women*. New York: Hart Publishing, 1974.

McCullough, David J. "Bone Dry? Prohibition New Mexico Style." *New Mexico Historical Review*, Jan 1988.

Milner, Clyde A., II, Carol A. O'Connor, and Martha A. Sandweiss (editors). *The Oxford History of the American West*, New York: Oxford University Press, 1994.

Monahan, Sherry. *The Wicked West: Boozers, Cruisers, Gamblers, and More*. Tucson: Rio Nuevo Publishers, 2005

Moore, Lucy. *Anything Goes: A Biography of the Roaring Twenties*. New York: Overlook Press, 2010.

Moore M.H. and, D.R. Gerstein (eds). *Alcohol and Public Policy: Beyond the Shadow of Prohibition*. Washington, D.C. : National Academies Press, 1981.

Morgan, Lael. *Good Time Girls*. Kenmore: Epicenter Press, 1998.

Morgan, Lael. *Wanton West: Madams, Money, Murder, and the Wild Women of Montana's Frontier*. Chicago: Chicago Review Press, 2011.

Musto, David F. (editor). *Drugs in America: A Documentary History*. New York: New York University Press, 2002.

Noel, Thomas J. *The City and the Saloon: Denver, 1858–1916*. Lincoln: University of Nebraska Press, 1982.

Okrent, Daniel. *Last Call: The Rise and Fall of Prohibition*. New York: Scribner's, 2010.

Ormes, Manly D., and Eleanor R. Ormes. *The Book of Colorado Springs*. Colorado Springs: Dentan Printing, 1933.

Palmer, Charles F. *Inebriety: Its Source, Prevention, and Cure*. New York: Fleming H. Revell, 1898.

Panati, Charles. *Sexy Origins and Intimate Things*. New York: Penguin Books, 1998.

Parker, Watson. *Deadwood: The Golden Years*. Lincoln: University of Nebraska Press, 1981.

Parkhill, Forbes. *The Wildest of the West*. New York: Henry Holt, 1951.

Rickey, Don, Jr., *Forty Miles a Day on Beans and Hay*. Norman: University of Oklahoma Press, 1963.

Rose, Al. *Storyville, New Orleans*. University: University of Alabama Press, 1974.

Rose, Mark E., and Cheryl J. Cherpitel. *Alcohol: Its History, Pharmacology and Treatment*. Center City: Hazelden, 2011.

Sax, N. Irving. *Dangerous Properties of Industrial Materials.* New York: Van Nostrand Reinhold, 1975.

Secrest, Clark. *Hell's Belles: Denver's Brides of the Multitudes.* Aurora: Hindsight Historical Publications, 1996.

Smith, Duane A. *Rocky Mountain Mining Camps.* Lincoln: University of Nebraska Press, 1967.

Sprague, Marshall. *Newport in the Rockies.* Denver: Sage Books, 1961.

Wagner, Heather L. *Alcohol.* Philadelphia: Chelsea House, 2003.

Walker, Clifford J. *One Eye Closed, The Other Red: The California Bootlegging Years.* Barstow, CA: Back Door Publishing, 1999.

West, Elliott. *The Saloon on the Rocky Mountain Mining Frontier.* Lincoln: University of Nebraska Press, 1976.

Zeitz, Joshua. *Flapper.* New York: Three Rivers Press, 2006.

# Index

Numbers in *bold italic* refer to pages with illustrations